Automatic Defense Against
Zero-day Polymorphic Worms
in Communication Networks

Automatic Defense Against Zero-day Polymorphic Worms in Communication Networks

Mohssen Mohammed • Al-Sakib Khan Pathan

CRC Press
Taylor & Francis Group
Boca Raton London New York

CRC Press is an imprint of the
Taylor & Francis Group, an **informa** business

AN AUERBACH BOOK

CRC Press
Taylor & Francis Group
6000 Broken Sound Parkway NW, Suite 300
Boca Raton, FL 33487-2742

First issued in paperback 2019

© 2013 by Taylor & Francis Group, LLC
CRC Press is an imprint of Taylor & Francis Group, an Informa business

No claim to original U.S. Government works

ISBN-13: 978-1-4665-5727-7 (hbk)
ISBN-13: 978-0-367-38003-8 (pbk)

Library of Congress Cataloging-in-Publication Data

Mohammed, Mohssen, 1982-
    Automatic defense against zero-day polymorphic worms in communication networks / Mohssen Mohammed, Al-Sakib Khan Pathan.
      pages cm
    Includes bibliographical references and index.
    ISBN 978-1-4665-5727-7 (hardback)
    1. Computer viruses. 2. Computer algorithms. 3. Computer networks--Security measures. 4. Machine theory. I. Pathan, Al-Sakib Khan. II. Title.

QA76.76.C68M64 2013
005.8--dc23   2012044400

Visit the Taylor & Francis Web site at
http://www.taylorandfrancis.com

and the CRC Press Web site at
http://www.crcpress.com

Dedication

To my father, Mohammed Zain Elabdeen Mohammed;
my sister, Maali Mohammed Zain Elaabdeen; faculty of
Mathematical Science, University of Khartoum, Khartoum,
Sudan, I especially would like to thank Dr. Mohsin Hashim
and Dr. Eihab Bashier, and Dr. Lorenzo Cavallaro, Information
Security Group, Royal Holloway, University of London.

Mohssen Mohammed

To my father, Abdus Salam Khan Pathan; my mother,
Delowara Khanom; and my loving wife, Labiba Mahmud.

Al-Sakib Khan Pathan

Contents

Preface

Internet worms pose a major threat to Internet infrastructure security, and their destruction is truly costly. A computer worm is a kind of malicious program that self-replicates automatically within a computer network. Worms are in general a serious threat to computers connected to the Internet and proper functioning of the computers. These malicious programs can spread by exploiting low-level software defects and can use their victims for illegitimate activities, such as corrupting data, sending unsolicited electronic mail messages, generating traffic for distributed denial-of-service (DoS) attacks, or stealing information. Today, the speed at which the worm propagates poses a serious security threat to the Internet.

A polymorphic worm is a kind of worm that is able to change its payload in every infection attempt, so it can evade the intrusion detection systems (IDSs) and damage data, delay the network, cause information theft, and contribute to other illegal activities that lead, for example, even to significant financial loss. To defend the network against the worm, IDSs such as Bro and Snort are commonly deployed at the edge of the network and the Internet. The main principle of these IDSs is to analyze the traffic to compare it against the signatures stored in their databases. Whenever a novel worm is detected in the Internet, the common approach is that the experts from the security community analyze the worm code manually and produce a signature. The signature is then distributed, and each IDS updates its database with this new signature.

This approach of creating a signature is human intensive and very slow, and when we have threats of worms that replicate very fast (that take as little as a few seconds to bring down the entire network) like zero-day polymorphic worms, the need for an alternative is recognized. The alternative approach is to find a way to automatically generate signatures that are relatively faster to generate and are of acceptable quality. This book focuses on how we can automatically generate signatures for unknown polymorphic worms.

Usually, to know how to generate signatures automatically for polymorphic worm attacks, reading a good number of books and information sources is necessary. To really understand the subject matter, a reader usually needs to read a wide range of books, such as the following:

a. Books about computer networking
   - To generate signatures for polymorphic worms, a strong background in computer networking is needed. Especially, knowledge is needed about network topologies, network routing protocols, network IP (Internet Protocol) addresses, and other network-related mechanisms.

b. Books about network security
   - Such books give general information about how to secure the communications in the network. Worm tackling may come as a part of such a book, but concrete information about unknown or zero-day worms may be missing.

c. Books about IDSs
   - Such books give information about how the IDSs work, what the types of IDSs are, what types of signatures are used in the IDSs, and so on.

d. Books about intrusion prevention systems (IPSs)
   - These types of books can give information about how the IPSs work, the differences between the IDSs and IPSs, and so on.

e. Books about the honeypot
   - Such books give information about what the honeypot is, where we can use it, the importance of the honeypot, how we can collect polymorphic worms using it, and so on.

f. Books about polymorphic worms
- These books provide information about the polymorphic worm attacks, how the polymorphic worms change their payloads, how they are launched in the Internet, and the like.

g. Books about string-matching algorithm

h. Books about statistical method

i. Books about artificial intelligence systems

j. Books about machine learning

To generate signatures for polymorphic worm attacks, we need some algorithms. All the books in categories g–j can help find suitable algorithms to generate good signatures for polymorphic worms.

To know, find, and read all these books or documents is time consuming and difficult. Our own experience shows that considerable effort is needed to reach even a minimum level of understanding of the functions of worms and then tackle them when they are polymorphic and unknown. Hence, keeping this personal experience in mind, the objective of our book is to combine all the knowledge of these sources in a single volume.

This is not a dense book considering its number of pages, but we have written it in a reasonable manner to address all the critical issues regarding the topic. We have included the core information and tried to explain exactly what is needed to automatically generate signatures for unknown polymorphic worms. We hope that our book will fill the existing void in the field of automatic handling of zero-day polymorphic worms.

The target audiences of this book are researchers, postgraduate students, industry experts, and academics working on malware detection in communication networks, especially polymorphic worm detection. We hope that this book will reduce the time for the practitioners and students in searching information for doing research in this area. It will directly provide valuable information in a single volume for their convenience.

So, this book is expected to be useful in terms of saving time and money. For the benefit of the readers, we have included the latest information along with future views and visions so that the information could be used for several years. As some fundamental data and practical information are combined for general readers, we hope it will also serve the purpose of providing general information about worms that will be useful well into the future.

To emphasize the danger of polymorphic worms, it should be noted that they can create serious problems for Internet security as they can be used to incur delay in a network, steal information, delete information, launch flooding attacks against servers, and so on. Polymorphic worm attacks are considered one of the top global attacks against Internet security, and their destruction is often extremely costly (or nearly impossible). We have extensively surveyed the currently available books and documents in the relevant areas. Our finding showed that at present there is no suitable alternative to this book. There are some network security-related books that have much less information on the topic, but they are not sufficient. So, we have taken this initiative to make things easier for researchers and common readers. We should add that the book requires some knowledge of the topic for in-depth understanding; otherwise, the preliminary chapters should be easily accessible for any reader in the area.

Before ending the preface of this book, we must give thanks to the Almighty, who gave us time to complete this work and kept us fit for work throughout the working period. Special thanks must be given to our family members who supported us working late into the night on many occasions. Special thanks to Richard O'Hanley for his kind support throughout the development of the book. Last but not least, we would like to thank the publication staff for their prompt replies to various queries and cordial cooperation.

Mohssen Mohammed, PhD
Al-Imam Muhammad ibn Saud Islamic University
College of Computer and Information Sciences
Riyadh, Saudi Arabia
Email: m_zin44@hotmail.com

Al-Sakib Khan Pathan, PhD
International Islamic University Malaysia
Jalan Gombak 53100, Kuala Lumpur, Malaysia
Email: sakib@iium.edu.my, sakib.pathan@gmail.com

About the Authors

Mohssen Mohammed received his BSc (Honors) degree in computer science from Computer Man College for Computer Studies (Future University), Khartoum, Sudan, in 2003. In 2006, he received the MSc degree in computer science from the Faculty of Mathematical Sciences—University of Khartoum, Sudan. In 2012, he received a PhD degree in electrical engineering from Cape Town University, South Africa. He has published several papers at top international conferences, such as GLOBECOM and MILCOM. He has served as a technical program committee member in numerous international conferences, like ICSEA 2010, ICNS 2011. He received the University of Cape Town prize for International Scholarship for Academic Merit (2007, 2008, and 2009). From 2005 to 2012, he worked as part of the permanent academic staff at the University of Juba, South Sudan. Currently, he is working as assistant professor in the College of Computer Science and Information Sciences, Al-Imam Muhammad ibn Saud Islamic University, Riyadh, Saudi Arabia. His research interests include network security, especially intrusion detection and prevention systems, honeypots, firewalls, and malware detection methods.

Al-Sakib Khan Pathan received the PhD degree in computer engineering in 2009 from Kyung Hee University, South Korea. He received a BSc degree in computer science and information technology from Islamic University of Technology (IUT), Bangladesh, in 2003. He is currently an assistant professor in the Computer Science Department at the International Islamic University Malaysia (IIUM), Malaysia. Until June 2010, he served as an assistant professor in the Computer Science and Engineering Department in BRAC University, Bangladesh. Prior to holding this position, he worked as a researcher at Networking Lab, Kyung Hee University, South Korea, until August 2009. His research interests include wireless sensor networks, network security, and e-services technologies. He is a recipient of several awards/best paper awards and has several publications in these areas. He has served as a chair, organizing committee member, and technical program committee member in numerous international conferences/workshops like HPCS, ICA3PP, IWCMC, VTC, HPCC, IDCS, and others. He is currently serving as the editor-in-chief of IJIDCS, an area editor of IJCNIS, editor of IJCSE, Inderscience, associate editor of IASTED/ACTA Press IJCA and CCS, guest editor of some special issues of top-ranked journals, and editor/author of five published books. He also serves as a referee of some renowned journals. He is a member of the Institute of Electrical and Electronics Engineers (IEEE) in the United States; the U.S. IEEE Communications Society; IEEE ComSoc Bangladesh Chapter; and several other international organizations.

1

THE FUNDAMENTAL CONCEPTS

1.1 Introduction

Network security comprises a wide range of concepts, provisions, and policies adopted by a network administrator or some management authority to prevent and monitor unauthorized access, misuse, modification, or denial of a computer network and network-accessible resources. It includes various notions of confidentiality, integrity, authentication, authorization, and nonrepudiation. The general understanding may cover very wide areas and multifaceted topics under this umbrella term. However, in this book, we give our notion of network security to describe various aspects of the theme we cover. This chapter covers mainly two parts:

- The importance of security in our lives and network security concepts.
- What we mean by automated signature generation for zero-day polymorphic worms and what is needed to generate signatures for polymorphic worms

1.1.1 Network Security Concepts

This part discusses the following:

- The importance of security in our lives, in computers, and in other fields
- Network security concepts

1.1.1.1 Importance of Security in Our Lives   Security is one of the most important things in our lives. If there is no security guarantee for our lives, our lives become measurable and we are under constant struggle for survival. For example, if we have an apparently rich country but this country faces various crimes such as robbery, theft, murder, and so on at a large scale, then we say such a country cannot guarantee its citizens protection of their lives and thus it becomes a low-class country for living. So, ensuring security in the country is one of the paramount requirements. If security and thus social stability and better life are ensured, then we may be able to develop the resources of the country. Otherwise, it would be too difficult a job to develop the country as constant crimes would hamper the required pace of development. From this premise, we can deduce a principle: In each field, we must provide security before the development initiatives because without security we cannot basically think of proper solutions for various issues associated with the system or the given environment.

This book is about automatic defense against zero-day polymorphic worms in communication networks in the network security field, mainly associated with computer-related topics. In today's world, the Internet has reached the core of many people's lives and provides a huge number of activities for everyday people; now, using the Internet it is even possible to connect people anywhere on the globe for research work, bank transactions, bidding, business, loans, e-meetings, and so on. Such trendy applications and technologies take a good amount of time but are of great help for performing everyday tasks. The reality is that if there is no Internet security, all of these activities would simply fail. For instance, if you have a lot of money in your bank account and like to make bank transactions, then you may have two options to do this:

- Manually through the bank, which may take more than one day to have a full transfer.
- Online, through the Internet, which would take just a few minutes.

If there is no Internet security available to do this transaction, what will be your choice? Definitely, you will choose the manual option because if you choose the second one, you may lose all of your money as hackers may intercept the communication and cause your money to be diverted to illegitimate recipients. So, we must first provide Internet security, then develop new techniques for any such case. Side by side, we also should keep in mind that it is not possible to guarantee 100%

"security" for any system in the world, but we must provide as much security as possible. Taking this point as a rule, we proceed.

1.1.1.2 Network Security Concepts This book is about signature generation for zero-day polymorphic worms. To understand various concepts and schemes presented in this book, we should discuss some preliminary concepts in the network security field. This addresses the following:

- Introduction to network security
- Introduction to vulnerabilities, threats, and attacks
- Attack examples
- Vulnerability analysis
- Analysis tools

1.1.1.2.1 Introduction to Network Security The use of the Internet continues to grow exponentially each and every year. As personal and business-critical applications become more prevalent on the Internet, there are many immediate benefits. However, these network-based applications and services can pose great security risks to individuals as well as to the information resources of companies. In many cases, the rush to become connected comes at the expense of adequate network security. The most important things that should be protected are information that is considered an asset. Without adequate protection or network security, many individuals, businesses, and governments are at risk of losing that asset.

Network security is the process by which digital information assets are protected. The main goals of security are to protect confidentiality, maintain integrity, and ensure availability. With this in mind, it is imperative that all networks must be protected as much as possible from threats and vulnerabilities for a business to achieve its fullest potential.

A threat refers to anything that has the potential to cause serious harm to a computer system. A threat is something that may or may not happen but has the potential to cause serious damage. Threats can lead to attacks on computer systems, networks, and more. Typically, these threats are persistent due to vulnerabilities, which can arise from misconfigured hardware or software, poor network design, inherent technology weaknesses, or end-user carelessness.

We should mention that security risks cannot be eliminated or prevented completely. However, effective risk management and assessment can significantly minimize the existing security risks. An acceptable level of risk depends on how much risk the business is willing to assume. Generally, the risk is worth assuming if the benefits of implementing the risk-reducing safeguards far exceeds the cost.

To protect the network from unauthorized access, we must apply a security model to the network so that it can be protected. In the following, we discuss the general types of security model as viewed in Rufi [1].

1.1.1.2.1.1 General Types of Security Models   With all security designs, some trade-off occurs between user productivity and security measures. The goal of any security design is to provide maximum security with minimum impact on user access and productivity. There are many security measures, such as network data encryption, that do not restrict access and productivity. On the other hand, cumbersome or unnecessarily redundant verification and authorization systems can frustrate users and prevent access to critical network resources. We should know that a network is a tool designed to enhance production. If the security measures that are put in place become too cumbersome, they will actually decrease rather than enhance productivity.

We should mention that networks are used as productivity tools, and they should be designed in a way so that business needs to dictate the security policy. A security policy should not determine how a business operates. As organizations are constantly subject to change, security policies must be systematically updated to reflect new business directions, technological changes, and resource allocations.

There are three general types of security models: open, restrictive, and closed. Figure 1.1 shows a conceptual diagram for these. As shown in the figure, our inclination is often some kind of restriction for either enterprise or application security.

Next, we give more details about these security models.

1.1.1.2.1.2 Open Security Model   Today's Internet and network technologies have expanded to numerous dimensions. When a simple definition like "Internet is the network of networks" is given, it does not tell how complex and dynamic the coverage of networks could

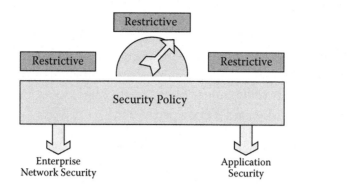

Figure 1.1 Network security policies.

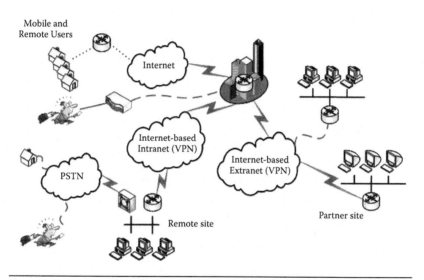

Figure 1.2 Open security model for a dynamic open network model.

be. Figure 1.2 shows a diagram that depicts a typical scenario of such openness and diversity of network technologies bound together under the concept of Internet or other concepts that are derived from it. For instance, the Internet-based intranet or extranet, commonly termed a VPN (virtual private network), is a technology for using the Internet or another intermediate network to connect computers to isolated remote computer networks that would otherwise be inaccessible. Such networks also could include wireless network connectivity. Various remote sites could use other kinds of technologies, such as a PSTN (public switched telephone network), which consists of telephone lines, fiber-optic cables, microwave transmission links, cellular networks, communications satellites, and undersea telephone cables, all interconnected by switching centers, thus allowing any telephone in the world to communicate with any other. Given this dynamism in the open network's infrastructure, a common consensus of security objectives is literally impossible to reach. Here comes the notion of the open security model as we perceive it.

We define an open security model as a setting or set of security policies and principles that could be generally applicable for an open network model as presented in Figure 1.2. The common objective is that all the transactions and communications would meet the basic idea of security: Authenticity will be ensured, authorization will be maintained, data integrity could be verified, confidentiality will be ensured, and nonrepudiation could be confirmed. However, which portion needs what level of security (or security parameters) should be a matter of open standards and requirements.

1.1.1.2.1.3 Closed Security Model   In a closed network, there are a limited number of parties involved, and often there might be some kind of central network administrator who could be given sufficient power to administer the network on various policies. A closed network model is shown in Figure 1.3. In such a setting, it is possible to have strict regulations on who could participate, who could not, the methods of authentication, the mechanisms and protocols

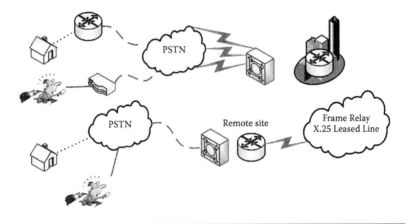

Figure 1.3   A closed network in which a closed security model is applicable.

of communications, the validity of a participating node, and so on. Hence, the closed security model is locally applicable for a particular small portion of a network and more reserved in terms of principles than those in an open network. For instance, in Figure 1.3, any of the PSTNs can be administered with its own set of security rules.

1.1.1.2.1.4 *Restrictive Security Model* The restrictive security model is basically a concept applicable for a network of any size. The idea behind this is a restrictive set of rules that is applied on the network that can be meaningful to various kinds of nodes and players in the network. As a general restriction of security policy, each of the participants can be treated as a legitimate entity unless proven as a rogue unit in the network.

1.1.1.2.2 Trends that Affect Security There are many trends that affect security [2]:

- Increased network attacks
- Increased sophistication of attacks
- Increased dependence on the network
- Lack of trained personnel
- Lack of awareness
- Lack of security policies
- Wireless access
- Legislation
- Litigation

1.1.1.2.3 Why Do We Need Internet Security? Each time we communicate over the Internet using a computer or any electronic device, security risks are involved in the event. If a proper protection mechanism is absent, the level of risk increases. Thus, with the use of appropriate Internet security, the computer's Internet account and files are protected from any kind of mischief and intrusion by unknown/illegitimate users. Basically, Internet security works well by protecting the computer through passwords, changing file permissions, and backing up the computer's data.

When it comes to the use of various IT (information technology) systems, Internet security is considered the most important parameter to business users because it makes them feel secure and confident against any criminal cyberattacks knowing that when the IT system is attacked, it can be damaging to the business. This implies that business users need to be vigilant about any attack that may come their way.

Before any Internet security solution can fully work, it should be thoroughly checked and should pass in some major aspects, like penetration testing, intrusion detection, and incidence response. Also, it must legally comply with the enforced law of the country.

1.1.1.2.4 Malicious Programs   In a computer system, there might be various kinds of programs running. Of those, some may be useful, and some may be deliberately written to cause harm. Again, there are a number of useful programs that contain features with hidden malicious intentions. Let us explore some of the programs that may have malicious features [3]; also, sometimes they could be used for positive purposes, like finding loopholes, flaws, and vulnerabilities in the system:

- **Malware** is the general term used for any malicious software. It is commonly used to damage or infiltrate a computer program or any other programmable device and system, such as the home or office computer system, networks, mobile phones, personal digital assistants (PDAs), automated devices, robots, or any other devices that are sufficiently complex.
- **Viruses** are programs that enable replication of their own structure or effect by incorporating themselves into the existing files or structures on a penetrated computer. Moreover, a virus usually contains a malicious or humorous payload designed to threaten or alter the actions or data of the host system or device without consent. The common example of it is by deleting or corrupting an owner's information.
- **Trojan horses** or Trojans are programs that steal information, alter it, or cause difficult problems on the computer or other programmable system or device by just pretending to do nothing.
- **Spyware** is a type of program that secretly keeps an eye on the keystrokes or any other activity on the computer system and reports the information to other parties without consent.

- **Worms** are programs that replicate themselves on an extensive computer network. Thus, worms also perform some malicious acts that can eventually affect the whole system of the economy.
- **Bots** are programs that use the resource of a computer system by taking it over in a network without consent and transmitting that information to others who control the bots.

To protect the computer or any other programmable device/system, antivirus programs and Internet security programs are commonly used to guard against any kind of malware. Such programs are commonly used to identify and extinguish viruses.

1.1.1.3 Introduction to Vulnerabilities, Threats, and Attacks   To fully understand Internet worm detection, we must know the following terms well:

Asset: People, property, and information [4]. People may include employees and customers along with other invited persons, such as contractors or guests. Property assets consist of both tangible and intangible items that can be assigned a value. Intangible assets include reputation and proprietary information. Information may include databases, software code, critical company records, and many other intangible items (i.e., an asset is what we are trying to protect).

Vulnerability: Weaknesses or gaps in a security program that can be exploited by threats to gain unauthorized access to an asset (i.e., a vulnerability is a weakness or gap in our protection efforts).

Threat: Anything that can exploit a vulnerability, intentionally or accidentally, and obtain, damage, or destroy an asset [5] (i.e., a threat is what we are trying to protect against).

Attack: An attack is a deliberate trial or attempt by any entity to cause harm to any system exploiting the discovered (or available) vulnerabilities.

Next, we discuss three terms—vulnerability, threat, and attack—with more details as defined in Reference 1.

1.1.1.3.1 Vulnerability   Security vulnerability is among the foremost concerns for network and security professionals as it provides a critical threat to the efficiency and effectiveness of an organization. It is extremely important to identify network security vulnerabilities proactively before a hacker does it to plan an attack on the organization. Network security vulnerabilities are significant threats to control measures of an organization.

It is extremely critical for organizations to focus on standardization and management compliance efforts. Network security vulnerability needs to be identified and removed to bridge the gap between an organization's current and desired stage. Organizations often use vulnerability scanners to identify vulnerabilities of their host systems and network assets. A vulnerability scanner identifies not only hosts and open ports on those hosts but also associated vulnerabilities on them.

Therefore, network security vulnerabilities are critical for identification by an administrator. Secure Auditor is an award winning network vulnerability assessment software used by a wide range of customers. It is a network vulnerability scanner that identifies network security vulnerabilities in information assets. It scans your network to detect, assess, and correct security vulnerabilities. Network security scanning by Secure Auditor ensures compliance and provides solutions for vulnerability issues, patch management, and network auditing.

Networks are typically plagued by one or all of three primary vulnerabilities or weaknesses:

- Technological weaknesses
- Configuration weaknesses
- Security policy weaknesses

The following examines each of these weaknesses.

1.1.1.3.1.1 Technological Weaknesses   There are many intrinsic security weaknesses in computer and network technologies. These include Transmission Control Protocol/Internet Protocol (TCP/IP) weaknesses, operating system weaknesses, and network equipment weaknesses. Table 1.1 describes these three kinds of weaknesses.

1.1.1.3.1.2 Configuration Weaknesses   Network administrators or network engineers need to learn what the configuration weaknesses are and correctly configure their computing and network devices. Table 1.2 lists some common configuration weaknesses.

Table 1.1 Network Security Weaknesses

WEAKNESS	DESCRIPTION
TCP/IP protocol weaknesses	HTTP (Hypertext Transfer Protocol), FTP (File Transfer Protocol), and ICMP (Internet Control Message Protocol) are inherently insecure.
	Simple Network Management Protocol (SNMP), Simple Mail Transfer Protocol (SMTP), and SYN floods are related to the inherently insecure structure on which TCP was designed.
Operating system weaknesses	The UNIX, Linux, Macintosh, Windows NT, 9x, 2K, XP, and OS/2 operating systems all have security problems that must be addressed.
	These are documented in the CERT archives at http://www.cert.org
Network equipment weaknesses	Various types of network equipment, such as routers, firewalls, and switches, have security weaknesses that must be recognized and protected against. These weaknesses include the following: • Password protection • Lack of authentication • Routing protocols • Firewall holes

Table 1.2 Configuration Weaknesses

WEAKNESS	HOW THE WEAKNESS IS EXPLOITED
Unsecured user accounts	User account information might be transmitted insecurely across the network, exposing usernames and passwords to snoopers.
System accounts with easily guessed passwords	This common problem is the result of poorly selected and easily guessed user passwords.
Misconfigured Internet services	A common problem is to turn on JavaScript in Web browsers, enabling attacks by way of hostile JavaScript when accessing untrusted sites. IIS (Internet Information Services), Apache, FTP, and Terminal Services also pose problems.
Unsecured default settings within products	Many products have default settings that enable security holes.
Misconfigured network equipment	Misconfigurations of the equipment itself can cause significant security problems. For example, misconfigured access lists, routing protocols, or SNMP community strings can open large security holes. Misconfigured or lack of encryption and remote-access controls can also cause significant security issues, as can the practice of leaving ports open on a switch (which could allow the introduction of noncompany computing equipment).

1.1.1.3.1.3 Security Policy Weaknesses   Security policy weaknesses can create unforeseen security threats. Many security risks can be present in the network if users do not follow the security policy properly or the policy itself is weak. Table 1.3 lists some common security policy weaknesses and how those weaknesses are exploited.

Table 1.3 Security Policy Weaknesses

WEAKNESS	HOW THE WEAKNESS IS EXPLOITED
Unwritten policy	An unwritten policy cannot be consistently applied or enforced.
Politics	Political battles and turf wars can make it difficult to implement a consistent security policy.
Lack of continuity	Poorly chosen, easily cracked, or default passwords can allow unauthorized access to the network.
Logical access controls not applied	Inadequate monitoring and auditing allow attacks and unauthorized use to continue, wasting company resources. This could result in legal action or termination against IT technicians, IT management, or even company leadership who allow these unsafe conditions to persist. Lack of careful and controlled auditing can also make it hard to enforce policy and to stand up to legal challenges for "wrongful termination" and suits against the organization.
Software and hardware installation and changes do not follow policy	Unauthorized changes to the network topology or installation of unapproved applications create security holes.
Disaster recovery plan nonexistent	The lack of a disaster recovery plan allows chaos, panic, and confusion to occur when someone attacks the enterprise.

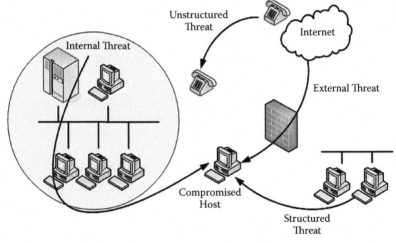

Figure 1.4 Variety of threats.

1.1.1.3.2 Threats There are four primary classes of threats to network security, as Figure 1.4 depicts. The list that follows describes each class of threat in more detail [1]:

- **Unstructured threats:** An unstructured threat refers to a computer attack from novice hackers, often called script kiddies, who use software created by more advanced hackers to gain information from or access to a system or launch a denial-of-service (DoS) attack. Unstructured threats are the most prevalent threats to a company or organization's computer system.

- **Structured threats:** Unlike unstructured threats, structured threats come from hackers who are more highly motivated and technically competent. These people know system vulnerabilities and can understand and develop exploit code and scripts. They understand, develop, and use sophisticated hacking techniques to penetrate unsuspecting businesses. These groups are often involved with the major fraud and theft cases reported to law enforcement agencies.

- **External threats:** External threats come from individuals or organizations working outside a company. They do not have authorized access to the computer systems or network. They work their way into a network mainly from the Internet or dial-up access servers.

- **Internal threats:** Internal threats occur when someone has authorized access to the network with either an account on a server or physical access to the network. According to the Federal Bureau of Investigation (FBI), internal access and misuse account for 60 percent to 80 percent of reported incidents.

As the types of threats, attacks, and exploits have evolved, various terms have been coined to describe different groups of individuals. Some of the most common terms are as follows:

- *Hacker*: Hacker is a general term that has historically been used to describe a computer programming expert. More recently, this term is commonly used in a negative way to describe an individual who attempts to gain unauthorized access to network resources with malicious intent.

- *Cracker*: Cracker is the term that is generally regarded as the more accurate word used to describe an individual who attempts to gain unauthorized access to network resources with malicious intent.

- *Phreaker*: A phreaker is an individual who manipulates the phone network to cause it to perform a function that is normally not allowed. A common goal of phreaking is breaking into the phone network, usually through a pay phone, to make free long-distance calls.

- *Spammer*: A spammer is an individual who sends large numbers of unsolicited e-mail messages. Spammers often use viruses to take control of home computers to use these computers to send out their bulk messages.
- *Phisher*: A phisher uses e-mail or other means in an attempt to trick others into providing sensitive information, such as credit card numbers or passwords. The phisher masquerades as a trusted party that would have a legitimate need for the sensitive information.
- *White hat*: White hat is a term used to describe individuals who use their abilities to find vulnerabilities in systems or networks and then report these vulnerabilities to the owners of the system so that they can be fixed.
- *Black hat*: Black hat is another term for individuals who use their knowledge of computer systems to break into the systems or networks that they are not authorized to use.

1.1.1.3.3 Attacks   There are four primary classes of attacks:

- Reconnaissance
- Access
- Denial of service
- Worms, viruses, and Trojan horses

This section covers each attack class in more detail [1, 6].

- **Reconnaissance:** Reconnaissance attacks are used to gather information about a target network or system. Such attacks may seem harmless at the time and may be overlooked by security administrators as "network noise" or pestering behavior, but it is usually the information gained through reconnaissance attacks that is used in subsequent access or DoS attacks.

    Several means may be used to gather information about an organization and could include automated and manual technological attacks as well as human social attacks. Examples might include Internet Control Message Protocol (ICMP) ping sweeps against a network or Simple Network

Management Protocol (SNMP) walking techniques to gather network map and device configuration data. Likewise, application-level scanners could be used to search for vulnerabilities such as Web server CGI (Common Gateway Interface) or ASP (Active Server Pages) weaknesses.

No specific damage may be caused by the reconnaissance attack, but it is akin to burglars staking out a neighborhood, watching for times of inactivity, and occasionally testing windows and doors for access.

Reconnaissance attacks are quite common and should be considered a serious threat to an organization as they may give potential attackers the information required to perform access or DoS attacks.

- **Access:** System access is the ability of an unauthorized intruder to gain access to a device for which the intruder does not have an account or a password. Entering or accessing systems to which one does not have authority to access usually involves running a hack, script, or tool that exploits a known vulnerability of the system or application being attacked.
- **Denial of Service (DoS):** A DoS implies that an attacker disables or corrupts networks, systems, or services with the intent to deny services to intended users. DoS attacks involve either crashing the system or slowing it to the point that it is unusable. But, DoS can also be as simple as deleting or corrupting information. In most cases, performing the attack simply involves running a hack or script. The attacker does not need prior access to the target because a way to access it is all that is usually required. For these reasons, DoS attacks are the most feared.
- **Worms, Viruses, and Trojan Horses:** Malicious software is inserted onto a host to damage a system; corrupt a system; replicate itself; or deny services or access to networks, systems, or services. It can also allow sensitive information to be copied or echoed to other systems.

Trojan horses can be used to ask the user to enter sensitive information in a commonly trusted screen. For example, an attacker might log in to a Windows box and run a program that looks like the true Windows log-on screen, prompting a user to type his or her username and password. The program would then send the information to the attacker and then give the Windows error for a bad password. The user would then log out, and the correct Windows log-on screen would appear; the user is none the wiser that the password has just been stolen.

1.1.1.4 Attack Examples   There are many types of attacks that are used today. This section covers some of those in details as described in Rufi [1].

1.1.1.4.1 Reconnaissance Attacks   Reconnaissance attacks can consist of the following:

- Packet sniffers
- Port scans
- Ping sweeps
- Internet information queries

1.1.1.4.2 Access Attacks   Access attacks exploit known vulnerabilities in authentication services, File Transfer Protocol (FTP) services, and Web services to gain entry to Web accounts, confidential databases, and other sensitive information.

Access attacks can consist of the following:

- Password attacks
- Trust exploitation
- Port redirection
- Man-in-the-middle attacks
- Social engineering
- Phishing

1.1.1.4.3 Denial-of-Service Attacks   The following are some examples of common DoS threats:

- *Ping of death*: This attack modifies the IP portion of the header, indicating that there are more data in the packet than there actually are, causing the receiving system to crash.
- *SYN flood attack*: This attack randomly opens many TCP ports, tying up the network equipment or computer with so many

bogus requests that sessions are denied to others. This attack is accomplished with protocol analyzers or other programs.

- *Packet fragmentation and reassembly*: This attack exploits a buffer-overrun bug in hosts or internetworking equipment.
- *E-mail bombs*: Programs can send bulk e-mails to individuals, lists, or domains, monopolizing e-mail services.
- *CPU (central processing unit) hogging*: These attacks constitute programs such as Trojan horses or viruses that tie up CPU cycles, memory, or other resources.
- *Malicious applets*: These attacks are Java, JavaScript, or ActiveX programs that act as Trojan horses or viruses to cause destruction or tie up computer resources.
- *Misconfiguring routers*: Misconfiguring routers to reroute traffic disables Web traffic.
- *The chargen attack*: This attack establishes a connection between user datagram protocol (UDP) services, producing a high character output. The host chargen service is connected to the echo service on the same or different systems, causing congestion on the network with echoed chargen traffic.
- *Out-of-band attacks such as WinNuke*: These attacks send out-of-band data to port 139 on Windows 95 or Windows NT machines. The attacker needs the victim's IP address to launch this attack.

1.1.1.4.4 Distributed Denial-of-Service Attacks   Distributed denial-of-service (DDoS) attacks are designed to saturate network links with spurious data. These data can overwhelm an Internet link, causing legitimate traffic to be dropped. DDoS uses attack methods similar to standard DoS attacks but operates on a much larger scale. Typically, hundreds or thousands of attack points attempt to overwhelm a target.

Examples of DDoS attacks include the following:

- Smurf
- Tribe Flood Network (TFN)
- Stacheldraht

1.1.1.5 Vulnerability Analysis   Before adding new security solutions to an existing network, you need to identify the current state of the network and organizational practices to verify their current compliance with the requirements. This analysis can help us with the opportunity to identify possible improvements and the potential need to redesign a part of the system or to rebuild a part of the system from scratch to satisfy the requirements. This analysis can be broken down into the following steps [1]:

1. Policy identification
2. Network analysis
3. Host analysis

The rest of this section investigates each of these steps in more depth.

1.1.1.5.1 Policy Identification   If a security policy exists, the designer should analyze it to identify the security requirements, which will influence the design of the perimeter solution. Initially, the designer should examine two basic areas of the policy:

- The policy should identify the assets that require protection. This helps the designer provide the correct level of protection for sensitive computing resources and to identify the flow of sensitive data in the network.
- The policy should identify possible attackers. This gives the designer insight into the level of trust assigned to internal and external users, ideally identified by more specific categories such as business partners, customers of an organization, and outsourcing IT partners.

The designer should also be able to evaluate whether the policy was developed using correct risk assessment procedures. For example, did the policy development include all relevant risks for the organization and not overlook important threats? The designer should also reevaluate the policy mitigation procedures to determine whether those satisfactorily mitigate expected threats. This ensures that the policy, which the designer will work with, is current and complete.

Organizations that need a high level of security assurance will require defense-in-depth mechanisms to be deployed to avoid single points of failure. The designer also needs to work with the organization to determine how much investment in security measures is acceptable for the resources that require protection.

The result of policy analysis will be as follows:

- The evaluation of policy correctness and completeness
- Identification of possible policy improvements, which need to be made before the security implementation stage

1.1.1.5.2 Network Analysis Many industry best practices, tools, guides, and training are available to help secure network devices. These include tools from Cisco, such as AutoSecure and Cisco Output Interpreter, and from numerous Web resources. Third-party resources include the U.S. National Security Agency (NSA) Cisco Router Security Recommendation Guides and the Center for Internet Security (CIS) Router Audit Tool (RAT) for auditing Cisco router and PIX Security Appliance configuration files [7].

1.1.1.5.3 Host Analysis The hosts that are on the network need to be considered when designing a network security solution. Determining the role in the network of each host will help decide the steps that will be taken to secure it. The network could have many user workstations and multiple servers that need to be accessed from both inside and outside the network.

The types of applications and services that are running on the hosts need to be identified, and any network services and ports that are not necessary should be disabled or blocked. All operating systems should be patched as needed. Antivirus software should be installed and kept current. Some servers may be assigned static routable IP addresses to be accessible from the Internet. These hosts in particular should be monitored for signs of malicious activity.

1.1.1.6 Analysis Tools There are many tools that are available that can help us to determine vulnerabilities in endpoint devices, such as network hosts and servers. You can obtain these tools from either the company that creates the operating system or a third party. In many cases, these tools are free. Here, we discuss some of the most commonly used analysis tools.

1.1.1.6.1 Knoppix STD Knoppix Security Tools Distribution (STD) is a Linux LiveCD distribution that contains many valuable security tools. The LiveCD is a bootable CD-ROM that contains the

Linux operating system, along with software applications, that can be run from memory without installation on the hard drive. After the LiveCD is ejected from the CD-ROM drive, the system can be rebooted to return to the original operating system. Knoppix STD contains many useful features, such as the following:

- Encryption tools
- Forensics tools
- Firewall tools
- Intrusion detection tools
- Network utilities
- Password tools
- Packet sniffers
- Vulnerability assessment tools
- Wireless tools

Many additional versions of LiveCD are available. If one distribution does not support a particular system or piece of hardware, it might be necessary to try another distribution. Most LiveCD releases are available as free downloads that the end user can burn to a CD.

1.1.1.6.2 Microsoft Baseline Security Analyzer   You can use the Microsoft Baseline Security Analyzer (MBSA) to scan hosts running Windows 2000, Windows XP, and Windows Server 2003 operating systems to determine potential security risks. MBSA scans for common system misconfigurations and missing security updates. MBSA includes both a graphical interface and a command line interface (CLI) that can perform local or remote scans. After a system scan, the MBSA provides a report outlining potential vulnerabilities and the steps required to correct them. This tool is available as a free download from Microsoft.

1.1.2 Automated Signature Generation for Zero-day Polymorphic Worms

In Section 1.1.1, we explained the importance of security in each relevant field and explored various concepts in the network security field. Now, we explain what we mean by "automated signature generation for zero-day polymorphic worms" and what we need to generate signatures for polymorphic worms.

1.1.2.1 Automated Signature Generation for Zero-day Polymorphic Worms

A. What is a signature? A human being has many features, like color, type of hair, weight, height, types of eyes, and so on. If you want to make a security system to identify humans, which human features would you use? Some fixed features of humans may be available to you, like DNA, fingerprints, or the like because someone cannot change these fixed features but might be able to change other features. These fixed features are called signatures (more specifically here, human signatures). Similar to this idea, we have almost the same concept in the field of Internet worm detection. To identify Internet worms, we must obtain fixed features in their payloads that are called worm signatures.

B. What are Internet worms? An Internet worm is a computer worm that is a stand-alone malware computer program that replicates itself in order to spread to other computers, without requiring any human intervention, by sending copies of its code in network packets and ensuring the code is executed by the computers that receive it. Internet worms can be used to incur delays in a network, steal credit card information, and for other damaging activities [8, 9]. A polymorphic worm is a computer worm that changes its payloads in every infection attempt to avoid detection by security systems [10].

C. What are zero-day polymorphic worms? Zero-day polymorphic worms or zero-day attacks mean unknown polymorphic worms or attacks (never faced before or never understood before). This book especially focuses on ways of generating signatures for zero-day polymorphic worms automatically without any human interaction.

1.1.2.2 What Do We Need to Generate Signatures for Zero-day Polymorphic Worms? Automated signature generation for zero-day polymorphic worms is a very challenging task that needs extensive background and experience in this field. If you are a PhD student or researcher and would like to work in this field, you must follow these two steps:

- First, you must collect zero-day polymorphic worm payloads.
- Then, you should generate signatures for the collected polymorphic worms.

Next, we present some more details of these steps; throughout the rest of the book, we explore these further. We place these points here just to highlight the difficulty and challenges faced in working in this area:

- First, you must collect zero-day polymorphic worm payloads. To do so, you should come up with a new method of collecting zero-day polymorphic worms, which is no easy task. To find a new method, you should read well and grasp these topics:
  - Internet worms
  - Computer networking: routers, firewalls, and the like
  - Honeypots
- Intrusion detection and prevention systems (IDPSs)

After you have read and understood these topics well, you should search for related works that have already been done in this area. Only after having sufficient background information and in-depth knowledge will it be possible to propose a new method of collecting zero-day polymorphic worms.

- After the previous step (i.e., having collected zero-day polymorphic worms and gaining sufficient knowledge), you should generate signatures for these polymorphic worms. To do so, you must have a sound background in various relevant algorithms (e.g., string-matching algorithms, supervised machine learning algorithms, unsupervised machine learning algorithms, and so on). If all these algorithms are understood well, you should read more related works that have been done in this area (regarding algorithms). Then, you should try to develop new algorithms to generate signatures for zero-day polymorphic worms.

1.2 Our Experience and This Book's Objective

From our experiences in this field, we so far have not found a single book that covers all the relevant topics associated with automated signature generation for zero-day polymorphic worms. In fact, we have found that often researchers waste their time simply trying to know what they should read and understand to generate signatures for zero-day polymorphic worms. That is why this book aims at putting all critical information together. Subsequent chapters explain various aspects and facets of this field and include practical examples whenever possible or relevant.

References

1. Rufi, A. *Network Security 1 and 2 Companion Guide* (Cisco Networking Academy). Indianapolis, IN: Cisco Press, October 5, 2006.
2. Lee, H. *CCNP Security (V1.0): Module 1—Modern Network Security Threats*. Indianapolis, IN: Cisco Academic Press, pp. 1–57. Available at http://ebookbrowse.com/ccnp-security-mod01-v1-0-modern-network-security-threats-pdf-d337996243 (accessed August 12, 2012).
3. Douglas, T.L. Why do we need Internet security? Available at http://ezinearticles.com/?Why-Do-We-Need-Internet-Security?&id=4193610 (accessed August 11, 2012).
4. Karim, H.V. *Strategic Security Management: A Risk Assessment Guide for Decision Makers*. Oxford, UK: Butterworth-Heinemann, October 26, 2006.
5. Threat Analysis Group. Threat, vulnerability, risk—commonly mixed up terms. Available at http://www.threatanalysis.com/blog/?p=43 (accessed August 11, 2012).
6. Sweeney, M., Baumrucker, C.T., Burton, J.D., and Dubrawsky, I. *Cisco Security Professional's Guide to Secure Intrusion Detection Systems*. Waltham, MA: Syngress, November 20, 2003.
7. Network analysis. Available at http://itt.century.edu/Cisco/SC/en_NS1_v20/en-knet-20EVFmBZeHAAMmcVYw/ccna3theme/ccna3/CHAPID=knet-EVFmBZcYAQIBR0SQ/RLOID = knet-EVFHgn-JABQUlAwUQ/RIOID=knet-EVFHgnIUCAVoIQFw/knet/EVFmBZ-cYAQIBR0SQ/resourcecontent.html (accessed August 12, 2012).
8. Costa, M. End-to-End Containment of Internet Worm Epidemics. PhD thesis, Churchill College, University of Cambridge, October 2006.
9. Sellke, S.H., Shroff, N.B., and Bagchi, S. Modeling and automated containment of worms. *IEEE Transactions on Dependable and Secure Computing*, 2008, Volume 5, Issue 2, pp. 71–86.
10. Newsome, J., Karp, B., and Song, D. Polygraph: Automatically generating signatures for polymorphic worms. *Proceedings of the 2005 IEEE Symposium on Security and Privacy*, May 2005, pp. 226–241.

2

COMPUTER NETWORKING

2.1 Computer Technologies

The computer, an electronic device, was first invented as a programmable machine designed to sequentially and automatically perform a sequence of arithmetic or logical operations, which were generally termed *computing*. The very first device called a *computer* was of huge size, occupying the space of a room in a building. With the passage of time, the size has shrunk, but the power of computing has increased to a great extent. Today, computer technologies not only mean the technologies associated with formal computing machines, but also multifaceted technical innovations, equipment, methods, and applications. A wide range of technical devices in our daily life use computing power now. For example, a cell phone could also have a calculator that can perform advanced scientific calculations like a personal computer. Operating systems are also used in smart phones and similar devices. Even a watch, a car, a door locking system, an elevator, and many other everyday devices could have computing capability. Hence, today's computer technologies mean a vast range of technologies that use computing power for their daily operations.

When it comes to the notion of using actual computers in a system, major computer technologies include the conceptual subject areas: computer networking, software engineering, artificial intelligence, database management system, supply chain management system, wireless communications, signal processing, numerical computations, number theory, quantum computing, computer security, cryptography, bioinspired computing, computer architecture, pervasive computing, and other emerging technologies like cloud computing, future Internet (FI), Internet of things (IoT), near-field communication (NFC), and so on. In this chapter, we briefly look into the basic issues of computer networking. Based on the structure of the networks, the strategies of dealing with worms should be different; hence, we need to know these or revise our understanding.

2.2 Network Topology

Network topology means the pattern or the model by which various elements of a network are interconnected. The elements could be computers, switches, routers, hubs, printers, phones, and other communications devices. For the interconnection, a wireless or wired medium could be used. Network topologies may be either physical or logical. Physical topology is defined by the physical design of a network, including the devices, location, and cable installation. Logical topology refers to how data are actually transmitted or circulated in a network. Physical topology could be understood by examining the structure or formation of the network; however, for understanding the logical topology, we need to understand which path the data follow while traveling through the network links. In other words, physical topology is the actual visible model of the network, and logical topology is the conceptual connectivity pattern of the communications devices.

In broad terms, mainly four topologies are recognized: (1) bus topology, (2) ring topology, (3) star topology, and (4) mesh topology. However, in this book, we note a wide range of topologies that should be clearly distinguished without resorting to grouping them under the banner of any of the four mentioned categories. Instead of using the term *hybrid topology*, we prefer to allow the readers to clearly identify some topologies [1] that should be studied distinctively in any form of computer networking. It should be noted that both physical and logical topologies are considered here, and we do not classify the mentioned terms under physical or logical as some of them contain both notions in the structure and in the operational method.

2.2.1 Point-to-Point Topology

When two endpoints are directly connected with a permanent link, it is called a point-to-point topology. Switched point-to-point topologies are the basic model of conventional telephony. Figure 2.1 shows a diagram of point-to-point topology.

Figure 2.1 Point-to-point topology.

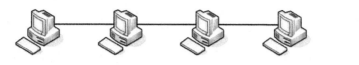

Figure 2.2 Daisy-chain topology.

2.2.2 Daisy-Chain Topology

Daisy chaining means connecting a device with another device in a sequence. In this topology, we basically extend the point-to-point topology by adding a number of devices (computers, switches, or other items) in a series. Figure 2.2 illustrates the daisy-chain topology. Such topology basically could take two shapes: linear and ring. Ring qualifies for being counted as a separate topology, which we present further in the chapter. In fact, many topologies are slight variants of other topologies, or the basic topologies are often present in the other complex topologies. Daisy chaining is also the basic method used for the bus topology (which is mentioned in the next section).

2.2.3 Bus (Point-to-Multipoint) Topology

When seen from the physical topology perspective, the bus topology is one of the major ones. A bus (or sometimes called a terminated bus) topology uses a single cable to which all of the nodes are connected. The cable is termed the *bus*. In the bus topology, as there is only one communication channel available, all the participating nodes compete with each other for the available bandwidth. In such a topology, a break of the cable at any point may disconnect the rest of the network. Figure 2.3 shows a bus topology.

2.2.4 Distributed Bus Topology

The distributed bus topology is a complex form of bus topology in which there is a main cable that connects several branch cables. It has

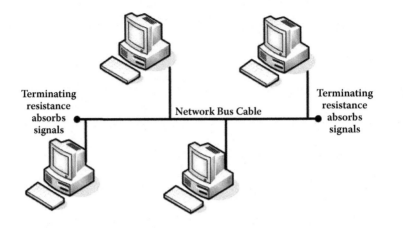

Figure 2.3   Bus topology.

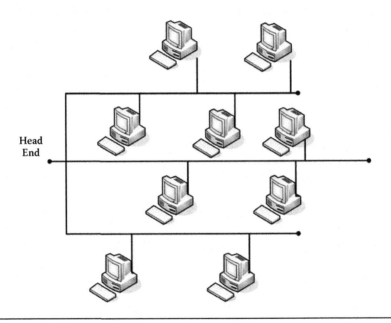

Figure 2.4   Distributed bus topology.

a head end, and each branch is terminated with absorber resistances. Figure 2.4 shows a diagram of such a topology. It should be noted that such a topology is susceptible to a single point of failure, and breaking the main cable disconnects the major portions of the network. In some scenarios, the topology could be useful.

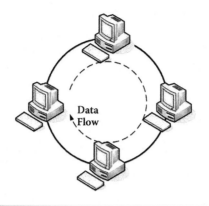

Figure 2.5   Ring topology.

2.2.5 Ring Topology

The ring topology uses daisy chaining of the devices in a circular fashion. The data within the topology flow circularly as shown in Figure 2.5. Each node in this topology checks a packet, and if it is not destined for itself, it forwards the packet to the next node. For a small-size network, this topology is suitable; in that case, it is relatively more robust than the bus topology.

2.2.6 Dual-Ring Topology

In a dual-ring topology, two concentric rings connect each node in a network instead of one network ring that is used in a ring topology. The redundant secondary ring in a dual-ring topology is used as a backup in case the primary ring fails. In these configurations, data move in opposite directions around the rings. Such a topology gives flexibility and robustness, so that each ring can operate independently of the other. When the primary one fails, the secondary ring is activated as shown in Figure 2.6.

2.2.7 Star Topology

In the star topology, there is a central entity that connects all the nodes with direct links. Figure 2.7 shows a diagram of the star topology. In fact, this is one of the topologies in which fault detection is the easiest. The number of node connections could be increased by increasing the connection links from the central entity. However,

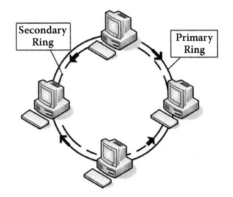

Figure 2.6 Dual-ring topology.

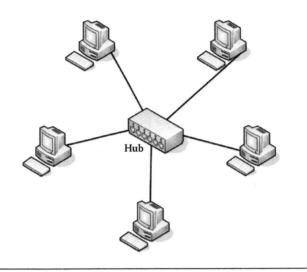

Figure 2.7 Star topology.

the scalability depends on the allowed limit of the link allowed with the central node. This topology is susceptible to a single point of failure as collapse of the hub (e.g., in Figure 2.7) breaks the entire network. However, a broken link with any node does not affect the link with another node, which is an advantage of this structure.

2.2.8 Star-Wired Bus Topology

In a star-wired bus topology, the nodes are connected with some kind of central entity in a star topology fashion; however, the difference is

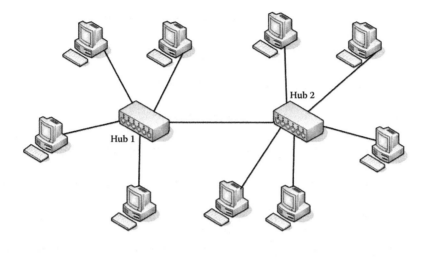

Figure 2.8   Star-wired bus topology.

that the central entities are again connected with each other. This is basically an extension of the star topology in a bus fashion to cover long distances. Figure 2.8 shows this topology.

2.2.9 Star-Wired Ring Topology

The star-wired ring topology physically looks like the star topology. However, the difference is that the data flow is in a circular fashion like that in a ring. Hence, the logical topology works like a ring topology. Figure 2.9 illustrates the star-wired ring topology; the dotted lines show the data flow through the central entity and the participating end nodes.

2.2.10 Mesh Topology

In a perfect mesh topology, each node is connected with every other node. This structure is robust and could sustain faults in multiple connections or links. Also, if one node goes down, other nodes could still communicate with multiple paths. A partial mesh topology has relatively fewer connections and a subset of a full mesh. Figure 2.10a and Figure 2.10b show the full-mesh and partial-mesh topologies, respectively.

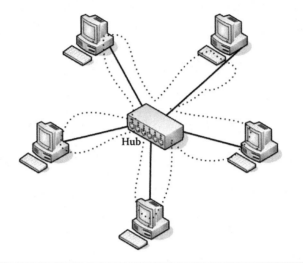

Figure 2.9   Star-wired ring topology.

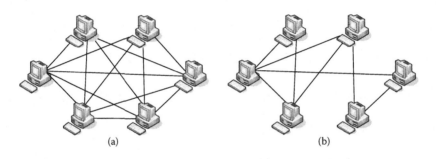

(a)   (b)

Figure 2.10   (a) Full-mesh topology; (b) partial-mesh topology.

2.2.11 Hierarchical or Tree Topology

In a hierarchical or tree topology, there are several levels of the connected components or the nodes. The higher node connects several nodes in the lower levels. A tree topology can be viewed as several star topologies connected in a hierarchical manner. Figure 2.11 shows a diagram of the tree topology. Of course, the number of connected nodes in the subsequent levels could be different, but overall the nodes have several layers where they exist, and the higher-level nodes support the lower-level nodes. The drawback of this topology is that if a higher-level node is down, the lower-level nodes depending on that higher-level node become disconnected from the main network.

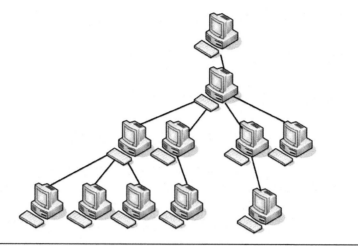

Figure 2.11   Hierarchical or tree topology.

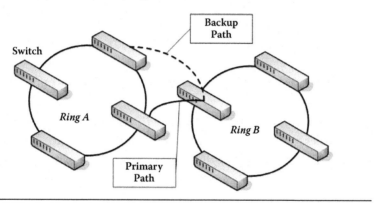

Figure 2.12   Dual-homing topology.

2.2.12 Dual-Homing Topology

The dual-homing topology adds reliability by allowing a device to be connected to the network by way of two independent connection points (points of attachment). One access point provides the operating connection; the other implements a standby or backup connection activated in the event of operating connection failure.

A dual-homing switch, with two attachments into the network, offers two independent media paths and two upstream switch connections. Loss of the link signal on the operating port connected upstream indicates a fault in that path, and traffic is quickly moved to the standby connection, accomplishing fault recovery. Figure 2.12 shows a diagram of the dual-homing topology.

After discussing various networking topologies, in the following sections we discuss some core definitions and terminologies that are essential for computer networking. Based on this knowledge, in further chapters we elaborate different aspects of dealing with worm technologies and their prevention mechanisms.

2.3 Internet Protocol

A protocol is the set of rules and principles for how the electronic devices communicate with each other by exchanging messages. Protocols may include various aspects like signaling, authentication, error detection, and error correction capabilities. The Internet Protocol, known in short as IP, is the protocol by which data are transmitted from one computing device to another over the Internet. Each computing device is termed a host or node, which is assigned at least one IP address that uniquely identifies it from all other computers or computing devices on the Internet.

The IP supports unique addressing for computers on a network. Most networks use the IP version 4 (IPv4) standard that features IP addresses 4 bytes (32 bits) in length. The newer IP version 6 (IPv6) standard features addresses 16 bytes (128 bits) in length. It should be noted here that IPv5 [2] was an experimental protocol based mostly on the OSI (Open System Interconnection) model that never materialized.

The IP is basically a connectionless protocol, which means that there is no continuous connection between the endpoints that are communicating. In this case, each traveling packet is treated as an independent unit of data without any relation to any other unit of data. The packets then are ordered the right way because of the TCP (Transmission Control Protocol), the connection-oriented protocol that keeps track of the packet sequence in a message. The TCP is discussed in the next section.

2.4 Transmission Control Protocol

The TCP is one of the core protocols of the IP Suite. TCP is one of the two original components of the suite, which complements the IP; therefore, the entire suite is commonly referred to as TCP/IP. TCP provides reliable, ordered delivery of a stream of bytes from a program on one computer to another program on another computer. This is the protocol on which major Internet applications such as the World Wide Web (WWW), e-mail, remote administration, and file transfer rely. Other applications, which do not require reliable data stream service, may use the User Datagram Protocol (UDP), which provides a datagram service that emphasizes reduced latency over reliability.

2.5 IP Routers

A router is a device that is used to route packets based on their logical addresses (host-to-host addressing). It connects LANs (local-area networks) and WANs (wide-area networks). Each router has a routing table that helps for decision making about choosing routes for packets that it handles. A routing table could be dynamic, which allows updates using various routing protocols. Figure 2.13 shows the use of a router in an internetworking scenario.

2.6 Ethernet Switch

An Ethernet switch or network switch is used to connect multiple computers with each other. The connection with a switch looks similar to an Ethernet hub in terms of appearance as it connects a LAN, but it has some kind of intelligence involved in the mechanism. A switch not only receives data packets but also has the ability to inspect them before allowing them to pass to the next connected computer. So, a switch is able to figure out the source and the contents of the data and identify the appropriate destination. As a result of this uniqueness, it sends the data to the relevant connected system only, thereby using less bandwidth at high-performance rates.

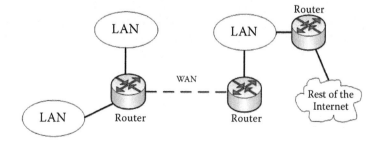

Figure 2.13   Router.

2.7 IP Routing and Routing Table

Internet Protocol routing is the process of selecting a path for network packets based on the destination IP addresses. Routing occurs at a sending TCP/IP host and at an IP router. In each case, the IP layer at the sending host or router must decide where to forward the packet. To make these decisions, the IP layer consults a routing table stored in the memory. Routing table entries are created by default when TCP/IP initializes, and entries can be added either manually or automatically.

A routing table or routing information base is a data table containing information about the routes to different network destinations (directly or indirectly), in some cases with distance information about the routes stored in the table. The router or any node using the TCP/IP has a routing table. Each table contains a series of default entries according to the configuration of the node, and additional entries can be added manually, for example, by administrators who use TCP/IP tools, or automatically, when nodes listen for routing information messages sent by routers [3].

When the IP forwards a packet, it extensively uses the routing table to determine

- The next-hop IP address
- Whether a packet is for a direct delivery, the next-hop IP address is the destination address in the IP packet, or whether it should be an indirect delivery (that is, the next-hop IP address is the IP address of a router)
- The next-hop interface
- That the interface identifies the physical or logical interface that forwards the packet.

A typical IP routing table entry includes the following fields:

- Destination address
- Prefix length corresponding to the address or range of addresses in the destination
- Next hop
- Interface

- Metric that indicates the cost of a route so that the IP can select the best possible route among many other routes to reach a particular destination; it may refer to the number of hops or links to reach the destination

2.8 Discussion on Router

As noted previously, routers basically direct network data messages, or packets, based on internal addresses and tables of routes, or known destinations that serve certain addresses. Directing data between portions of a network is the primary purpose of a router.

2.8.1 Access Mechanisms for Administrators

It is very important that a network administrator controls the access to a router to keep the networks safe from outside attacks. Here, we discuss this briefly. Some of the views and information were taken from Antoine, Bongiorni, and Borza [4]. So, for detailed knowledge, readers are encouraged to consult the official document.

There are two types of access:

- Local
- Remote

Local access usually involves a direct connection to a console port on the router with a dumb terminal or a laptop computer. Remote access typically involves allowing telnet or SNMP (Simple Network Management Protocol) connections to the router from some computer on the same subnet or a different subnet. It is recommended only to allow local access because during remote access, all telnet passwords or SNMP community strings are sent in the clear to the router. If an attacker can collect network traffic during remote access, then the attacker can capture passwords or community strings. However, there are some options if remote access is required. Two options are

1. Establishing a dedicated management network. The management network should include only identified administration hosts and a spare interface on each router. Figure 2.14 shows an example scenario.

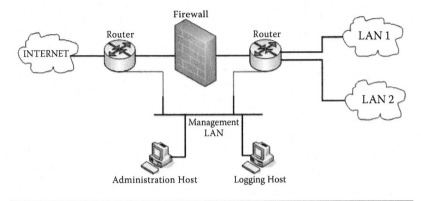

Figure 2.14 A sample management LAN (local-area network) for network administration.

2. Another method is to encrypt all traffic between the administrator's computer and the router.

In either case, packet filters can be configured to permit only the identified administration hosts management access to the router.

In addition to how administrators access the router, there may be a need to have more than one level of administrator or more than one administrative role. So, it is required to define clearly the capabilities of each level or role in the router security policy. For example, one role might be "network manager," and administrators authorized to assume that role may be able to view and modify the configuration settings and interface parameters. Another role might be "operators"; administrators authorized to assume that role might be authorized only to clear connections and counters. In general, it is best to keep the number of fully privileged administrators to a minimum, maybe only one. In fact, too many cooks spoil the broth. The same applies in case of network administration.

2.8.2 Security Policy for a Router

There are several important tips to remember when creating the security policy for a router [4]:

- Specify security objectives, not particular commands or mechanisms. When the policy specifies the security results to be achieved, rather than a particular command or mechanism, the policy is more portable across router software versions and between different kinds of routers.

- Specify policy for all the zones identified in Figure 2.14. Begin with physical security and work outward to security for the static configuration, the dynamic configuration, and traffic flow.
- Services and protocols that are not explicitly permitted should be denied. When representing the network policy in the router policy, concentrate on services and protocols that have been identified as explicitly needed for network operation; explicitly permit those and deny everything else.

In some cases, it may not be practical to identify and list all the services and protocols that the router will explicitly permit. A backbone router that must route traffic to many other networks cannot always enforce highly tailored policies on the traffic flowing through it because of performance concerns or differences in the security policies of the different networks served. In these types of cases, the policy should clearly state any limitations or restrictions that can be enforced. When drafting a policy, keep most of the directives and objectives high level; avoid specifying the particular mechanisms in the policy.

A security policy must be a living document. Make it part of the security practices of your organization to review the network security policy and the router security policy regularly. Update the router policy to reflect changes in the network policy or whenever the security objectives for the router change. It may be necessary to revise the router security policy whenever there is a major change in the network architecture or organizational structure of network administration. In particular, examine the router security policy and revise it as needed whenever any of the following events occur:

- New connections made between the local network and outside networks
- Major changes to administrative practices, procedures, or staff
- Major changes to the overall network security policy
- Deployment of substantial new capabilities (e.g., a new VPN [virtual private network]) or new network components (e.g., a new firewall)
- Detection of an attack or serious compromise

When the router security policy undergoes a revision, notify all individuals authorized to administer the router and all individuals authorized for physical access to it. Maintaining policy awareness is crucial for policy compliance.

Finally, some organizations have high-level policies that impose specific requirements on the contents of individual network security policies. Carefully check your router's security policy against any applicable high-level policy to ensure that it meets all the requirements.

2.8.3 Router Security Policy Checklist

The list that follows was designed in Antoine et al. [4] as an aid for creating router security policy. We cite the same here for readers. After drafting a policy, go through the list and check that each item is addressed in your policy.

2.8.3.1 Physical Security
- Designates who is authorized to install, deinstall, and move the router.
- Designates who is authorized to perform hardware maintenance and to change the physical configuration of the router.
- Designates who is authorized to make physical connections to the router.
- Defines controls on placement and use of the console and other direct-access port connections.
- Defines recovery procedures in the event of physical damage to the router or evidence of tampering with the router.

2.8.3.2 Static Configuration Security
- Designates who is authorized to log in directly to the router via the console or other direct-access port connections.
- Designates who is authorized to assume administrative privileges on the router.
- Defines procedures and practices for making changes to the router static configuration (e.g., logbook, change recording, review procedures).

- Defines the password policy for user/log-in passwords and for administrative or privilege passwords. Includes a list of conditions that require passwords to be changed (e.g., lifetime, staff changes, compromise).
- Designates who is authorized to log in to the router remotely.
- Designates protocols, procedures, and networks permitted for logging in to the router remotely.
- Defines the recovery procedures and identifies individuals responsible for recovery in the case of compromise of the router's static configuration.
- Defines the audit log policy for the router, including outlining log management practices and procedures and log review responsibilities.
- Designates procedures and limits on use of automated remote management and monitoring facilities (e.g., SNMP).
- Outlines response procedures or guidelines for detection of an attack against the router itself.
- Defines the management policy and update intervals for long-term secrets, such as those for routing protocols, NTP (Network Time Protocol), TACACS+ (Terminal Access Controller Access-Control System Plus), RADIUS (Remote Authentication Dial In User Service), and SNMP.
- Defines the key management policy for long-term cryptographic keys (if any).

2.8.3.3 Dynamic Configuration Security

- Identifies the dynamic configuration services permitted on the router and the networks permitted to access those services.
- Identifies the routing protocols to be used and the security features to be employed on each.
- Designates mechanisms and policies for setting or automating maintenance of the router's clock (e.g., manual setting, NTP).
- Identifies key agreement and cryptographic algorithms authorized for use in establishing VPN tunnels with other networks (if any).

2.8.3.4 Network Service Security

- Enumerates protocols, ports, and services to be permitted or filtered by the router, for each interface or connection (e.g. inbound and outbound), and identifies procedures and authorities for authorizing them.
- Describes security procedures and roles for interactions with external service providers and maintenance technicians.

2.8.3.5 Compromise Response

- Enumerates individuals or organizations to be notified in the event of a network compromise.
- Identifies relevant configuration information to be captured and retained.
- Defines response procedures, authorities, and objectives for response after a successful attack against the network, including provision for preserving evidence and for notification of law enforcement.

If such policy is employed, it is considered that the network security is given enough emphasis, and the network could be vulnerable to fewer potential commonly known attacks. This is because it is nearly impossible to keep a network free of any kind of attack. That is why we talk about minimizing security-related attacks rather than keeping them away completely.

2.9 Network Traffic Filtering

Network traffic filtering is a way of limiting the traffic by employing appropriate measures for checking which packets are allowed and which are not. This is a critical method used to enhance network security by using a different set of rules and criteria.

Here, we note two methods of traffic filtering: (1) packet filtering and (2) source routing.

2.9.1 Packet Filtering

Packet filtering is a method by which network packets are examined as they pass through routers or a firewall (see Figure 2.14) and it is determined whether the packets should pass or not. Packets may be filtered based on their protocol, sending or receiving port, sending or receiving IP address, or the value of some status bits in the packet. Packet filtering could be of two types: static or dynamic.

1. **Static Packet Filtering:** This method does not track the state of network packets and does not know whether a packet is the first, a middle packet, or the last packet. It does not need to know whether the traffic is associated with a response to a request or is the start of a request.

2. **Dynamic Packet Filtering:** This method tracks the state of connections to employ a stricter form of security. It can identify if someone is trying to fool the firewall or router. Dynamic filtering is especially important when UDP traffic is allowed to pass. It can notify if traffic is associated with a response or request.

2.9.2 Source Routing

Source routing allows a sender of a packet to partially or completely specify the route that the packet takes through the network. On the other hand, in nonsource routing protocols, routers in the network determine the path based on the packet's destination. It is somewhat good that the packets in source routing contain header information describing the route they are to take to the destination. However, this type of routing is also a security concern when an attacker may gain access to a network without going through the firewall. So, by disabling source routing on the routers' traffic filtering mechanism, network security could be enhanced.

2.10 Tools Used for Traffic Filtering or Network Monitoring

Traffic filtering basically is a combination of various strategies and policies that are used for filtering network traffic. However, there are some tools that help for better handling and categorizing of network traffic. These are known as network monitoring tools, network analyzers, or network traffic-filtering tools. Some commonly used tools are Ethereal, EtherDetect, and Wireshark. There are many other tools that may be released soon or are available on the market. Searching the Internet may provide more knowledge about the latest tools and trends.

2.10.1 Packet Capture

Packet capture is a task of capturing network packets that pass through a network. Packet capturing could be used for network traffic analysis and network monitoring. Critical information about the packets could be obtained by capturing; hence, it is a very important task in network traffic filtering. A packet capture mechanism could be present in different network devices, like routers, switches, load balancers, servers, and other network equipment. Packet capture could be used in different ways, as mentioned next.

2.10.1.1 Complete Packet Capture   Complete packet capture means capturing all packets that cross a network segment, regardless of source, protocol, or other distinguishing bits of data in the packet. Complete capture is the unrestricted, unfiltered, raw capture of all network packets.

2.10.1.2 Filtered Capture   Packet capture devices may have the ability to limit capture of packets by protocol, IP address, MAC (media access control) address, and so on. With the application of filters, only complete packets that meet the criteria of the filter (header and payload) are captured, diverted, or stored from the raw capture of all network packets.

2.11 Concluding Remarks

The intent of this chapter was to set the base of discussion for our book's subject matter. As many of these are commonly known, we have given here a snapshot of various terms and scenarios that may have our solutions and algorithms applied to them. For the general readers of the topic, this chapter could provide an overview of the basic computer networking terminologies. For the experts, this should be considered just a reminder of what is known regarding the current status of computer networking.

References

1. BICSI. *Network Design Basics for Cabling Professionals*. New York: McGraw-Hill, 2002.
2. Forouzan, B.A. *Data Communications and Networking*, 4th ed. New York: McGraw-Hill, 2007.
3. Microsoft. IP Routing, in *TCP/IP Fundamentals for Windows*, Chapter 5. Redmond, WA: Microsoft. Available at http://technet.microsoft.com/en-us/library/hh182191.aspx (accessed September 17, 2012).
4. Antoine, V., Bongiorni, R., Borza, A., et al. *Router Security Configuration Guide*, Report C4-040R-02. Ft. Meade, MD: U.S. National Security Agency. Available at http://www.nsa.gov/ia/_files/routers/C4-040R-02.pdf (accessed September 17, 2012).

3

INTRUSION DETECTION AND PREVENTION SYSTEMS (IDPSs)

3.1 Introduction

An intrusion detection system (IDS) is a device or software application that monitors network or system activities for malicious activities or policy violations and produces reports to the administrators. So, the main function of an IDS is detection by sending a report to the administrators; therefore, there is no prevention task in the IDS. The prevention can be done manually by the administrators after receiving the alert from the IDS. An intrusion prevention system (IPS) consists of network security appliances that monitor network or system activities for malicious activity, attempting to block or stop the activity, and report activity. So, the main function of an IPS is automatic prevention and sending a report to the administrators about the case. A combination of the IDS and IPS is called an intrusion detection and prevention system (IDPS). Most organizations now use IDPS products because they offer great defense mechanisms [1].

Let us give two real-life examples to explain more about the main difference between the IDS and the IPS.

EXAMPLE 3.1
Let us consider a big house with a security guard to protect it from attackers or unwanted outsiders. The security guard is always sitting at the main entrance of the house, and the house is equipped with a warning bell, which is activated at 1 a.m. and remains active until 8 a.m. The warning bell sends an alert if anyone tries to enter the house forcefully or by illegitimate means (i.e., anyone not coming through the main entrance, which is the legal way).

If the warning bell sends an alert, the security guard would go to see what exactly has happened. In fact, if the warning bell sends an alert, it may not always mean that there is an attacker trying to break into the house; it may be a member of the household (legitimate one). If an illegal person penetrates the house and the warning bell does not send an alert, this is considered a false negative. If the warning bell sends an alert for a legal person (by mistake), this is considered a false positive. From the example, the warning bell is acting as an IDS, and the security guard is working as the network administrator. So, what are the benefits of an IDS if it does not protect organizations from attacks automatically (i.e., just by sending the IDS alert)? This example answers this question: Without the warning bell, the security guard would not be able to know that someone was trying to penetrate the house. Therefore, the network administrators would not be able to know there are some attacks that have been launched without the IDS alert. We should mention here that some types of IDSs have limited capabilities to prevent attacks from entering an organization, but in general, the main function of the IDS is detection, not prevention.

EXAMPLE 3.2

We find in some countries that some people put a wire along the wall of their houses, which could be electrified by turning on an electrical switch. The house owner turns on the switch, say, for example, from 1 to 8 a.m. to prevent an attacker or burglar from entering the house. This example is similar to that of an IPS because this method can prevent the burglar from entering the house easily.

A combination of the two examples can be considered the mechanism of an IDPS. It should be noted here that we present Example 3.2 just to give the idea of the main function of an IPS. In a real-life situation, an electrified wire like that may cause a fatality, which is not supportable. The voltage level, however, could be set so that it does the work of preventing illegal entry to the house without causing any fatality. Of course, in practical situations it is better to avoid a mechanism that uses high voltage.

Figure 3.1 shows at a glance what this chapter covers. The numbers shown in the figure are not the section numbers, but just relate the

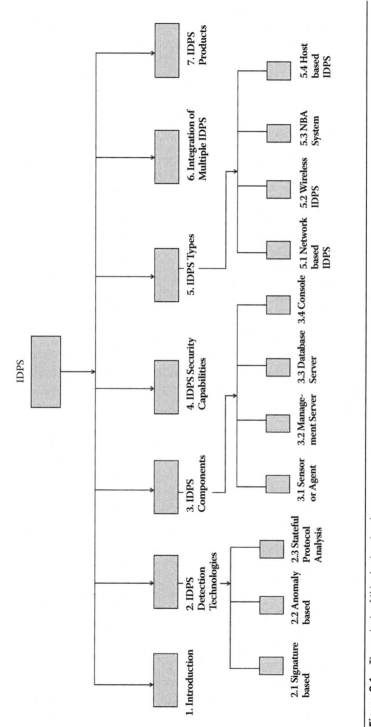

Figure 3.1   The contents of this chapter at a glance.

items. As can be seen, first we give an introduction to the IDPS. Then, we discuss the IDPS detection technologies, which are signature-based detection, anomaly-based detection, and stateful protocol analysis. Then, we give details about the IDPS components, which are sensors or agents, management server, database server, and console. After that, we discuss the IDPS security capabilities against authorized activities. Next, we discuss the types of IDPS technologies: network-based IDPS, wireless IDPS, NBA (network behavior analysis) system, and host-based IDPS. By the types of the IDPS technologies, we mean the level at which we put the IDPS product; for example, within a house we can put the warning bell on the house wall, which is similar to the network-based IDPS; also, we can put it in any of the rooms, which is similar to the host-based IDPS. Before concluding the chapter with some examples of IDPS products, we discuss the advantages of integrating multiple IDPS technologies and integrating different IDPS products.

The IDSs and IPSs [2] are considered as main defense methods against Internet worms and other types of security attacks. The main function of an IDS is to monitor the events occurring in a computer system or network and analyze them to detect unauthorized activities, consequently alerting the security administrators to take appropriate actions. On the other hand, the main function of an IPS is to identify unauthorized activities and to attempt to block or stop them. An IPS can be considered a relatively more sophisticated system put in place to block an attack from its initial trial.

To obtain good defense performance, the security experts often combine the IDS and IPS into a single system, the IDPS. The main functions of the IDPSs are focused on identifying possible incidents, logging information about them, attempting to stop them, and reporting them to security administrators.

The IDPSs generally do the following tasks on observing any event:

a. Record information related to observed events.
b. Notify security administrators of important observed events.
c. Provide reports to the security administrators.

There are several IDPSs that, after recording a suspicious activity (or a threat), can also respond by attempting to prevent the activity or threat from succeeding. There are several response techniques used by the IDPSs, involving such actions as stopping the attack itself, changing the security environment (e.g., reconfiguring a firewall), or changing the attack's content.

Organizations, banks, educational institutes, research labs, offices, or wherever computer systems are used for networking and communications recommend ensuring all IDPS components are secured appropriately. Securing IDPS components is a critical matter in many networking systems because the attackers may attempt to avoid attack detection by the IDPSs or they can try to gain access to sensitive information in the IDPSs, such as host configurations and known vulnerabilities. The IDPSs have several types of components, including [2, 3]

    a. Sensors or agents
    b. Management servers
    c. Database servers
    d. User and administrator consoles
    e. Management networks

All components' operating systems and applications should always be kept updated, and all software-based IDPS components should be developed in the most intricate way possible so that potential threats are diminished and the security protections may not be breached easily.

Specific protective actions of particular importance include creating separate accounts for each IDPS user and administrator, restricting network access to IDPS components, and ensuring that IDPS management communications are protected appropriately, such as encrypting them or transmitting them over a physically or logically separate network. Administrators should maintain the security of the IDPS components on a continuous basis, including verifying that the components are functioning as desired, monitoring the components for security issues, performing regular vulnerability assessments, responding appropriately to vulnerabilities in the IDPS components, and testing and deploying IDPS updates. Administrators should also back up configuration settings periodically and before applying updates ensure that the existing settings are not inadvertently lost.

To obtain more comprehensive and accurate detection and prevention of Internet worms and other attacks, different types of organizations need to consider using different types of IDPS technologies. There are four primary types of IDPS [2, 4] mechanisms available today:

1. Network based
2. Wireless
3. NBA based
4. Host based

Each of these mechanisms provides a different type of defense against malicious activities (i.e., the network-based mechanism can detect attacks that the host-based cannot/may not detect). For example, the network-based mechanism can detect attacks on the network level, whereas the host-based mechanism can detect attacks on the host level. To obtain a good and effective defense solution, a combination of network-based and host-based IDPS mechanisms is needed. If the organization determines that its wireless networks need additional monitoring, it can use the wireless IDPS technologies to obtain a good defense performance.

If organizations desire additional detection capabilities for denial-of-service (DoS) attacks, worms, and other threats, it is recommended to use the NBA technologies to achieve that goal. The organizations that plan to use multiple types of IDPS technologies or multiple products of the same type of IDPS are recommended to be aware of whether the IDPSs should be integrated.

There are two types of IDPS integrations [2]:

a. **Direct IDPS integration.** The process of a product feeding information to another product is called direct IDPS integration. Direct IDPS integration is the most suitable when an organization uses multiple IDPS products from a single vendor. For example, a network-based IDPS technology perhaps uses host-based IDPS data to determine whether an attack is detected successfully by the network-based IDPS technology, and a network-based IDPS technology could give network flow information to an NBA IDPS technology. The feeding information helps in improving detection accuracy, speeds up the analysis process, and helps in ordering the threats according to their priorities. The main drawback of using a fully integrated solution is that a failure or compromise could affect all the IDPS technologies negatively.

b. **Indirect IDPS integration.** Indirect IDPS integration is the process when many IDP products send their data to security information and event management (SIEM) software. The main function of the SIEM software is to import information from various security-related logs and correlate events among them. SIEM software commonly receives copies of the logs from the logging hosts over security network channels; then it normalizes the log data into standard fields and value (known as normalization), and it determines related events by matching Internet Protocol (IP) addresses, timestamps, usernames, and other characteristics. SIEM products can identify malicious activity such as attacks and malware infections as well as misuse and inappropriate usage of systems and networks.

SIEM software can complement IDPSs. For example, if an organization uses different IDPS technologies, the SIEM software can correlate events logged for these different IDPS technologies. SIEM software can identify incidents that a single device cannot; also, it can collect information related to an event in a single place for more efficient analysis. However, there is a significant limitation in the SIEM software, which is a delay between the time when an event begins and the time SIEM software sees the corresponding log data since log data are often transferred in batch mode to conserve resources. Resource consumption is also limited by SIEM products transferring only some event data from the original resources.

Organizations should define the requirements that the products should meet before evaluating IDPS products. To do this task, evaluators need to understand the characteristics of the organization's system and network environments. Then, evaluators can select a compatible IDPS that can monitor the events of interest on the systems or networks. Evaluators should explain well the goals and objectives they wish to achieve by using an IDPS, such as stopping common attacks, identifying misconfigured wireless network devices, and detecting misuse of the organization's system and network resources. In addition, evaluators should reconsider their existing security policies, which serve as a specification for many of the features that the IDPS products need to provide. Evaluators should also understand whether the organization is subject to oversight or review by another organization. If so, the evaluators should determine if that oversight authority requires IDPSs or other specific system security resources. Resource constraints should also be taken into account by evaluators. Moreover, the evaluators need to define specialized sets of requirements for the following:

- Security capabilities in depth, including the methodologies that they use to identify suspicious activity.
- Performance, including maximum capacity and performance features.
- Management, including design and implementation (e.g., reliability, interoperability, scalability, product security); operation and maintenance (including software updates); and training, documentation, and technical support.
- Life-cycle costs, both initial and maintenance costs.

When an organization evaluates IDPS products, it should consider using a combination of several sources of data on the products' characteristics and capabilities. Common product data sources include test lab or real-world product testing, vendor-provided information, third-party product reviews, and previous IDPS experience from individuals within the organization and trusted individuals at other organizations. When data are received from other parties, the organization should consider the fidelity because those data are often presented without an explanation of how they were generated. There are several significant challenges in performing in-depth, hands-on IDPS testing, such as the need for a considerable amount of resources and lack of a standard test methodology and test suites, which often makes it infeasible. However, limited IDPS testing is helpful for evaluating security requirements, performance, operation, and maintenance capabilities.

3.2 IDPS Detection Methods

The IDPS technologies use many methods to detect attacks. The primary methods are signature based, anomaly based, and stateful protocol analysis. Most IDPS technologies use more than one method to provide more accurate detection. Next, we present more details about the mentioned methods [2].

3.2.1 Signature-Based Detection

A signature is a pattern that corresponds to a known threat. A signature-based detection scheme monitors packets in the network and compares them against a database of signatures from known malicious threats. This method works similar to the way most antivirus software detect malware. The main disadvantage of this kind of method is that there would always be a lag between a new threat being discovered in the wild and the signature for detecting that threat being applied to an IPS. During that lag time, the IPS would be unable to detect the new threat.

The signature-based detection method is considered as the simplest detection method because it just compares the current unit of activity, such as a packet or a log entry, to a list of signatures using string comparison operations. Another limitation that these kinds of detection technologies have is their lack of understanding of many network or application protocols, and they cannot track and understand the state of complex communications. For example, signature-based detection methods cannot pair a request with the corresponding response, such as knowing that a request to a Web server for a particular page that generated a response status code of 403 means that the server refused to accept the request (in fact, a 403 error is equivalent to a blanket "NO" by the Web server—with no further discussion allowed). These methods also lack the ability to remember previous requests when processing the current request. This limitation prevents signature-based detection methods from detecting attacks comprised of multiple events if none of the events contains a clear indication of an attack [2, 5].

3.2.2 Anomaly-Based Detection

An anomaly-based detection method monitors network traffic and compares it against an established baseline. The baseline identifies what is "normal" for that network, what sort of bandwidth is generally used, what protocols are used, and what ports and devices generally connect to each other and alert the administrator or user when traffic is detected that is anomalous or significantly different from the baseline.

The major advantage of anomaly-based detection methods is that they can be effective at detecting previously unknown threats. For example, suppose that a computer becomes infected with a new type of malware. The malware could consume the computer's processing resources, send a large number of e-mails, initiate a large number of network connections, and show other behaviors that would be significantly different from the established profiles for the computer.

An initial profile is generated over a period of time (typically days, sometimes weeks), sometimes called a training period. There are two types of anomaly-based profiles: static and dynamic. Once generated, a static profile is unchanged unless the IDPS is specifically directed to generate a new profile. A dynamic profile is adjusted constantly as additional events are observed. The reality is that the systems and networks change over time, so the corresponding measures of normal behavior also change. A static profile will eventually become inaccurate; hence, it needs to be regenerated periodically. Dynamic profiles do not have this problem, but they are susceptible to evasion attempts from attackers. For example, an attacker can perform small amounts of malicious activities occasionally, then slowly increase the frequency and quantity of activities. If the rate of change is sufficiently slow, the IDPS might think the malicious activity is normal behavior and include it in its profile. Malicious activity might also be observed by an IDPS while it builds its initial profiles.

Inadvertently including malicious activity as part of a profile is a common problem with anomaly-based IDPS products (in some cases, administrators can modify the profile to exclude activity in the profile that is known to be malicious). To develop a good anomaly-based detection scheme, experts should study network activities well (such as the traffic rate, the number of packets for each protocol, the rate of connections, the number of different IP addresses, etc.), then put these activities in a profile. However, there is another critical problem associated with building profiles: It can be challenging in some cases to make them accurate because computing activities can be complex. For example, if a particular maintenance activity that performs large file transfers occurs only once a month, it might not be observed during the training period; when the maintenance occurs, it is likely to be considered a significant deviation from the profile and trigger an alert (which would be a false detection/false positive).

An IPS's evaluation tools are false negatives and false positives. A false negative occurs when an attack or an event either is not detected by the IDS or is considered benign by the analyst. A false positive occurs when an event is picked up by the IDS and declared as an attack but actually it is not or it is benign. The main disadvantage of the anomaly-based IDPS products is that they often produce many false positives because of benign activity that deviates significantly from profiles, especially in more diverse or dynamic environments. Another noteworthy problem with the use of anomaly-based detection techniques is that it is often difficult for analysts to determine why a particular alert was generated and to validate that an alert is accurate and not a false positive because of the complexity of events and number of events that may have caused the alert to be generated [2, 6].

3.2.3 Stateful Protocol Analysis

The stateful protocol analysis method identifies deviations of protocol states by comparing observed events with predetermined profiles of generally accepted definitions of benign activity. This method, unlike anomaly-based detection (which uses host- or network-specific profiles), relies on vendor-developed universal profiles that specify how particular protocols should and should not be used. The *stateful* in stateful protocol analysis means that the IDPS is capable of understanding and tracking the state of network, transport, and application protocols that have a notion of state. For example, when a user starts a File Transfer Protocol (FTP) session, the session is initially in the unauthenticated state. Unauthenticated users should only perform a few commands in this state, such as viewing help information or providing usernames and passwords. An important part of understanding state is pairing requests with responses, so when an FTP authentication attempt occurs, the IDPS can determine if it was successful by finding the status code in the corresponding response. Once the user has authenticated successfully, the session is in the authenticated state, and users are expected to perform any of several dozen commands. Performing most of these commands while in the unauthenticated state would be considered suspicious, but in the authenticated state, performing most of them is considered benign.

Unexpected sequences of commands can be identified by the stateful protocol, such as issuing the same command repeatedly or issuing a command without first issuing a command on which it is dependent. In addition, there is another state-tracking feature of stateful protocol analysis; for protocols that perform authentication, the IDPS can keep track of the authenticator used for each session and record the authenticator used for suspicious activity. This is helpful when investigating an incident. Some IDPSs can also use the authenticator information to define acceptable activity differently for multiple classes of users or specific users.

Stateful protocol analysis methods perform protocol analysis to detect attacks, which includes reasonableness checks for individual commands, such as minimum and maximum lengths for arguments. If a command typically has a username argument, and usernames have a maximum length of 20 characters, then an argument with a length of 1000 characters is suspicious. If the large argument contains binary data, then it is even more suspicious.

To detect unauthorized activities, stateful protocol analysis methods use protocol models, which are typically based primarily on protocol standards from software vendors and standards bodies (e.g., Internet Engineering Task Force [IETF] Request for Comments [RFC]). The protocol models also typically take into account variances in each protocol's implementation. Many standards are not exhaustively complete in explaining the details of the protocol, which causes variations among implementations. Also, many vendors either violate standards or add proprietary features, some of which may replace features from the standards. For proprietary protocols, complete details about the protocols are often not available, making it difficult for IDPS technologies to perform comprehensive, accurate analysis. As protocols are revised and vendors alter their protocol implementations, IDPS protocol models need to be updated to reflect those changes.

The main disadvantage of the stateful protocol analysis methods is that they are resource intensive because of the complexity of the analysis and the overhead involved in performing state tracking for many simultaneous sessions. Another disadvantage is that the stateful protocol analysis methods cannot detect attacks that do not violate the characteristics of generally acceptable protocol behavior, such as performing many benign actions in a short period of time to cause a DoS. Yet another problem is that the protocol model used by an IDPS might conflict with the way the protocol is implemented in particular versions of specific applications and operating systems or how differently client and server implementations of the protocol interact [2, 7].

3.3 IDPS Components

In this section, we mention typical components in an IDPS solution [2]. They are as follows:

- **Sensor or agent.** The main function of this component is to monitor and analyze activity. The term *sensor* is typically used for IDPSs that monitor networks, and the term *agent* is typically used for IDPS technologies that monitor only a single host.
- **Management server.** A management server is a device that receives information from sensors or agents and manages it. There are some management servers that perform analysis on the information received and can identify incidents that the individual sensor or agent cannot. Matching event information from multiple sensors or agents, such as finding events triggered by the same IP address, is known as correlation. Some small IDPS deployments do not use any management servers. In larger IDPS deployments, there are often multiple management servers, sometimes in tiers.
- **Database server.** A database server is a repository for event information recorded by sensors, agents, and management servers. Many IDPSs support the use of database servers.
- **Console.** A console is a program that provides an interface for the users and administrators of the IDPS. Console software is typically installed on standard desktop or laptop computers. Some consoles are used for IDPS administration only, such as configuring sensors or agents and applying software updates, whereas other consoles are used strictly for monitoring and analysis. Some IDPS consoles provide both administration and monitoring capabilities.

IDPS components can be connected with each other through regular networks or a separate network designed for security software management, known as a management network. If a management network is used, each sensor or agent host has an additional network interface known as a management interface that connects to the management network, and the hosts are configured so that they cannot pass any traffic between management interfaces and other network interfaces.

The management servers, database servers, and consoles are attached to the management network only. This architecture effectively isolates the management network from the production networks, concealing the IDPS from attackers and ensuring that the IDPS has adequate bandwidth to function under adverse conditions. If an IDPS is deployed without a separate management network, a way of improving IDPS security is to create a virtual management network using a virtual local-area network (VLAN) within the standard networks. Using a VLAN provides protection for IDPS communications, but not as much protection as a separate management network.

3.4 IDPS Security Capabilities

IDPS technologies offer extensive and accurate detection capabilities. To provide more accurate detection, IDPS products use a combination of detection techniques. The types of events detected and the typical accuracy of detection vary greatly depending on the type of IDPS technology. Most IDPSs require at least some tuning and customization to improve their detection accuracy, usability, and effectiveness. Examples of tuning and customization capabilities are as follows [2]:

- **Thresholds.** A threshold is a value that sets the limit between normal and abnormal behavior. Thresholds usually specify a maximum acceptable level, such as five failed connection attempts in 60 seconds or 100 characters for a filename length.
- **Blacklists and white lists.** A blacklist is a list of discrete entities, such as hosts, Transmission Control Protocol (TCP) or User Datagram Protocol (UDP) port numbers, Internet Control Message Protocol (ICMP) types and codes, applications, usernames, Uniform Resource Locators (URLs), filenames, or file extensions, that have been previously determined to be associated with malicious activity. Blacklists allow IDPSs to block activity that is highly likely to be malicious. Some IDPSs generate dynamic blacklists that are used to temporarily block recently detected threats (e.g., activity from an attacker's IP address). A white list is a list of discrete entities that are known to be benign. White lists are typically used on a granular basis, such as protocol by protocol, to reduce or ignore false positives involving known benign activity.

- **Alert settings.** Most IDPS technologies allow administrators to customize each alert type. Examples of actions that can be performed on an alert type include toggling it on or off and setting a default priority or severity level. Some products can suppress alerts if an attacker generates many alerts in a short period of time and may also temporarily ignore all future traffic from the attacker. This is to prevent the IDPS from being overwhelmed by alerts.
- **Code viewing and editing.** Some IDPS technologies permit administrators to see some or all of the detection-related code. This is usually limited to signatures, but some technologies allow administrators to see additional code, such as programs used to perform stateful protocol analysis. Viewing the code can help analysts determine why particular alerts were generated so they can better validate alerts and identify false positives. The ability to edit detection-related code and write new code (e.g., new signatures) is necessary to fully customize certain types of detection capabilities.

Most IDPSs offer multiple prevention capabilities to provide more accurate detection; the specific capabilities vary by IDPS technology type. IDPSs usually allow administrators to specify the prevention capability configuration for each type of alert. This usually includes enabling or disabling prevention, as well as specifying which type of prevention capability should be used. Some IDPS technologies offer information-gathering capabilities, such as collecting information on hosts or networks from observed activity. Examples include identifying hosts and the operating systems, applications that they use, and general characteristics of the network.

3.5 Types of IDPS Technologies

As mentioned, there are mainly four types of IDPS technologies:

- Network-based IDPSs
- Wireless IDPSs
- NBA systems
- Host-based IDPSs

In this section, we present details about these IDPS technologies.

3.5.1 Network-Based IDPSs

Network-based IDPSs are placed at a strategic point or points within the network to monitor traffic to and from all devices in the network. A network-based IDPS monitors and analyzes all inbound and outbound traffic for particular network segments or devices to identify suspicious activity; however, doing so might create a bottleneck that would impair the overall speed of the network. The IDPS network interface cards are placed into promiscuous mode so that they accept all packets that they see, regardless of their intended destinations. In fact, most of the IDPSs perform their analysis at the application layer, for example, Hypertext Transfer Protocol (HTTP), Simple Mail Transfer Protocol (SMTP), and Domain Name System (DNS). They also analyze activity at the transport (e.g., TCP, UDP) and network (e.g., Internet Protocol version 4 [IPv4]) layers to identify attacks at those layers and facilitate application-layer analysis. Some network-based IDPSs also perform limited analysis at the hardware layer, for example, Address Resolution Protocol (ARP).

Network-based IDPS sensors can be deployed in one of two modes: in line or passive.

- An in-line sensor is deployed so that the traffic that it monitors passes through it. Some in-line sensors are hybrid firewall/IDPS devices. The primary motivation for deploying sensors in line is to stop attacks by blocking traffic.
- A passive sensor is deployed so that it monitors a copy of the actual traffic; no traffic passes through the sensor. Passive sensors can monitor traffic through various methods, including a switch-spanning port, which can see all traffic going through the switch; a network tap, which is a direct connection between a sensor and the physical network medium itself, such as a fiber-optic cable; and an IDS load balancer, which is a device that aggregates and directs traffic to monitoring systems.

Most techniques having a sensor that prevents intrusions require that the sensor be deployed in in-line mode. Passive techniques typically provide no reliable way for a sensor to block traffic. In some cases, a passive sensor can place packets onto a network to attempt to disrupt a connection, but such methods are generally less effective than in-line methods. IP addresses are normally not assigned to the sensor network interfaces (which are used to monitor traffic), except for network interfaces that are also used for IDPS management. Operating a sensor without IP addresses assigned to its monitoring interfaces is known as stealth mode. It improves the security of the sensors because it conceals them and prevents other hosts from initiating connections to them. However, attackers may be able to identify the existence of a sensor and determine which product is in use by analyzing the characteristics of its prevention actions. Such analysis might include monitoring protected networks and determining which scan patterns trigger particular responses and what values are set in certain packet header fields.

3.5.1.1 Network-Based IDPS Security Capabilities against Malicious Activity Network-based IDPSs provide extensive and broad detection capabilities. Most IDPSs use a combination of signature-based, anomaly-based, and stateful protocol analysis detection techniques. These techniques are usually tightly interwoven; for example, a stateful protocol analysis engine might parse activity into requests and responses, each of which is examined for anomalies and compared against signatures of known bad activity.

Most types of events commonly detected by network-based IDPS sensors include application-, transport-, and network-layer reconnaissance and attacks. Many sensors can also detect unexpected application services, such as tunneled protocols, backdoors, and hosts running unauthorized applications. Also, some types of security policy violations can be detected by sensors that allow administrators to specify the characteristics of activity that should not be permitted, such as TCP or UDP port numbers, IP addresses, and Web site names. Some sensors can also monitor the initial negotiation conducted when establishing encrypted communications to identify client or server software that has known vulnerabilities or is misconfigured. Examples include secure shell (SSH), Transport Layer Security (TLS), and IP Security (IPsec).

Network-based IDPSs are associated with high rates of false positives and false negatives. These rates can only be reduced to some extent because of the complexity of the activities monitored. A single sensor may monitor traffic involving hundreds or thousands of internal and external hosts, which run a wide variety of frequently changing applications and operating systems. A sensor cannot understand everything it sees. Another common problem with detection accuracy is that the IDPS typically requires considerable tuning and customization to take into account the characteristics of the monitored environment. Also, security controls that alter network activity, such as firewalls and proxy servers, could cause additional difficulties for sensors by changing the characteristics of traffic.

Usually, network-based schemes can collect limited information on hosts and their network activity. Examples of these are a list of hosts on the organization's network, the operating system versions and application versions used by these hosts, and general information about network characteristics, such as the number of hops between devices. This information can be used by some IDPSs to improve detection accuracy. For example, an IDPS might allow administrators to specify the IP addresses used by the organization's Web servers, mail servers, and other common types of hosts and specify the types of services provided by each host (e.g., the Web server application type and version run by each Web server). This allows the IDPS to better prioritize alerts; for instance, an alert for an Apache attack directed at an Apache Web server would have a higher priority than the same attack directed at a different type of Web server. Some network-based IDPSs can also import the results of vulnerability scans and use them to determine which attacks would likely be successful, if not blocked. This allows the IDPS to make better decisions on prevention actions and prioritize alerts more accurately.

Network-based IDPS sensors offer many prevention capabilities. A passive sensor can attempt to end an existing TCP session by sending TCP reset packets to both endpoints, to make it appear to each endpoint that the other is trying to end the connection. However, this technique often cannot be performed in time to stop an attack and can only be used for TCP; other, newer prevention capabilities are more effective. In-line sensors can perform in-line firewalling, throttle bandwidth usage, and alter malicious contents. Both passive and in-line sensors can reconfigure other network security devices to block malicious activity or route it elsewhere, and some sensors can run a script or program when certain malicious activity is detected to trigger custom actions.

3.5.1.2 Network-Based IDPS Limitations Although network-based IDPSs provide extensive detection capabilities, they do have some significant limitations. Attacks within encrypted traffic would not be detected by the network-based IDPSs, including virtual private network (VPN) connections, Hypertext Transfer Protocol over Secure Sockets Layer (HTTPS), and SSH sessions. To ensure that sufficient analysis is performed on payloads within encrypted traffic, IDPSs can be deployed to analyze the payloads before they are encrypted or after they have been decrypted. Examples include placing network-based IDPS sensors to monitor decrypted traffic and using host-based IDPS software to monitor activity within the source or destination host.

When a high load appears in a network, the network-based IDPSs may be unable to perform full analysis. This leads to some attacks going undetected, especially if stateful protocol analysis methods are in use. For in-line IDPS sensors, dropping packets also causes disruptions in network availability, and delays in processing packets could cause unacceptable latency. To avoid this, some in-line IDPS sensors can recognize high-load conditions and either pass certain types of traffic through the sensor without performing full analysis or drop low-priority traffic. Sensors may also provide better performance under high loads if they use specialized hardware (e.g., high-bandwidth network cards) or recompile components of their software to incorporate settings and other customizations made by administrators.

IDPS sensors can be avoided by various types of attacks. Attackers can generate large volumes of traffic, such as distributed denial-of-service (DDoS) attacks, and other anomalous activity (e.g., unusually fragmented packets) to exhaust a sensor's resources or cause it to crash. Another attack technique, known as blinding, generates traffic that is likely to trigger many IDPS alerts quickly. In many cases, the blinding traffic is not intended actually to attack any target. An attacker runs the "real" attack separately at the same time as the blinding traffic, hoping that the blinding traffic will either cause the IDPS to fail in some way or cause the alerts for the real attack to go unnoticed. Many sensors can recognize common attacks against them, alert administrators to the attack, and then ignore the rest of the activities.

3.5.2 Wireless IDPSs

A wireless IDPS monitors wireless network traffic and analyzes wireless networking protocols to identify malicious behavior. However, it cannot identify suspicious activity in the application- or higher-layer network protocols (e.g., TCP, UDP) that the wireless network traffic is transferring. It is most commonly deployed within the range of an organization's wireless network to monitor it, but it can also be deployed to locations where unauthorized wireless networking could be occurring.

Because of the transmission methods, wireless network attacks differ from those on wired networks. However, the basic components involved in a wireless IDPS are the same as the network-based IDPS: consoles, database servers, management servers, and sensors. A wireless IDPS monitors the network by sampling the traffic. There are two frequency bands to monitor (2.4 and 5 GHz), and each band includes many channels. A sensor is used to monitor a channel at a time, and it can switch to other channels as needed.

We should mention that most of the wireless local-area networks (WLANs) use the Institute of Electrical and Electronics Engineers (IEEE) 802.11 family of WLAN standards [8]. IEEE 802.11 WLANs have two main architectural components:

- A station, which is a wireless endpoint device (e.g., laptop computer, personal digital assistant)
- An access point, which logically connects stations with an organization's wired network infrastructure or other network

Some WLANs also use wireless switches, which act as intermediaries between access points and the wired network. A network based on stations and access points is configured in infrastructure mode; a network that does not use an access point, in which stations connect directly to each other, is configured in ad hoc mode. Nearly all organizational WLANs use infrastructure mode. Each access point in a WLAN has a name assigned to it called a service set identifier (SSID). The SSID allows stations to distinguish one WLAN from another.

Wireless sensors have several available forms. A dedicated sensor is usually passive, performing wireless IDPS functions but not passing traffic from source to destination. Dedicated sensors may be designed for fixed or mobile deployment, with mobile sensors used primarily for auditing and incident-handling purposes (e.g., to locate rogue wireless devices). Sensor software is also available bundled with access points and wireless switches. Some vendors also have host-based wireless IDPS sensor software that can be installed on stations, such as laptops. The sensor software detects station misconfigurations and attacks within range of the stations. The sensor software may also be able to enforce security policies on the stations, such as limiting access to wireless interfaces.

If an organization uses WLANs, it most often deploys wireless sensors to monitor the radio-frequency range of the organization's WLANs, which often includes mobile components such as laptops and personal digital assistants. Many organizations also use sensors to monitor areas of their facilities where there should be no WLAN activity, as well as channels and bands that the organization's WLANs should not use, as a way of detecting rogue devices.

3.5.2.1 Wireless IDPS Security Capabilities The main advantages of wireless IDPSs include detection of attacks, misconfigurations, and policy violations at the WLAN protocol level, primarily examining IEEE 802.11 protocol communication. The major limitation of a wireless IDPS is that it does not examine communications at higher levels (e.g., IP addresses, application payloads). Some products perform only simple signature-based detection, whereas others use a combination of signature-based, anomaly-based, and stateful protocol analysis detection techniques. Most of the types of events commonly detected by wireless IDPS sensors include unauthorized WLANs and WLAN devices and poorly secured WLAN devices (e.g., misconfigured WLAN settings). In addition, the wireless IDPSs can detect unusual WLAN usage patterns, which could indicate a device compromise or unauthorized use of the WLAN, and the use of wireless network scanners. Other types of attacks, such as DoS conditions, including logical attacks (e.g., overloading access points with large numbers of messages) and physical attacks (e.g., emitting electromagnetic energy on the WLAN's frequencies to make the WLAN unusable), can also be detected by wireless IDPSs. Some wireless IDPSs can also detect a WLAN device that attempts to spoof the identity of another device.

Another significant advantage is that most wireless IDPS sensors can identify the physical location of a wireless device by using triangulation—estimating the device's approximate distance from multiple sensors from the strength of the device's signal received by each sensor, then calculating the physical location at which the device would be, the estimated distance from each sensor. Handheld IDPS sensors can also be used to pinpoint a device's location, particularly if fixed sensors do not offer triangulation capabilities or if the device is moving.

Wireless IDPSs overcome the other types of IDPS by providing more accurate prevention; this is largely due to its narrow focus. Anomaly-based detection methods often generate high false positives, especially if threshold values are not properly maintained. Although many alerts based on benign activities might occur, such as another organization's WLAN being within range of the organization's WLANs, these alerts are not truly false positives because they are accurately detecting an unknown WLAN.

Some tuning and customization are required for the wireless IDPS technologies to improve their detection accuracy. The main effort required in the wireless IDPS is in specifying which WLANs, access points, and stations are authorized and in entering the policy characteristics into the wireless IDPS software. As wireless IDPSs only examine wireless network protocols, not the higher-level protocols (e.g., applications), generally there is not a large number of alert types and consequently not many customizations or tunings are available.

Wireless IDPS sensors provide two types of intrusion prevention capabilities:

- Some sensors can terminate connections through the air, typically by sending messages to the endpoints telling them to dissociate the current session and then refusing to permit a new connection to be established.
- Another prevention method is for a sensor to instruct a switch on the wired network to block network activity involving a particular device based on the device's media access control (MAC) address or switch port. However, this technique is only effective for blocking the device's communications on the wired network, not the wireless network.

An important consideration when choosing prevention capabilities is the effect that prevention actions can have on sensor monitoring.

For example, if a sensor is transmitting signals to terminate connections, it may not be able to perform channel scanning to monitor other communications until it has completed the prevention action. To mitigate this, some sensors have two radios—one for monitoring and detection and another for performing prevention actions.

3.5.2.2 Wireless IDPS Limitations The wireless IDPSs offer great detection capabilities against authorized activities, but there are some significant limitations. The use of evasion techniques is considered as one of the limitations of some wireless IDPS sensors, particularly against sensor channel-scanning schemes. One example is performing attacks in very short bursts on channels that are not currently being monitored. An attacker could also launch attacks on two channels at the same time. If the sensor detects the first attack, it cannot detect the second attack unless it scans away from the channel of the first attack.

Wireless IDPS sensors (physical devices) are also vulnerable to attack. The same DoS attacks (both logical and physical) that attempt to disrupt WLANs can also disrupt sensor functions. In addition, sensors are often particularly vulnerable to physical attacks because they are usually located in hallways, conference rooms, and other open areas. Some sensors have antitamper features, which are designed to look like fire alarms that can reduce the possibility of physically being attacked. All sensors are vulnerable to physical attacks, such as jamming that disrupts radio-frequency transmissions; there is no defense against such attacks other than to establish a physical perimeter around the facility so that the attackers cannot get close enough to the WLAN to jam it.

We should mention that the wireless IDPSs cannot detect certain types of attacks against wireless networks. An attacker can passively monitor wireless traffic, which is not detectable by wireless IDPSs. If weak security methods are used, for example, Wired Equivalent Privacy (WEP), the attacker can then perform off-line processing of the collected traffic to find the encryption key used to provide security for the wireless traffic. With this key, the attacker can decrypt the traffic that was already collected, as well as any other traffic collected from the same WLAN. As the wireless IDPSs cannot detect certain types of attacks against wireless networks, they cannot fully compensate for the use of insecure wireless networking protocols.

3.5.3 NBA Systems

An NBA system examines network traffic or traffic statistics to identify threats that generate unusual traffic flows, such as DDoS attacks, certain forms of malware, and policy violations. In fact, NBA systems have been known by many names, including network behavior anomaly detection (NBAD) software, NBA and response software, and network anomaly detection software. NBA solutions usually have sensors and consoles, and some products also offer management servers (which are sometimes called analyzers).

The NBA system has some sensors similar to network-based IDPS sensors that sniff packets to monitor network activity on one or a few network segments. These sensors may be active or passive and are placed similarly to network-based IDS sensors—at the boundaries between networks, using the same connection methods. Other NBA sensors do not monitor the networks directly but instead rely on network flow information provided by routers and other networking devices. *Flow* refers to a particular communication session occurring between hosts. Typical flow data include source and destination IP addresses, source and destination TCP or UDP ports or ICMP types and codes, the number of packets and number of bytes transmitted in the session, and timestamps for the start and end of the session.

3.5.3.1 NBA System Security Capabilities   NBA technologies can detect several types of malicious activities. Most NBA system products use primarily anomaly-based detection, along with some stateful protocol analysis techniques. Therefore, most NBA technologies offer no signature-based detection capability, other than allowing administrators to manually set up custom filters that are essentially signatures to detect or stop specific attacks. Most of the types of authorized activities detected by NBA sensors include network-based DoS attacks, network scanning, worms, the use of unexpected application services, and policy violations (e.g., a host attempting to contact another host with which it has no legitimate reason to communicate). The NBA sensors have the ability to determine the origin of an attack. For example, if worms infect a network, NBA sensors can analyze the worms' flows and find the host on the organization's network that first transmitted the worms.

As mentioned, the NBA sensors are anomaly detection based, so they work primarily by detecting significant deviations from normal behavior; they are most accurate in detecting attacks that generate large amounts of network activity in a short period of time (e.g., DDoS attacks) and attacks that have unusual flow patterns (e.g., worms spreading among hosts). Attacks that are conducted slowly are less accurately detected by NBA sensors because they cannot detect many attacks until they reach a point at which their activity is significantly different from what is expected. The point during the attack at which the NBA software detects it may vary considerably depending on an NBA product's configuration. Configuring sensors to be more sensitive to anomalous activities will cause alerts to be generated more quickly when attacks occur, but more false positives are also likely to be triggered. Conversely, if sensors are configured to be less sensitive to anomalous activity, there will be fewer false positives, but alerts will be generated more slowly, allowing attacks to occur for longer periods of time. False positives can also be caused by benign changes in the environment. For example, if a new service is added to a host and hosts start using it, an NBA sensor is likely to detect this as anomalous behavior.

NBA technologies depend mainly on observing network traffic and developing baselines of expected flows and inventories of host characteristics. NBA products provide automatic updates to their baseline, which speeds up the prevention against unauthorized activities. Administrators might adjust thresholds periodically (e.g., how much additional bandwidth usage should trigger an alert) to take into account changes to the environment.

We mentioned that the NBA system is anomaly based, but a few NBA products offer limited signature-based detection capabilities. The supported signatures tend to be very simple, primarily looking for particular values in certain IP, TCP, UDP, or ICMP header fields. The signature-based capability is most helpful for in-line NBA sensors because they can use the signatures to find and block attacks that a firewall or router might not be capable of blocking. However, even without a signature capability, an in-line NBA sensor might be able to detect and block the attack because of its flow patterns.

NBA technologies overcome the other technologies by offering extensive information-gathering capabilities because knowledge of the characteristics of the organization's hosts is needed for most of the NBA product's detection techniques. In addition, NBA sensors can automatically create and maintain lists of hosts communicating on the organization's monitored networks. They can monitor port usage, perform passive fingerprinting, and use other techniques to gather detailed information on the hosts. Information typically collected for each host includes IP address, the type and version of the operating system, the network services the host provides, and the nature of the host's communications with other hosts. NBA sensors constantly monitor network activity for changes to this information. Additional information on each host's flows is also collected on an ongoing basis.

NBA sensors provide various intrusion prevention capabilities, including sending TCP reset packets to endpoints, performing in-line firewalling, and reconfiguring other network security devices. Most NBA system implementations use prevention capabilities in a limited fashion or not at all because of false positives; erroneously blocking a single flow could cause major disruptions in network communications. Prevention capabilities are most often used for NBA sensors when blocking a specific known attack, such as a new worm [9].

3.5.3.2 NBA System Limitations NBA technologies overall have great prevention capabilities against authorized activities, but also have significant limitations. One of the most important limitations is the delay in detecting attacks. Some delay is inherent in anomaly detection methods that are based on deviations from a baseline, such as increased bandwidth usage or additional connection attempts. Generally, NBA technologies often have additional delay caused by their data sources, especially when they rely on flow data from routers and other network devices. These data are often transferred to the NBA system in batches, as frequently as every minute or two, often much less frequently. Therefore, this delay is considered as a significant limitation on the NBA technologies because attacks that occur quickly, such as malware infestations and DoS attacks, may not be detected until they have already disrupted or damaged systems. To solve the delay problem, the NBA system can use sensors (software or hardware components) that do their own packet captures and analysis instead of relying on flow data from other devices. However, performing packet captures and analysis is much more resource intensive than analyzing flow data. A single sensor can analyze flow data from many networks or perform direct monitoring (packet captures) itself generally for a few networks at the most. More sensors may be needed to do direct monitoring instead of using flow data [10].

3.5.4 Host-Based IDPS

Host-based systems monitor the characteristics of a single host and the events occurring within that host for suspicious activity. Examples of the types of host characteristics that a host-based IDPS might monitor are network traffic for that host, system logs, running processes, application activity, file access and modification, and system and application configuration changes. Host-based IDPSs are most commonly deployed on critical hosts such as publicly accessible servers and servers containing sensitive information. In addition, most host-based IDPSs have detection software known as agents installed on the hosts of interest. Each agent monitors activity on a single host and may perform prevention actions. Some agents monitor a single specific application service, for example, a Web server program; these agents are also known as application-based IDPSs.

Host-based IDPS agents are deployed to critical hosts, such as publicly accessible servers and servers containing sensitive information, although they can be deployed to other types of hosts as well. Some organizations use agents mainly to analyze activity that cannot be monitored by other security controls. For example, network-based IDPS sensors cannot analyze the activity within encrypted network communications, but host-based IDPS agents installed on endpoints can see the unencrypted activity. The network architecture for host-based IDPS deployments is typically simple. Since the agents are deployed on existing hosts on the organization's networks, the components usually communicate over those networks instead of using a separate management network.

To provide more accurate intrusion prevention capabilities, most IDPS agents alter the internal architecture of hosts. This is typically done through a shim, which is a layer of code placed between existing layers of code. A shim intercepts data at a point where it would normally be passed from one piece of code to another. The shim can then analyze the data and determine whether it should be allowed or denied. Host-based IDPS agents may use shims for several types of resources, including network traffic, file system activity, system calls, Windows registry activity, and common applications (e.g., e-mail, Web). Some agents monitor activity without using shims, or they analyze artifacts of activity, such as log entries and file modifications. Although these methods are less intrusive to the host, they are also generally less effective at detecting attacks and often cannot perform prevention actions.

3.5.4.1 Host-Based IDPS Security Capabilities   Host-based IDPSs offer good prevention against several types of malicious activities. A combination (signature based and anomaly based) often is used by the host-based IDPSs. The signature-based mechanism is used to identify known attacks, whereas the anomaly based is used to identify previously unknown attacks.

There are many types of events detected by host-based IDPSs, but this detection is based on the detection techniques that the IDPSs use. Some host-based IDPS products offer several of these detection techniques; others focus on a few or one. In the following, we mention some specific techniques that are commonly used in host-based IDPSs:

- **Code Analysis.** Agents might analyze attempts to execute malicious code. One technique is executing code in a virtual environment or sandbox to analyze its behavior and compare it to profiles of known good and bad behavior. Another technique is looking for the typical characteristics of stack and heap buffer overflow exploits, such as certain sequences of instructions and attempts to access portions of memory not allocated to the process. System call monitoring is another common technique; it involves knowing which applications and processes should be performing certain actions.

- **Network Traffic Analysis.** This is often similar to what a network-based IDPS does. Some products can also analyze wireless traffic. Another capability of traffic analysis is that the agent can extract files sent by applications such as e-mail, Web, and peer-to-peer file sharing, which can then be checked for malware.

- **Network Traffic Filtering.** Agents often include a host-based firewall that can restrict incoming and outgoing traffic for each application on the system, preventing unauthorized access and acceptable use policy violations (e.g., use of inappropriate external services).

- **File System Monitoring.** File system monitoring can be performed using several different techniques. File integrity checking involves generating cryptographic checksums for critical files and comparing them to reference values to identify which files have been changed. File attribute checking is the process of checking critical files' security attributes, such as ownership and permissions, for changes. Both file integrity and file attribute checking are reactive, detecting attacks only after they have occurred. Some agents have more proactive capabilities, such as monitoring file access attempts, comparing each attempt to an access control policy, and preventing attempts that violate policy.
- **Log Analysis.** Some agents can monitor and analyze operating system and application logs to identify malicious activity. These logs may contain information on system operational events, audit records, and application operational events.

As the host-based IDPSs provide extensive knowledge of hosts' characteristics and configurations, an agent can often determine whether an attack would succeed if not stopped. Agents can use this knowledge to select preventive actions and to prioritize alerts.

Like any other IDPS technology, host-based IDPSs often cause false positives and false negatives. However, the accuracy of detection is more challenging for host-based IDPSs because they detect events but do not have knowledge of the context under which the events occurred. For example, a new application may be installed; this could be done by malicious activity or done as part of normal host operations. The event's benign or malicious nature cannot be determined without additional context. Therefore, organizations that would like to use a host-based IDPS are recommended to use a host-based product that uses combinations of several detection techniques, which achieve more accurate detection than products that use one or a few techniques. As each technique can monitor different aspects of a host, using more techniques allows agents to have a more complete picture of the events, including additional context.

Considerable tuning and customization are required to achieve better prevention by the host-based IDPSs. For example, many rely on observing host activity and developing profiles of expected behavior. Others need to be configured with detailed policies that define exactly how each application on a host should behave. The policies need to be updated as the host environment changes so that these changes are taken into account. Some products permit multiple policies to be configured on a host for multiple environments; this is mostly helpful for hosts that function in multiple environments, such as a laptop used both within an organization and from external locations.

Host-based IDPS agents provide several intrusion prevention capabilities, based on the detection techniques they use. For example, code analysis techniques can prevent malicious code from being executed, and network traffic analysis techniques can stop incoming traffic from being processed by the host and can prevent malicious files from being placed on the host. Network traffic-filtering techniques can block unwanted communications. File system monitoring can prevent files from being accessed, modified, replaced, or deleted, which could stop installation of malware, including Trojan horses and rootkits, as well as other attacks involving inappropriate file access. Other host-based IDPS detection techniques, such as log analysis, network configuration monitoring, and file integrity and attribute checking, generally do not support prevention actions because they identify events after they have occurred [11].

3.5.4.2 Host-Based IDPS Limitations   Host-based IDPSs also have some significant limitations. Although agents generate alerts on a real-time basis for most detection techniques, some techniques are used periodically to identify events that have already happened. Such techniques might only be applied hourly or even just a few times a day, causing significant delay in identifying certain events. In addition, many host-based IDPSs are intended to forward their alert data to the management servers on a periodic basis, such as every 15–60 minutes, to reduce overhead. This can cause delays in initiating response actions, which especially increases the impact of incidents that spread quickly, such as malware infestations. Host-based IDPSs can consume a considerable amount of resources on the hosts that they protect, particularly if they use several detection techniques and shims. Host-based IDPSs can also cause conflicts with existing security controls, such as personal firewalls, particularly if those controls also use shims to intercept host activity.

3.6 Integration of Multiple IDPSs

Integration of multiple IDPS technologies and that of different IDPS products offers a good prevention mechanism for organizations. Next, we discuss the advantages of integration.

3.6.1 Multiple IDPS Technologies

We mentioned that there are four primary types of IDPS technologies: network based, wireless, NBA, and host based. Each of these types has different prevention capabilities from other types from unauthorized activities. For example, some of these types can detect an attack that others cannot. Therefore, detecting as many attacks as possible will result in a better defense. Accordingly, using multiple types of IDPS technologies can achieve more comprehensive and accurate detection and prevention of malicious activity. For most of the environments, a combination of network-based and host-based IDPSs is needed at a minimum. Wireless IDPSs may also be needed if WLAN security or rogue WLAN detection is a concern. NBA products can also be deployed to achieve stronger detection capabilities for DoS attacks, worms, and other threats that cause anomalous network flows.

In fact, some organizations use multiple products of the same IDPS technology type to get more prevention and detection against malicious activities because each product can detect attacks that another product cannot. Therefore, using multiple products can offer more comprehensive and accurate defense. For the organizations that would like to use multiple products of the same IDPS technology type, we recommend using one monitoring device for multiple products. One monitoring device makes it easier for analysts to confirm the validity of alerts and identify false positives and provides redundancy. Because using many monitoring devices will result in a difficult analysis scenario, this also will be time and resource consuming [2].

3.6.2 Integration of Different IDPS Products

Different IDPS products function completely independently of each other. One of the most important advantages of using different IDPS products is that if one of them is compromised or fails, the other will not be affected, which means there are other products still defending against malicious activity. However, if the products are not integrated, the effectiveness of the entire IDPS implementation may be somewhat limited. Data cannot be shared by the products, and extra effort will be needed to monitor and manage multiple sets of products. IDPS products can be directly or indirectly integrated [2].

3.7 IDPS Products

All the previous sections were concerned with the IDPS. Implementation of these concept will result in IDPS products. There are many IDPS products in the world, and each has relative advantages over others. Therefore, in this section, we mention some of these products so that researchers can be familiar with these products, use them, modify their open source, and can start a new IPDS product for research [2].

3.7.1 Common Enterprise Network-Based IDPSs

Table 3.1 presents common enterprise network-based IDPSs.

3.7.2 Common Enterprise Wireless IDPSs

Table 3.2 presents common enterprise wireless IDPSs.

3.7.3 Common Enterprise NBA Systems

Table 3.3 shows NBA IDPSs.

3.7.4 Common Enterprise Host-Based IDPSs

Common enterprise host-based IDPSs are shown in Table 3.4.

Table 3.1 Network-Based IDPSs

PRODUCT LINE	VENDOR	URL
Attack Mitigator	Top Layer Networks	http://www.toplayer.com/content/products/index.jsp
BBX	DeepNines	http://www.deepnines.com/products.htm
Bro	Vern Paxson	http://bro-ids.org/
Check Point IPS-1	Check Point Software Technologies	http://www.checkpoint.com/corporate/nfr/index.html
Cisco IPS	Cisco Systems	http://www.cisco.com/en/US/products/hw/vpndevc/index.html
Cyclops	e-Cop.net	http://www.e-cop.net/
DefensePro	Radware, Ltd.	http://www.radware.com/content/products/dp/default.asp
Enterasys Intrusion Prevention System	Enterasys Networks, Inc.	https://www.enterasys.com/products/advanced-security-apps/dragon-intrusion-detection-protection.aspx
eTrust Intrusion Detection	Computer Associates	http://www3.ca.com/solutions/Product.aspx?ID = 163
Juniper Networks IDP	Juniper Networks	https://www.juniper.net/products/intrusion/
IntruShield	McAfee, Inc	http://www.mcafee.com/us/products/network-security/network-intrusion-prevention.aspx
Managed IDPS	StillSecure	http://www.stillsecure.com/services/idps.php
iPolicy	iPolicy Networks	http://www.ipolicynetworks.com/products/ipf.html
Proventia	Internet Security Systems	http://www.iss.net/products/product_sections/Intrusion_Prevention.html
SecureNet	Intrusion	http://www.intrusion.com/
Snort	Sourcefire	http://www.snort.org/
Sourcefire	Sourcefire	http://www.sourcefire.com/products/is.html
StoneGate	StoneSoft Corporation	http://www.stonesoft.com/en/products_and_solutions/products/ips/
Symantec Network Security	Symantec Corporation	http://www.symantec.com/enterprise/products/index.jsp
UnityOne	TippingPoint Technologies	http://reviews.cnet.com/firewall/tippingpoint-unityone-ips-1200/4505-3269_7-31424832

Table 3.2 Wireless IDPSs

PRODUCT LINE	VENDOR	URL
AirDefense	AirDefense	http://www.airdefense.net/products/index.php
AirMagnet	AirMagnet	http://www.airmagnet.com/products/
AiroPeek	WildPackets	http://www.wildpackets.com/products/airopeek/overview
BlueSecure	BlueSocket	http://www.bluesocket.com/products/centralized_intrusion.html
Highwall	Highwall Technologies	http://www.highwalltech.com/products.cfm
Red-Detect	Red-M	http://www.red-m.com/products-services/our-approach/manage/
RFProtect	RFProtect Wireless Intrusion Protection	http://www.arubanetworks.com/products/arubaos/rfprotect-wireless-intrusion-protection
SpectraGuard	AirTight Networks	http://www.airtightnetworks.net/products/products_overview.html

Table 3.3 NBA IDPSs

PRODUCT LINE	VENDOR	URL
Arbor Peakflow	Arbor Networks	http://www.arbornetworks.com/products
Cisco Guard, Cisco Traffic Anomaly Detector	Cisco Systems	http://www.cisco.com/en/US/products/hw/vpndevc/index.html
The V-Flex Platform	VANTOS	http://www.vantos.com/products.html[a]
OrcaFlow	Cetacea Networks	http://www.glopeda.com/detail/1796/cetacea-networks-orcaflow.html[b]
Profiler	Mazu	http://www.mazunetworks.com/products/index.php
Proventia Network Anomaly Detection System (ADS)	Internet Security Systems	http://www.iss.net/products/Proventia_Network_Anomaly_Detection_System/product_main_page.html
QRadar	NDM Technologies	http://www.ndm.net/siem/ibm-q1-labs/qradar-risk-manager
StealthWatch	Lancope	http://www.lancope.com/products/

[a] When some private companies are sold, others acquire their products.
[b] The name of the tool/software/solution is important to note because some companies are sold, have become inactive, or been renamed, and their products sold to others.

Table 3.4   Host-Based IDPSs

PRODUCT LINE	VENDOR	URL
Blackice	Internet Security Systems	http://www.iss.net/products/product_sections/Server_Protection.html
		http://www.iss.net/products/product_sections/Desktop_Protection.html
Blink	eEye Digital Security	http://www.eeye.com/html/products/blink/index.html
Cisco Security Agent	Cisco Systems	http://www.cisco.com/en/US/products/sw/secursw/ps5057/index.html[a]
Deep Security	Third Brigade	http://www.thirdbrigade.com/
DefenseWall HIPS	SoftSphere Technologies	http://www.softsphere.com/programs/
Intrusion SecureHost	Intrusion	http://www.intrusion.com/
McAfee Host Intrusion Prevention	McAfee	http://www.mcafee.com/uk/products/host-ips-for-desktop.aspx
Primary Response SafeConnect 2.1	AVG	http://www.smartdevicecentral.com/article/Primary+Response+SafeConnect+21/196106_1.aspx
Proventia	Internet Security Systems	http://www.iss.net/products/product_sections/Server_Protection.html
		http://www.iss.net/products/product_sections/Desktop_Protection.html
Intrusion SecureHost	Intrusion	http://www.intrusion.com/
RealSecure	Internet Security Systems	http://www.iss.net/products/product_sections/Server_Protection.html
		http://www.iss.net/products/product_sections/Desktop_Protection.html
SecureIIS Web Server Protection	eEye Digital Security	http://www.eeye.com/html/products/secureiis/index.html
Symantec Critical System Protection	Symantec	http://www.symantec.com/enterprise/products/index.jsp

[a] Although this product is not supported by the URL, it is important to know the product name in order to find some information written or noted in research papers and other documents. Otherwise, this product name would not be familiar.

3.8 Concluding Remarks

As new network technologies, topologies, and structures are developing, different kinds of attack strategies are also being devised. The hackers are not sitting idle, and each day hundreds of experts may try to put their expertise to negative use. Hence, different kinds of detection and prevention schemes will be needed to deal with different network scenarios. A constant learning process and setting the defense strategy accordingly could ensure secure functionality of a network.

References

1. Alsafi, H.M., Abduallah, W.M., and Pathan, A.-S.K. IDPS: An integrated intrusion handling model for cloud computing environment. *International Journal of Computing and Information Technology*, 2012, Volume 4, Issue 1, pp. 1–16.
2. Scarfone, K., and Mell, P. *Guide to Intrusion Detection and Prevention Systems (IDPS)*. National Institute of Standards and Technology Special Publication 800-94, 127 pp. Gaithersburg, MD: National Institute of Standards and Technology, February 2007. Available at csrc.nist.gov/publications/nistpubs/800-94/SP800-94.pdf (accessed August 11, 2012).
3. Abduvaliyev, A., Pathan, A.-S.K., Zhou, J., Roman, R., and Wong, W.-C. Intrusion detection and prevention in wireless sensor networks. In *Wireless Sensor Networks: Current Status and Future Trends*, S. Khan, A.S. Khan Pathan, and N.A. Alrajeh, eds. Boca Raton, FL: Auerbach, CRC Press, Taylor & Francis Group, 2012.
4. Vacca, J.R. *Managing Information Security*. Waltham, MA: Syngress, March 29, 2010.
5. Frederick, K.K. Network intrusion detection signatures, part three. *SecurityFocus*, 2002. Available at http://www.symantec.com/connect/articles/network-intrusion-detection-signatures-part-three (accessed August 11, 2012).
6. Bace, R. *Intrusion Detection*. Indianapolis, IN: New Riders, 2000.
7. Frederick, K.K. Network intrusion detection signatures, part five. *SecurityFocus*, 2002. Available at http://www.symantec.com/connect/articles/network-intrusion-detection-signatures-part-five (accessed August 11, 2012).
8. Pathan, A.-S.K., Monowar, M.M., and Fadlullah, Z.M. *Building Next-Generation Converged Networks: Theory and Practice*. Boca Raton, FL: CRC Press, Taylor & Francis Group, 2013.
9. Marchette, D.J. *Computer Intrusion Detection and Network Monitoring: A Statistical Viewpoint (Information Science and Statistics)*. New York: Springer, June 26, 2001.

10. Rash, M., Orebaugh, A.D., Clark, G., Pinkard, B., and Babbin, J. *Intrusion Prevention and Active Response: Deploying Network and Host IPS.* Waltham, MA: Syngress, April 26, 2005.
11. Northcutt, S., Zeltser, L., Winters, S., Kent, K., and Ritchey, R.W. *Inside Network Perimeter Security,* 2nd ed. Indianapolis, IN: Sams, March 14, 2005.

4

HONEYPOTS

4.1 Definition and History of Honeypots

4.1.1 Honeypot and Its Working Principle

It would be best to first define the term *honeypot* and then talk about its history for an appropriate sequence of reading and understanding relevant critical information. There are many definitions of honeypot [1]. In other words, there is no clearly standardized definition. Different researchers may have their own definitions of what a honeypot is. This situation has created a great deal of confusion and miscommunication. Some think that a honeypot is a tool for deception, whereas others consider it as a weapon to lure hackers, and still others believe that it is simply another intrusion detection tool. Some believe a honeypot should emulate vulnerabilities. Others see it as simply a jail. There are also some who view honeypots as controlled production systems that attackers can break into. These various viewpoints have caused a lot of misunderstanding about what a honeypot is and thus have caused a barrier to realizing its true value.

The formal definition of a honeypot given by Lance Spitzner [1] is "A Honeypot is a security resource whose value lies in being probed, attacked, or compromised."

We now ask a series of questions to give explanations about a honeypot's definition. First, why do we need to make a honeypot? The answers are as follows:

- A honeypot collects information about who is trying to compromise our system. How? The honeypot has tools that can keep traces of the source and destinations.
- A honeypot can provide us with the information about which tools and tactics have been used by the attacker to

compromise our system. Such information can be found in the techniques that have been used inside a honeypot, such as firewall logs, intrusion detection systems (IDSs), and system logs. By obtaining this information, we can avoid such attacks in the future. How? We improve our system against these known attacks. This point (i.e., collecting information about tools and tactics) is considered as the most important goal of a honeypot because anyone likes to make a system as complex as possible so that it becomes more difficult for attackers to compromise the system.

- By using a honeypot, we can have zero-day attacks (unknown attacks). We should mention that most honeypot users are researchers because the honeypot provides them with extensive information about various attacks and their patterns. There are other people as well who make honeypots for other goals, like finding a solution for an attack in a company, simply as a test, for a demonstration of the concept, and so on.

An interesting fact about the honeypot is that a honeypot has no value if it is not attacked by the attacker. This is because the honeypot must be compromised to capture information about the attacker. Otherwise, it has no utility as it cannot provide the required information. This point explains why we need a honeypot. Then, we can ask another question: How can we apply a honeypot so the system is attacked? There are several ways:

1. First, we should put a honeypot in our real network as a real machine or as software in a device.
2. We should separate the honeypot from other machines in the network using firewalls, routers, or other defense mechanisms. Why should we make such separation between the honeypot and other machines? This safeguards other machines from the attackers.
3. If we need to improve our defense systems, then in the honeypot we should use the same defense systems that we are using in the other protected machines. Using the same defense systems in the honeypot helps us to know how the attackers can compromise these defense systems so we can improve them. For example, if we want to discover zero-day attacks,

we should use an updated intrusion detection and prevention system (IDPS) and an antivirus program and add supporting defense mechanisms because these defense systems can filter out the known attacks; then just unknown attacks will compromise our honeypot (which is our expectation). Therefore, we can reduce the heavy loads for our honeypot.

4. Based on need, we can use weak defense systems in the honeypot or we may not use any defense system at all if we would like to trace an attacker and obtain information about how it causes damage. For example, if a government wants to trace who will try to compromise its systems, then the government can use a honeypot with weak defense systems or no defensive mechanism. Therefore, the attacker will be lured and can easily compromise the government systems. Then, the government can trace this attacker. We should note that in this case, the attacker can at least guess it is a honeypot because if a device with weak defense systems is set up, especially in a government institution, it is highly likely to be a honeypot. The attackers are not stupid. Hence, such a trap may not always work to entice the attackers when it comes to a government institution's machines or computers.

5. We should inform all the people in an organization when we set up a honeypot so that they do not try to access it. Therefore, anything going out or coming in to the honeypot should be considered attacks. After a considerable amount of time, we can go to the honeypot and check what it has captured. Also, in real time, we can see what exactly is happening in the honeypot.

As should be apparent from these descriptions, honeypots are different from most security tools. Most of the security technologies in use today are designed to address specific problems. For example, a firewall is a technology that protects your organization by controlling what traffic can flow where. These are used as an access control tool. Firewalls are most commonly deployed around an organization's perimeter to block unauthorized activity. Network IDSs are designed to detect attacks by monitoring either system or network activity.

Honeypots are different because they are not limited to solving a single, specific problem. Instead, honeypots are a highly flexible tool that can be applied to a variety of different situations. This is why the definition of honeypot may at first seem vague because honeypots can be used to achieve so many different goals and can come in a variety of different forms. For example, honeypots can be used to deter attacks, a goal shared with firewalls. Honeypots also can be used to detect attacks, similar to the functionality of an IDS. Honeypots can be used to capture and analyze automated attacks, such as worms, or act as early indication and warning sensors. Honeypots also have the capability to analyze the activities of the blackhat community, capturing the keystrokes or conversations of attackers. How you use honeypots is up to you. It depends on what you are trying to achieve. Chapter 5 has greater details on the different goals you can accomplish with a honeypot. However, all the possible manifestations share one common feature: Their value lies in being probed, attacked, or compromised.

It is important to note that honeypots do not contain valuable data. Instead, they contain some kind of fake data. Therefore, honeypots are security resources that have no production value; no person or resource should be communicating with them. As such, any activity sent their way is "suspect" by nature. Any traffic sent to the honeypot is most likely a probe, scan, or attack. Any traffic initiated by the honeypot means the system has most likely been compromised, and the attacker is making outbound connections.

Let us give a practical example to complete the understanding of the definition of honeypot. Let us consider that there is a house with three rooms. We assume that this house is targeted by the attackers. The house owner needs to know who the attacker is and how the attacker compromises the house defense systems (i.e., doors locks, money storage, window grills, etc.). The house owner has put all the valuable things in the first two rooms and has set a (hidden) camera inside the third room and another camera (hidden) in the front of the room to monitor the attackers. The other defense systems used for the third room are the same as the defense systems used in the first two rooms, but the third room does not contain any valuable things. In this scenario, when an attacker breaks in or comes to the third room, the camera would capture all the attacker's activities. So, in this case, the third room is working the same as a honeypot does because this room gives a free movement option for the attacker but records all the attacker's moves.

4.1.2 History of Honeypots

In this section, we present a brief history of honeypots [1].

- 1990/1991—First public works documenting honeypot concepts: Clifford Stoll's *The Cuckoo's Egg* [2] and Bill Cheswick's "An Evening with Berferd" [3].
- 1997—Version 0.1 of Fred Cohen's Deception Toolkit was released, one of the first honeypot solutions available to the security community [2, 3].
- 1998—Development began on CyberCop Sting, one of the first commercial honeypots sold to the public. CyberCop Sting introduces the concept of multiple virtual systems bound to a single honeypot.
- 1998—Marty Roesch and GTE Internetworking begin development of a honeypot solution that eventually became NetFacade. This work also began the concept of Snort [1, 4].
- 1998—BackOfficer Friendly (BOF) is released—a free, simple-to-use, Windows-based honeypot.
- 1999—Formation of the Honeynet Project and publication of the "Know Your Enemy" series of papers. This work helped increase awareness and validated the value of honeypots and honeypot technologies [1, 5].
- 2000/2001—Use of honeypots to capture and study worm activity. More organizations adopting honeypots for both detecting attacks and for doing research on new threats.
- 2002—A honeypot is used to detect and capture in the wild a new and unknown attack, specifically the *Solaris dtspcd* exploit.

4.1.2.1 Early Publications   Surprisingly little, if any, material can be found before 1990 concerning honeypot concepts. The first resource was a book written by Clifford Stoll, *The Cuckoo's Egg* [2]. The second was the white paper, "An Evening with Berferd in which a Cracker Is Lured, Endured, and Studied" [3], by security icon Bill Cheswick. This does not mean that honeypots were not invented until 1990;

they were undoubtedly developed and used by a variety of organizations well before that time. A great deal of research and deployment occurred within military, government, and commercial organizations, but little of it was public knowledge before 1990.

In *The Cuckoo's Egg* [2], Clifford Stoll discusses a series of true events that occurred over a 10-month period in 1986 and 1987. Stoll was an astronomer at Lawrence Berkeley Lab who worked with and helped administer a variety of computer systems used by the astronomer community. A 75-cent accounting error led him to discover that an attacker, code named "Hunter," had infiltrated one of his systems. Instead of disabling the attacker's accounts and locking him out of the system, Stoll decided to allow the attacker to stay on his system. His motives were to learn more about the attacker and hunt him down. Over the following months, he attempted to discover the attacker's identity while protecting the various government and military computers the attacker was targeting. Stoll's computers were not honeypots; they were production systems used by the academic and research communities. However, he used the compromised systems to track the attacker in a manner similar to the concept of honeypots and honeypot technologies. Stoll's book is not technical; it reads more like a Tom Clancy spy novel. What makes the book unique and important for the history of honeypots are the concepts Stoll discusses in it.

The most fascinating thing in the book is Stoll's approach to gaining information without the attacker realizing it [2]. For example, he creates a bogus directory on the compromised system called SDINET, for Strategic Defense Initiative Network. He wanted to create material that would attract the attention of the attacker. He then filled the directory with a variety of interesting-sounding files. The goal was to waste the attacker's time by compelling the attacker to look through a lot of files. The more time the attacker spent on the system, the more time authorities had to track down the attacker. Stoll also included documents with different values. By observing which particular documents the attacker copied, he could identify the attacker's motives. For example, Stoll provided documents that included those that appeared to have financial value and those that had government secrets. The attacker bypassed the financial documents and focused on materials about national security. This indicated that the attacker's motives were not financial gain but access to highly secret documents.

Bill Cheswick's "An Evening with Berferd in which a Cracker Is Lured, Endured, and Studied" was released in 1990 [3]. This paper is more technical than *The Cuckoo's Egg* [2]. It was written by security professionals for the security community. Like *The Cuckoo's Egg*, everything in Cheswick's paper is nonfiction. However, unlike the book, Cheswick builds a system that he wants to be compromised—which should be the first documented case of a true honeypot. In the paper, he discusses not only how the honeypot was built and used but also how a Dutch hacker was studied as he attacked and compromised a variety of systems.

Cheswick initially built a system with several vulnerabilities (including Sendmail) to determine what threats existed and how they operated. His goal was not to capture someone specific but rather to learn what threatening activity was happening on his networks and systems.

Cheswick's paper [3] explains not only the different methodologies he used in building his system (he never called it a honeypot) but also how these methodologies were used. In addition to a variety of services that appeared vulnerable, he created a controlled environment called a "jail," which contained the activities of the attacker. He provided step-by-step information on how an intruder (called Berferd) attempts to infiltrate the system and what Cheswick was able to learn from the attacker. We see how Berferd infiltrated a system using a Sendmail vulnerability and then gained control of the system. Cheswick describes the advantages and disadvantages of his approach. (This paper is on the CD-ROM that accompanies this book.)

Both Stoll's book and Cheswick's paper are good-read documents. However, none of the resources describes how to design and deploy honeypots in detail. And, neither provides a precise definition of honeypots or explores the value of honeypot technologies.

4.1.2.2 Early Products The first public honeypot solution, called Deception Toolkit (DTK) [6], was developed by Fred Cohen. Version 0.1 was released in November 1997, seven years after *The Cuckoo's Egg* [2] and "An Evening with Berferd" [3]. DTK was one of the first free honeypot solutions one could download, install, and try. It is a collection of PERL scripts and C code that is compiled and installed on a Unix system. DTK is similar to Bill Cheswick's Berferd system in that it emulates a variety of known Unix vulnerabilities. When attacked, these emulated vulnerabilities log the attacker's behavior and actions and reveal information about the attacker. The goal of DTK is not only to gain information but also to deceive the attacker and psychologically confuse the attacker. DTK introduced honeypot solutions to the security community.

Following DTK, in 1998, development began on the first commercial honeypot product, CyberCop Sting. Originally developed by Alfred Huger at Secure Networks Incorporated, it was purchased by NAI in 1998. This honeypot had several features different from DTK. First, it ran on Windows NT systems and not Unix. Second, it could emulate different systems at the same time, specifically a Cisco router, a Solaris server, and an NT system.

Thus, CyberCop Sting could emulate an entire network, with each system having its own unique services devoted to the operating system it was emulating. It would be possible for an attacker to scan a network and find a variety of Cisco, Solaris, and NT systems. The attacker could then telnet to the Cisco router and get a banner saying the system was Cisco, FTP (File Transfer Protocol) to the Solaris server and get a banner saying the system was Solaris, or make an HTTP (Hypertext Transfer Protocol) connection to the NT server. Even the emulated Internet Protocol (IP) stacks were modified to replicate the proper operating system. This way, if active fingerprinting measures were used, such as Nmap [7], the detected operating system would reflect the services for that IP address. The multiple honeypot images created by a single CyberCop Sting installation greatly increased the chance of the honeypots being found and attacked. This improved detection of and alerting to the attacker's activity.

For its time and development, CyberCop Sting was a cutting-edge and advanced honeypot. Also, it was easy to install, configure, and maintain, making it accessible to a large part of the security community. However, as a commercial product, it never really took off and has now been discontinued. Since its demise, several excellent commercial honeypot products have been released, including NetSec's Specter [8] and Recourse's Mantrap [9], both of which we discuss in detail further in the book.

In 1998, Marty Roesch, while working at GTE Internetworking, began working on a honeypot solution for a large government client. Roesch and his colleagues developed a honeypot system that would simulate an entire class C network, up to 254 systems, using a single host to create the entire network. Up to seven different types of operating systems could be emulated with a variety of services. Although the resulting commercial product, NetFacade [4], has seen little public exposure, an important side benefit of this honeypot solution is that Roesch also developed a network-based debugging tool, which eventually led to his open source IDS, Snort [10].

The year 1998 also saw the release of BOF, a Windows- and Unix-based honeypot developed by Marcus Ranum and released by Network Flight Recorder. What made BOF unique is that it was free, was extremely easy to use, and could run on any Windows-based desktop system. All you had to do was download the tool and install it on your system, and you instantly had your own personal honeypot. Though limited in its capabilities, BOF was many people's first introduction to the concepts of honeypot technologies.

In 1999, the Honeynet Project was formed [11]. As a nonprofit research group of 30 security professionals, this group is dedicated to researching the blackhat community and sharing what they learn. Their primary tool for learning is the honeynet, an advanced type of honeypot. Over several years, the Honeynet Project demonstrated the capabilities and value of honeypots, specifically honeynets, for detecting and learning about attacks and the attackers themselves. All of the group's research methods, specifically how they designed and deployed honeypots, were publicly documented and released for the security community in a series of papers known as "Know Your Enemy." In 2001, they released the book *Know Your Enemy* [5] that documented their research works and findings. This helped develop the awareness, credibility, and value of honeypots.

4.1.2.3 Recent History: Honeypots in Action During 2000 and 2001, there was a sudden growth in both Unix-based and Windows-based worms. These worms proved to be extremely effective. Their ability to exponentially spread across the Internet astounded the Internet community. One of the challenges that various security organizations faced was obtaining a copy of the worm for analysis and understanding how it worked. Obtaining copies of the worm from compromised production systems was difficult because of data pollution or, as in the case of the CodeRed worm [12], because the worms only resided in the system's memory. Honeypots proved themselves a powerful solution in quickly capturing these worms, once again proving their value to the security community.

One example was the capture and analysis of the Leaves worm by Incidents.org. On June 19, 2001, a sudden rise of scans for the Sub7 Trojan was detected. Sub7 was a Trojan that took over Windows systems, giving an attacker total remote control of the system. The Trojan listened on the default port 27374. The attacker controlled the compromised system by connecting to this port with special client software. A team of security experts from Incidents.org attempted to find the reason for the activity.

On June 21, Johannes Ullrich of the SANS Institute deployed a honeypot he had developed to emulate a Windows system infected with the Sub7 Trojan. Within minutes, this honeypot captured an attack, giving the Incidents team the ability to analyze it. They discovered that a worm was pretending to be a Sub7 client and attempting to infect systems already infected by the Sub7 Trojan. This saved the attacker from the trouble of hacking into systems since the systems were already attacked and compromised. Matt Fearnow and the Incidents.org team were able to do a full analysis of the worm, which was eventually identified as the W32/Leaves worm, and forward the critical information to the National Infrastructure Protection Center (NIPC). Other organizations also began using honeypots for capturing worms for analysis, such as Ryan Russel at SecurityFocus.com for analysis of the CodeRed II worm. These incidents again helped develop awareness of the value of honeypots within the security community and security research.

The first recorded instance involving honeypot technologies in capturing an unknown exploit occurred on January 8, 2002. A Solaris honeypot captured a dtspcd exploit, an attack never seen before. On November 12, 2001, the CERT Coordination Center, a security research organization, released an advisory for the Common Desktop Environment (CDE) Subprocess Control Service [13] or, more specifically, dtspcd. The security community was aware that the service was vulnerable. An attacker could theoretically remotely attack and gain access to any Unix system running the dtspcd service. However, no actual exploit was known, and it was believed that there was no exploit being used in the wild. When a honeypot was used to detect and capture a dtspcd attack, it confirmed that exploit code did exist and was being used by the blackhat community. CERT was able to release an advisory [14] based on this information, warning the security community that the vulnerability was now being actively attacked and exploited. This demonstrated the value of honeypots in not only capturing known attacks, such as by a worm, but also detecting and capturing unknown attacks.

4.1.3 Types of Honeypots

There are mainly two types of honeypots:

* Production honeypots
* Research honeypots

The concept of these types came from Marty Roesch, developer of Snort. It evolved during his work and research at GTE Internetworking. Production honeypots protect an organization; research honeypots are used to learn.

Production honeypots are easy to use, capture only limited information, and are used primarily by companies or corporations. These honeypots are placed inside the production network with other production servers by an organization to improve their overall state of security. They add value to the security of a specific organization and help mitigate risk. Normally, production honeypots give less information about the attacks or attackers than research honeypots do.

As mentioned, production honeypots usually are easier to build and deploy than research honeypots because they require less functionality. Production honeypots are relatively simple and generally have less risk. One of the disadvantages of the production honeypots is that they generally give us less information about the attacks or the attackers than research honeypots do. We may learn about which systems the attackers are coming from or what exploits they launch, but we will most likely not learn how they communicate among each other or how they develop their tools.

Research honeypots are often complex to deploy. The main goals of the research honeypots are to gather extensive information about the motives and tactics of the blackhat community targeting different networks. It should be mentioned that the research honeypots do not add direct value to a specific organization; instead, they are used to research the threats that the organizations face and to learn how to better protect against those threats. Research honeypots are complex to deploy and maintain, capture extensive information, and are used primarily by research, military, or government organizations.

To obtain extensive information about the attackers, we need to use research honeypots; there is no other alternative. These honeypots give attackers real operating systems and applications with which to interact. This helps us potentially to learn who the attackers are, how they communicate, or how they develop or acquire their tools, but we should mention that the research honeypots have great risks as well and require more time and effort to administer. In fact, research honeypots could potentially reduce the security of an organization since they require extensive resources and maintenance efforts.

4.2 Types of Threats

A honeypot is a kind of security solution. Therefore, it is better to explain what the problem is, that is, explain the attacker. By understanding who the threat is and how the attacker operates, we can easily understand the solution better, which is the concept of a honeypot.

4.2.1 Script Kiddies and Advanced Blackhat Attacks

There are two types of attackers: script kiddies and advanced blackhat. It does not matter if these threats are coming from the outside, such as the Internet, or from the inside, such as a disgruntled employee. Most threats tend to fall into one of these two categories.

Script kiddies. These types of attackers usually depend on scripted attacks. Sometimes, these attackers have certain requirements, such as hacking systems with a fast connection to the Internet or a large hard drive for storing files. In general, however, all they care about are numbers. They tend to be less sophisticated, but they are far more numerous, representing the vast majority of probes, scans, and attacks you see today.

To compromise a device using script kiddies is very simple, and the attacker only needs to follow a number of steps to reach its intended goal. Without script kiddies, the task is much more complicated and may only be performed by experts. For example, there would be the following steps:

- First, an attacker has to identify a vulnerability within an operating system or application. This is not an easy task. It requires extensive knowledge of how operating systems work, such as memory management, kernel mechanisms, and file systems' functionality. To identify vulnerabilities in an application, an attacker would have to learn how an application operated and interacted with both the input and output of information. It could take days, weeks, even months to identify vulnerabilities.

- After a vulnerability is identified, an attacker would have to develop a tool to exploit it. This requires extensive coding skills, potentially in several different computer programming languages.

- After the exploit is developed, the attacker has to find vulnerable systems. Often, one scanning tool is used to find systems that are accessible on the Internet, using such functionality as an ICMP (Internet Control Message Protocol) ping or a full TCP (Transmission Control Protocol) connection. These tools are used to develop a database of systems that are accessible. Then, the attacker has to determine what services existed on the reachable systems—that is, what was actually running on the targets. Furthermore, the attacker has to determine if any of these services were vulnerable.

- The next step would be launching the exploit against the victim, hacking into and gaining control of the system. Finally, various other tools (often called rootkits) should be used to take over and maintain control of a compromised system.

Each of these steps just described requires the development of a unique tool, and using all those tools takes a lot of time and resources. Once the attack is launched, the tools are often manually operated, requiring a great deal of work from an experienced attacker.

The steps mentioned are too difficult and need great experience from the attackers, which means there could be only a few people who could do these successfully. Unfortunately, today the story is different. With almost no technical skills or knowledge, anyone can simply download tools from the Internet that can do all the work for them. Sometimes, these tools combine all of the activities we described into a fully automated weapon that only needs to be pointed at certain systems or even at an entire network. This is as simple as just clicking a button or pressing a key on the keyboard. An attacker simply downloads these tools, follows the instructions, launches the attacks, and happily hacks his or her way into hundreds or even thousands of systems. These tools are rapidly spreading across the Internet, giving access to thousands of attackers, who may do such tasks just for fun. What used to be a highly complex development process is now extremely simple.

Attackers can download the automated tools from a variety of resources or exchange them with their friends. IRC (Internet Relay Chat) and the World Wide Web (WWW) enabled blackhats to instantly share new attack tools around the world. Then, they simply learn the command line syntax for the tool. For attackers who are unfamiliar with command line syntax, a variety of tools has been designed for Windows with point-and-click capabilities. Some of the exploits even come with well-written, step-by-step instructions.

Advanced blackhat. These types of attackers focus on targets of choice and may want to compromise a specific system or systems of high value. These individuals are most likely highly experienced and knowledgeable attackers. Their attack is usually financially or nationally motivated, such as state-sponsored terrorism. They have a specific target they want to compromise, and they focus only on that one. Although less common and fewer in number, these attackers are far more dangerous due to their advanced skill level. Not only can they penetrate highly secured systems, their actions are difficult to detect and trace. Advanced blackhats make little "noise" when attacking systems, and they excel at covering their tracks. Even if you have been successfully attacked by such a skilled blackhat, you may never even be aware of it.

While script kiddies and automated attacks represent the largest percentage of attackers, the smaller, more dangerous percentage of attackers are the skilled ones that do not want anyone to know about their existence. These advanced blackhats do not release their tools. They only attack and compromise systems of high value (i.e., systems of choice). When these attackers are successful, they do not tell the world about it. Instead, they silently infiltrate organizations, collecting information, users' accounts, and access to critical resources. Often, organizations have no idea that they have been compromised. Advanced attackers can spend months, even years, within a compromised organization without anyone finding out.

These attackers are interested in a variety of targets. It could be an online banking system, where the attacker is after the database containing credit card information for millions of individuals. It could be a case of corporate espionage; perhaps the attacker is attempting to infiltrate a car manufacturer and obtain research designs for future cars. Or, it can be as sinister as a foreign government attempting to access highly confidential government secrets, potentially compromising the security of a country.

These individuals are highly trained and experienced, and they are far more difficult to detect than script kiddies. Even after they have successfully penetrated an organization, they will take advanced steps to ensure that their presence or activity cannot be detected. Very little is known about these attackers. Unlike unskilled attackers, advanced blackhats do not share the same tools or techniques. Each one tends to develop personal skills, methods, and tool sets specialized for specific activities. As such, when the tools and methods of one advanced attacker are discovered, the information gained may not apply to other advanced blackhats.

We should mention that every computer connected to the Internet is exposed to a great danger. This danger may cost you all your life; for example, what would happen if an attacker uses your hard drive to store all of the stolen credit card information that he or she has collected? If the competent authorities for credit cards prosecute thieves, track the attacker traces, and find that the credit card information is in your computer, what will you do? It may happen that the amount of money that was stolen from the credit cards is too much. In such an embarrassing case, how can you deny the charge against you? Therefore, everyone should take care about this great issue and try to make his or her computer as secure as possible.

4.2.2 Attackers' Motivations

Understanding the motivation of the attackers will help us to understand threats better. The following information on attacks will help in understanding why an attacker would target and attempt to compromise a system.

4.2.2.1 Denial-of-Service Attack Denial-of-service (DoS) attacks are those designed to take out the computer systems or networks of a victim. This is commonly done by flooding the intended target (such as a Web server) with a barrage of network traffic. The more traffic that is thrown at a victim, the more effective the attack is. Attackers will often compromise hundreds, if not thousands, of systems to be used for attacks. The more computers they own, the more traffic they can launch at a target. Many blackhats use DoS attacks to take out other blackhats. One example is IRC wars; one individual attempts to knock out another individual from an IRC channel using DoS attacks [15].

4.2.2.2 BOTs Bots are automated robots that act on behalf of an individual in a preprogrammed fashion. They are most commonly used to maintain control of IRC. The more computers one hacks into, the more bots one can launch, and the more one can control specific IRC channels. Using many bots protects individuals from losing control of an IRC from DoS attacks.

4.2.2.3 Phishing Phishing is a way of attempting to acquire information (and sometimes, indirectly, money) such as usernames, passwords, and credit card details by masquerading as a trustworthy entity in an electronic communication. Communications purporting to be from popular social Web sites, auction sites, online payment processors, or information technology (IT) administrators are commonly used to lure the unsuspecting public. Phishing is typically carried out by e-mail spoofing or instant messaging, and it often directs users to enter details at a fake Web site whose look and feel are almost identical to the legitimate one. Phishing is an example of social engineering techniques used to deceive users and exploit the poor usability of current Web security technologies. Attempts to deal with the growing number of reported phishing incidents include legislation, user training, public awareness, and technical security measures [16].

4.3 The Value of Honeypots

We know now from all this discussion that there is no specific definition of honeypot. Therefore, the value of a honeypot depends on what your problem is or why you need to build honeypots. The answer highlights the value of honeypots. Therefore, the value of honeypots basically depends on your goals.

There are advantages and disadvantages of honeypots that affect their value. In this section, we show their advantages and disadvantages. Moreover, we present the differences between production and research honeypots and their respective roles.

4.3.1 Advantages of Honeypots

There are many advantages of using honeypots; this section focuses on some of them [1].

- **Data Value.** One of the challenges the security community faces is gaining value from data. Organizations collect vast amounts of data every day, including firewall logs, system logs, and intrusion detection alerts. The sheer amount of information can be overwhelming, making it extremely difficult to derive any value from the data. Honeypots, on the other hand, collect few data, but what they do collect is normally of high value. The honeypot concept of no expected production activity dramatically reduces the noise level. Instead of logging gigabytes of data every day, most honeypots collect several megabytes of data per day, if even that much. Any data logged are most likely a scan, probe, or attack—information of high value.

Honeypots can give you the precise information you need in a quick and easy-to-understand format. This makes analysis much easier and reaction time much quicker. For example, the Honeynet Project, a group researching honeypots, collects on average less than 1 megabyte of data per day. Even though this is a very small amount of data, it contains primarily malicious activities. These data can then be used for statistical modeling, trend analysis, detecting attacks, or even analyzing attackers. This is similar to a microscope effect. Whatever data you capture is placed under a microscope for detailed scrutiny.

- **Resources.** Another challenge most security mechanisms face is resource limitations or even resource exhaustion. Resource exhaustion is when a security resource can no longer continue to function because its resources are overwhelmed. For example, a firewall may fail because its connections table is full, it has run out of resources, or it can no longer monitor connections. This forces the firewall to block all connections instead of just blocking unauthorized activity. An IDS may have too much network activity to monitor, perhaps hundreds of megabytes of data per second. When this happens, the IDS sensor's buffers become full, and it begins dropping packets. Its resources have been exhausted, and it can no longer effectively monitor network activity, potentially missing attacks. Another example is centralized log servers. They may not be able to collect all the events from remote systems, potentially dropping and failing to log critical events.

Because they capture and monitor little activity, honeypots typically do not have problems of resource exhaustion. As a point of contrast, most IDS sensors have difficulty monitoring networks that have gigabits speed. The speed and volume of the traffic are simply too great for the sensor to analyze every packet. As a result, traffic is dropped, and potential attacks are missed. A honeypot deployed on the same network does not share this problem. It only captures activities directed at itself, so the system is not overwhelmed by the traffic. Where the IDS sensor may fail because of resource exhaustion, the honeypot is not likely to have a problem. A side benefit of the limited resource requirements of a honeypot is that you do not have to invest a great deal of money in hardware for it. Honeypots, in contrast to many security mechanisms such as firewalls or IDS sensors, do not require the latest cutting-edge technology, vast amounts of RAM or chip speed, or large disk drives. You can use leftover computers found in your organization or that old laptop your boss no longer wants. This means that not only can a honeypot be deployed on your gigabit network but also it can be a relatively cheap computer.

- **Simplicity.** Simplicity is the biggest single advantage of honeypots. There are no fancy algorithms to develop, no signature databases to maintain, no rule bases to misconfigure. You just take the honeypot, drop it somewhere in your organization, and sit back and wait. While some honeypots, especially research honeypots, can be more complex, they all operate on the same simple premise: If somebody or someone connects to the honeypot, check it out. As experienced security professionals will tell you, the simpler the concept, the more reliable it is. With complexity come misconfigurations, breakdowns, and failures.

- **Fewer false positives.** We mentioned that any interaction with the honeypots will be considered suspicious. Moreover, when all people in an organization are informed that there is a honeypot set up in the organization (i.e., some devices are acting as honeypots), nobody will try to access them.

- **Do not require known attack signatures, unlike an IDS.** Honeypots do not require a known attack signature to detect suspicious activities. All activities in honeypots will be stored as suspicious.

4.3.2 Disadvantages of Honeypots

While it is true that honeypots have great advantages, they also have several disadvantages [1]. A critical point to remember is that honeypots do not replace any security mechanisms; they only work with and enhance your overall security architecture. Let us see now some of the significant disadvantages:

- **Only monitor interactions made directly with the honeypot.** This is considered as the greatest disadvantage of honeypots. They only see what activity is directed against them. If an attacker breaks into your network and attacks a variety of systems, your honeypot will be unaware of the activity unless it is attacked directly. If the attacker has identified your honeypot for what it is, the attacker can avoid that system and infiltrate your organization, with the honeypot never knowing something bad happened. As noted, honeypots have a microscope effect on the value of the data you collect, enabling you to focus closely on data of known value. However, like a microscope, the honeypot's limited field of view can exclude events happening all around it.
- **Risk.** Honeypots can be used by expert attackers to attack other systems. Therefore, they can even be great threats for your network.
- **Fingerprinting.** Another disadvantage, found especially in many commercial versions, is fingerprinting. Fingerprinting is when an attacker can identify the true identity of a honeypot because it has certain expected characteristics or behaviors. For example, a honeypot may emulate a Web server. Whenever an attacker connects to this specific type of honeypot, the Web server responds by sending a common error message using standard HTML (Hypertext Markup Language). This is the exact response we would expect from any Web server. However, if the honeypot has a weakness in it and misspells one of the HTML commands, such as spelling the word *length* as *legnht*, then this misspelling becomes a fingerprint for the honeypot. This is because any attacker can quickly identify such types of mistakes in the Web server

emulation. Also, an incorrectly implemented honeypot can identify itself. For example, a honeypot may be designed to emulate an NT IIS Web server, but it also has certain characteristics that identify it as a Unix Solaris server. These contradictory identities can act as a signature for a honeypot. There is a variety of other methods to fingerprint a honeypot discussed in other parts of this book.

If a blackhat identifies an organization using a honeypot on its internal networks, the blackhat could spoof the identity of other production systems and attack the honeypot. The honeypot would detect these spoofed attacks and falsely alert administrators that a production system is attacking it, sending the organization on a wild goose chase. Meanwhile, in the midst of all the confusion, an attacker could focus on real attacks.

Fingerprinting is an even greater risk for research honeypots. A system designed to gain intelligence can be devastated if detected. An attacker can feed bad information to a research honeypot as opposed to avoiding detection. This bad information would then lead the security community to make incorrect conclusions about the blackhat community.

Although these disadvantages seem to diminish the value of honeypots, some organizations might want to use them positively to scare away or confuse attackers. Once a honeypot is attacked, it can identify itself and then warn the attacker in hopes of scaring the attacker off. However, in most situations, organizations do not want their honeypots to be detected.

4.3.3 Roles of Honeypots in Network Security

We have discussed the advantages and disadvantages of honeypots. To see what the greatest value of the honeypots could be, we must apply them to security. We may analyze how they add value to security and reduce an organization's overall risk.

Security was broken into three categories by Bruce Schneier in *Secrets and Lies* [17]: prevention, detection, and response. Here, we discuss how honeypots can or cannot add value to each of them.

4.3.3.1 Prevention In network security, prevention means keeping the bad guy out (i.e., preventing the bad guy (or gal) from entering your network). Honeypots add a little value to prevention. Moreover, we know that honeypots can be used by the attackers to attack other systems in your organizations. The good news is that there are many methods that can be used by the honeypots to prevent the attackers from entering your organization. When attackers know that an organization has applied honeypots, they will worry about being detected and will waste time and resources attacking the honeypots. This method, discussed previously, is known as prevention by deception or deterrence. The deception concept is to make attackers waste time and resources attacking honeypots, as opposed to attacking production systems. The deterrence concept is that if attackers know there are honeypots in an organization, they may be scared off. Perhaps they will not want to be detected, or they will not want to waste their time or resources.

We should mention that deception and deterrence fail to prevent the most common of the attacks, especially targets of opportunity. This is because targets-of-opportunity attackers use automated tools to compromise as many systems as possible. These attackers do not spend time analyzing the systems they target. Deception or deterrence will not prevent these attacks because there is no conscious individual to deter or deceive. Finally, we can say that there is no real prevention by honeypots or limited prevention can be provided by them.

4.3.3.2 Detection Detection means the act of monitoring, detecting, and alerting unauthorized activity. In the IDPS chapter (Chapter 3), we explained what the main difference between detection and prevention is and gave real-life examples. In addition to those concepts, prevention means to prevent unauthorized activities from entering your organization, but in case of detection, unauthorized activities can enter your organization, and the system sends an alert in real time to the administrators. Consequently, the administrators will check whether these activities are authorized. If they are unauthorized, then the administrators will deny them or purge them.

The security community has designed several technologies for doing detection tasks; one of them is an IDS, for example. An IDS is a great security solution that is designed to detect unauthorized activities in the network or on individual machines.

After these descriptions about detection, one question comes forward: Do honeypots add value in detecting unauthorized or suspicious activity? The answer is, Yes. Honeypots add great value in detection, which we now explore.

There are mainly three common challenges of the detection environment:

- False positives
- False negatives
- Data aggregation

False positives happen when the IDS falsely alerts concerning suspicious or malicious activity, typically because of flawed traffic modeling or weak rules, signatures, or anomalies specified. False negatives are when the system fails to detect an attack. The third challenge is data aggregation, centrally collecting all the data used for detection and then corroborating those data into valuable information.

A single false positive is not a problem. The problem occurs when a system sends too many false positives (i.e., hundreds or even thousands of times a day). So, too many false positives are a big problem because the administrator should take care of all these false positives to check whether they are truly false positives or not. This adds to the burden of tasks of an administrator as we know that a person in that role has too many tasks to perform each day, including taking care of the IDS. If an IDS has a huge number of false positives, an administrator is supposed to give most of his or her time for this issue and ignore all the other issues. Often, some people say that an IDS is good if it has a few false positives, and they seem not to care about the danger of false negatives. Our view in this matter is that both false positives and false negatives are equally crucial for an organization because a successful false negative will make a big problem in an organization, such as information theft, network delay, system down, and so on. Again, the false positives cause a problem that can occupy an administrator and drain the administrator's resources.

It is well understood that there is not a single man-made system in the world that is 100% perfect. But, our goal is to design and develop any system to be as flawless as possible to the best of our abilities. A perfect system needs godly inputs and supports, which would be free from any error, which is not applicable for human beings. So, a good IDS also should have a few false positives and false negatives.

The third challenge is data aggregation. Modern technology is extremely effective at capturing extensive amounts of data. Network intrusion detection systems (NIDS), system logs, application logs—all of these resources are good at capturing and generating gigabytes of data. The challenge is how to aggregate all these data so that they have value in detecting and confirming an attack. New technologies are constantly being devised to pull all these data together to create value to potentially detect attacks. At the same time, new technologies are being developed that can generate more new forms of data. So, here the problem is that the technology is advancing too rapidly, and the solutions for aggregating data cannot keep up with the pace of data production.

To make a good environment for detection, we must address these three challenges. The honeypots can address these challenges in style. Let us see how:

- **False positives.** Most honeypots have no production traffic and will not run any legitimate production services. So, there is little activity to generate false positives.
- **False negatives.** Honeypots address false negatives because they are not easily evaded or defeated by new exploits. Moreover, as we know that there is little or no production activity within the honeypots, they reduce false negatives by capturing absolutely everything that enters and leaves the system. This means that all the activities that are captured are most likely the suspects.
- **Data aggregation.** Honeypots address this issue by capturing high-value data. They usually generate only several megabytes of data a day, most of which are of high value. Also, honeypots can capture zero-day attacks (i.e., unknown attacks), which are not detected by other security tools. This makes them extremely handy for use in network systems.

One example of using a honeypot for detection would be its deployment within a DMZ, often called the demilitarized zone. This is a network of untrusted systems normally used to provide services to the Internet, such as e-mail or Web server. These are usually the systems at great risk since anyone on the Internet can initiate a connection to them, so they are highly likely to be attacked and potentially compromised. Detection of such activity is critical. The problem is that such attacks are difficult to detect because there are so many production activities going on. All of this traffic can generate a significant number of false positives. Administrators may quickly ignore alerts generated by traffic within the DMZ. Also, because of the large amount of traffic generated, data aggregation becomes a challenge. However, we do not want to miss any attacks, specifically false negatives. Hence, such implementation is often welcome.

4.3.3.3 Response   Once an attack is detected, we need the ability to respond to this attack. A honeypot can help protect an organization in such a response event. One of the greatest challenges that organizations face today is how to respond to an attack. There is often little information regarding the attackers, how they got in, or how much damage they have already done. In an attack situation, detailed information about the attacker's activities is critical. The main problem of attack response is that often the compromised system is a production system and is running essential services. Hence, it is difficult to shut it down or take it offline. Even if the system is taken offline, the logs and data entries are so great that it can be difficult to determine what normal day-to-day activities are and what the attacker's activities are.

Honeypots can help address both problems. Honeypots make an excellent incident response tool as they can quickly and easily be taken offline for a full forensic analysis without having an impact on day-to-day production operations. Also, the only activity a honeypot captures is unauthorized or malicious activity (as mentioned). This makes hacked honeypots much easier to analyze than hacked production systems as any data we retrieve from a honeypot are most likely related to the attacker. The precious gift they (i.e., honeypots) provide here is quickly giving organizations some kind of in-depth information that the organizations need to respond to an attack effectively. Generally, high-interaction honeypots make the best solution for response. We discuss this in Section 4.4.2.

4.4 Honeypot Types Based on Interaction Level

Level of interaction gives us a scale with which we could measure and compare honeypots. The more a honeypot can do and the more an attacker can do to a honeypot, the greater the information that can be derived from it. However, by the same token, the more an attacker can do to the honeypot, the more potential damage an attacker can incur. Based on interaction levels, honeypots fall into three categories [1]: low-interaction honeypots, high-interaction honeypots, and medium-interaction honeypots.

4.4.1 Low-Interaction Honeypots

Low-interaction honeypots are the simplest in terms of implementation and typically are the easiest to install, configure, deploy, and maintain because of their simple design and basic functionality. These honeypots merely emulate a variety of services. So, the attacker is limited to interacting with these predesignated services. For example, a low-interaction honeypot could emulate a standard Unix server with several running services, such as telnet and FTP. An attacker could telnet to the honeypot, get a banner that states the operating system, and perhaps obtain a log-in prompt. The attacker can then attempt to log in by brute force or by guessing the passwords. The honeypot would capture and collect these attempts, but we should mention that there is no real operating system for the attacker to log in to, so the attacker's interaction is limited to log-in attempts.

In fact, the main function of the low-interaction honeypots is detection, specifically of unauthorized scans or unauthorized connection attempts. As mentioned, low-interaction honeypots offer a limited functionality; most of this can be emulated by a program. The program is simply installed on a host system and configured to offer whatever services the administration wants, and the honeypot is ready. This makes both deployment and maintenance of the honeypot easy. All that the administrator has to do is to maintain patch levels of the program and monitor any alerting mechanisms.

Low-interaction honeypots have the lowest risk because there are no real operating systems for the attacker to interact with (i.e., all of the services are emulated, not real). So, these honeypots cannot be used to harm or monitor other systems. Low-interaction honeypots log only limited information and are designed to capture known activities. An attacker can detect a low-interaction honeypot by executing a command that the emulation does not support.

One of the advantages of this approach is that the activities of the attacker are naturally "sandboxed" within the boundaries of the software running on a host operating system. The honeypot can pretend to be, for example, a Solaris server, with TCP/IP stack characteristics of a Solaris system emulated to fool operating system fingerprinting and services that one would expect to see on such a server running Solaris. However, because these services are incompletely implemented, exploits written to compromise a Solaris server will at best result in a simulated compromise of the honeypot. That is, if the exploit is known and handled by the honeypot, the actual host operating system is not compromised. For the worst case, the exploit will fail because the exploit is unknown or the vulnerability is not implemented in the honeypot.

Another advantage of the low-interaction honeypot is that the attacker is also restricted from attacking other hosts from the honeypot system. This is again because the compromise of the server is emulated.

The use of low-interaction honeypots also has some disadvantages, which come from the advantages. By definition, no low-interaction emulation of an operating system and its services will be complete. The responses an attacker would expect for known vulnerabilities and exploits are emulated, so a low-interaction honeypot will not respond accurately to exploits we have not included in the emulated responses. The so-called zero-day exploits would fall into this category. These exploits are kept private by the attackers, and it is therefore difficult to prepare your honeypot for these kinds of exploits [18].

4.4.2 High-Interaction Honeypots

The high-interaction honeypots are different from low-interaction honeypots in terms of implementation and collecting information. High-interaction honeypots utilize actual operating systems rather than emulations. As actual operating systems are used in the high-interaction honeypots, the attacker obtains a more realistic experience, and we are able to gather more information about intended attacks. This makes high-interaction honeypots useful when one wishes to capture details of vulnerabilities or exploits that are not yet known to the public. These vulnerabilities or exploits are used only by a small number of attackers who discovered the vulnerability and wrote an exploit for it. Such exploits are known as *zero–day* exploits. It is important to find and publicize these vulnerabilities quickly so that system administrators can filter or work around these problems. Also, vendors can develop and release software patches to fix these vulnerabilities [18].

The high-interaction honeypots are dangerous because the attackers can use these systems to harm other systems. So, most often high-interaction honeypots are placed within a controlled environment, such as behind a firewall. The ability to control the attacker comes not from the honeypot itself but from the network access control device—in many cases the firewall. The firewall allows the attacker to compromise one of the honeypots sitting behind the firewall, but it does not let the attacker use the honeypot to launch attacks from behind the firewall. Such architecture is complex to deploy and maintain, especially if you do not want the attacker to realize that he or she is being monitored and controlled. A great deal of work goes into building a firewall with proper rule bases.

As mentioned, the high-interaction honeypots need extensive control mechanisms; these can be extremely difficult and time consuming to install and configure. To implement high-interaction honeypots, a variety of different technologies should be combined, such as firewalls and IDSs. All of the technologies have to be properly customized for the high-interaction honeypot. Maintenance is also time consuming because we must update firewall rule bases and IDS signature databases and monitor the honeypot activity around the clock. Because of these complexities, the high-interaction honeypots are high risk. The more interaction we allow the attacker, the more that can go wrong. However, once implemented correctly, a high-interaction honeypot can give valuable insights about attackers that no other honeypot can.

4.4.3 Medium-Interaction Honeypots

Medium-interaction honeypots [19] try to combine the benefits of both approaches (low interaction and high interaction) with regard to botnet detection and malware collection while removing their shortcomings.

The key feature of medium-interaction honeypots is application-layer virtualization. The medium-interaction honeypots do not aim at fully simulating a full operational system environment or implement all details of an application protocol. What the medium-interaction honeypots do is provide sufficient responses that known exploits await on certain ports that will trick them into sending their payload.

Once the payload has been received, the shellcode is extracted and analyzed. The medium-interaction honeypot then emulates the actions the shellcode would perform to download the malware. Therefore, the honeypot has to provide some virtual file system as well as virtual standard Windows download utilities. The honeypot can then download the malware from the serving location and store it locally or submit it somewhere else for analysis.

4.5 An Overview of Five Honeypots

In this section, we present an overview of five notable honeypots [1]. These examples can give the readers some idea about what honeypot products are available (the open source products and the commercial versions).

4.5.1 *BackOfficer Friendly*

BackOfficer Friendly or BOF was developed by Marcus Ranum and the folks at Network Flight Recorder. BOF is commonly called a simple, free honeypot solution. BOF is considered a low-interaction honeypot designed to run on almost any Windows system.

BOF is simple so that anyone can install it on a system; also, it is easy to configure and requires low maintenance. Because it is simple, its capabilities are also severely limited. It has a small set of services that simply listen on ports, with notably limited emulation capabilities.

4.5.2 *Specter*

Specter is developed and sold by NetSec, and it is considered a commercially supported honeypot. Specter is also considered a low-interaction honeypot like BOF, but it has more functionality and capabilities than BOF. In fact, Specter is not only emulated services, but also has the ability to emulate different operating systems and vulnerabilities. It also has extensive alerting and logging capabilities. Moreover, Specter is easy to deploy and simple to maintain and is low risk because it only emulates services with limited interaction. However, compared to medium- and high-interaction honeypots, it is limited in the amount of information that it can gather. Specter is primarily a production honeypot.

4.5.3 Honeyd

Honeyd is considered to be an open source, low-interaction honeypot. The main functions of Honeyd are to

- detect,
- capture, and
- alert to suspicious activity.

Honeyd was developed by Niels Provos in April 2002. It introduced several new concepts for honeypots. First, it does not monitor a single IP address for activity; instead, it monitors networks of millions of systems. When it detects probes against a system that does not exist, it dynamically assumes the identity of the victim and then interacts with the attacker, exponentially increasing the honeypot's ability to detect and capture attacks. It can emulate hundreds of operating systems, at both the application and IP stack levels. As an open source solution, Honeyd is free technology, giving you full access to the source code. You can customize your own solutions or use those developed by other members of the security community. Designed for the Unix platform, Honeyd is relatively easy to install and configure, relying primarily on a command line interface.

4.5.4 ManTrap

ManTrap is considered a medium- to high-interaction honeypot, and it is a commercial honeypot sold by Recourse. ManTrap does not emulate any services like BOF, Specter, and Honeyd. Instead, it takes an operating system and creates up to four virtual operating systems. This gives the administrator extensive control and data-capturing capabilities over the virtual operating systems. Organizations can even install production applications that they want to test, such as DNS (Domain Name System), Web servers, or even a database. These virtual operating systems have almost the exact same interaction and functionality as standard production systems. Thus, a great deal can be learned from the attacker.

ManTrap is fairly easy to deploy and maintain as a commercial product. It can also capture an incredible amount of information. Not only does ManTrap detect scans and unauthorized connections, but also it can capture unknown attacks, blackhat conversations, or new vulnerabilities. However, its versatility comes at the cost of increased risk. As the honeypot has a full operating system for the attacker to work with, the honeypot can be used to attack other systems and execute unauthorized activity.

One limitation of ManTrap is that it is currently limited to the Solaris operating system. At the time of writing this book, other versions for other operating systems were under development, but they had not yet been released. As technology moves forward at great speed, readers are suggested to look for the latest product version. ManTrap has the flexibility to be used as either a production or research honeypot, although it is most commonly used for production purposes.

4.5.5 Honeynets

Honeynets are high-interaction honeypots. In fact, it is difficult to envisage any other honeypot solution that can offer a greater level of interaction than honeynets do. The concept of a honeynet is simple: building a network of standard production systems, just as we would find in most organizations today, and putting this network of systems behind some type of access control device (such as a firewall) and watching what happens. Attackers can probe, attack, and exploit any system within the honeynet, giving them full operating systems and applications for interaction. No services are emulated, and no caged environments are created. The systems within a honeynet can be anything: a Solaris server running an Oracle database, a Windows XP server running an IIS Web server, a Cisco router, and so on. In short, the systems within a honeynet are true production systems [1].

The complexity of a honeynet is not in the building of the honeypots themselves (they can easily be nothing more than default installations) but rather in building the controlled network that both controls and captures all the activities that are happening to and from the honeypots. As such, honeynets are some of the most difficult honeypots to both deploy and maintain. This complexity makes the honeynet the highest-risk honeypot solution. One of the most important advantages of honeynets is that they can also capture the greatest level of information on almost any platform that may exist. Honeynets are primarily used for research purposes. Because of the incredible amount of work involved, they have little value as production honeypots.

4.5.5.1 Virtual Honeynets   A virtual honeynet is a solution that allows you to run everything you need on a single computer. We use the term *virtual* because different operating systems have the "appearance" of running on their own independent computers, which are not real machines. These solutions are possible because of virtualization software that allows running multiple operating systems at the same time on the same hardware. Virtual honeynets are not a radically new technology; they simply take the concept of honeynet technologies and implement them into a single system. This implementation has its unique advantages and disadvantages over traditional honeynets [11].

The advantages of a virtual honeynet include reduced cost and easier management, as everything is combined in a single system. Instead of deploying many computers with a full honeynet, you can do it with only one computer. However, this simplicity comes at a cost. First, you are restricted as to what types of operating systems you can deploy by the hardware and virtualization software. For example, most virtual honeynets are based on the Intel X86 chip, so you are restricted to operating systems based on that architecture. You most likely cannot deploy an Alteon switch, VAX, or Cray computer within a virtual honeynet. Second, virtual honeynets come with a risk. Specifically, an attacker may be able to compromise the virtualization software and take over the entire honeynet, giving the attacker control over all the systems. Finally, there is the risk of fingerprinting. Once the bad guys (or gals) have hacked the systems within your virtual honeynet, they may be able to determine what systems are running in a virtual environment.

We have broken virtual honeynets into two categories: self-contained and hybrid. Of the two, self-contained is the more common. We first define these two different types and then cover the different ways that virtual honeynets can be deployed.

Self-Contained Virtual Honeynet. A self-contained virtual honeynet is an entire honeynet network condensed onto a single computer. The entire network is virtually contained on a single, physical system. A honeynet network typically consists of a firewall gateway for data control and data capture and the honeypots within the honeynet. Some advantages of this type of virtual honeynet are as follows:

- *Portable*: Virtual honeynets can be placed on a laptop and taken anywhere. The Honeynet Project demonstrated this functionality at the Blackhat Briefings in August 2002.
- *Plug and catch*: You can take the one box and just plug it in to any network and be ready to catch those blackhats. This makes deployment much easier as you are physically deploying and connecting only one system.
- *Cheap in money and space*: You only need one computer, so it cuts down on your hardware expenses. It also has a small footprint and only takes one outlet and one port. For those of us with limited space and power, this is a lifesaver.

There are some disadvantages as well:

- *Single point of failure*: If something goes wrong with the hardware, the entire honeynet could be out of commission.
- *High-quality computer*: Even though a self-contained honeynet only requires one computer, it will have to be a powerful system. Depending on your setup, you may need a great deal of memory and processing power.
- *Security*: Since everything might be sharing the same hardware, there is a danger of an attacker getting at other parts of the system. Much of this depends on the virtualization software, discussed in a further section.
- *Limited software*: Since everything has to run on one box, you are limited in the software you can use. For instance, it is difficult to run Cisco IOS (Internetwork operating system) on an Intel chip.

Hybrid Virtual Honeynet. A hybrid virtual honeynet is a combination of the classic honeynet and virtualization software. Data capture, such as firewalls, and data control, such as IDS sensors and logging, are on a separate, isolated system. This isolation reduces the risk of compromise. However, all the honeypots are virtually run on a single box. The advantages to this setup are as follows:

- *Secure*: As we saw with the self-contained virtual honeynets, there is a danger of an attacker getting to the other parts of the honeynet (like the firewall). With hybrid virtual honeynets, the only danger would be the attacker accessing the other honeypots.
- *Flexible*: You are able to use a wide variety of software and hardware for the data control and data capture elements of the hybrid network. An example would be that you can use the OpenSnort sensor on the network or a Cisco pix appliance. You can also run any kind of honeypot you want because you can just drop another computer on the network (in addition to your virtual honeypot's box).

Some disadvantages are the following:

- *Not portable*: Since the honeynet network will consist of more than one box, it makes it more difficult to move.
- *Expensive in time and space*: You will have to spend more in terms of power, space, and possibly money since there is more than one computer in the network.

4.5.5.2 Virtualization Software   Hybrid virtual honeynets can allow you to leverage the flexibility of classic honeynets and let you increase the amount of honeypots by using virtualization software. Now that we have defined the two general categories of virtual honeynets, let us highlight some of the possible ways to implement a virtual honeynet. Here, we outline three different technologies that will allow you to deploy your own. Undoubtedly, there are other options, such as Bochs; however, the Honeynet Project has used and tested all three methods given here. No one solution is better than another. Instead, each has its own unique advantages and disadvantages; it is up to you to decide which solution works best. The three options we cover are VMware Workstation, VMware GSX Server, and User Mode Linux.

- VMware Workstation

VMware Workstation is a long-used and -established virtualization option. It is designed for the desktop user and is available for Linux and Windows platforms. Advantages of using VMware Workstation as a virtual honeynet are the following:

1. **Wide range of operating system support**: You are able to run a variety of operating systems within the virtual environment (called GuestOSs), including Linux, Solaris, Windows, and FreeBSD honeypots.
2. **Networking options**: Workstation provides two ways to handle networking. The first is Bridged, which is useful for hybrid virtual honeynet networks because it lets a honeypot use the computer's card and appear to be any other host on the honeynet network. The second option is host-only networking; this is good for self-contained virtual honeynets because you are able to better control traffic with a firewall.
3. **VMware Workstation creates an image of each guest operating system**: These images are simply a file, making them highly portable. This means that you can transfer them to other computers. To restore a honeypot to its original condition, you can just copy a backup into its place.
4. **Ability to mount VMware virtual disk images**: You are able to mount a VMware image just like you would mount a drive using vmware-mount.pl.
5. **Easy to use**: VMware Workstation comes with a graphical interface (both Windows and Linux) that makes installing, configuring, and running the operating systems simple.
6. **Is a commercial product**: VMware Workstation comes with support, upgrades, and patches.

Some disadvantages are the following:

1. **Cost**: VMware Workstation cost about $250 per license in December 2012 (price may vary over time). This might be a bit much for the hobbyist or the unemployed student.
2. **Resource requirements**: VMware Workstation must run under an X environment, and each virtual machine will need its own window. So, on top of the memory you allocate for the GuestOSs, you have the overhead of the X system.

3. **Limited amount of GuestOSs**: With VMware, you can only run a small number of virtual machines, about one to four. This might make for a limited honeynet.

4. **Closed source**: Since VMware is closed source, you cannot really make any custom adjustments.

5. **Fingerprinting:** It may be possible to fingerprint the VMware software on a honeypot, especially if the "VMware tools" are installed on the systems. This could give the honeypots away to the blackhat. However, VMware Workstation does have options that can make fingerprinting more difficult, such as the ability to set the media access control (MAC) address for virtual interfaces.

VMware products also have some nice features, like the ability to suspend a virtual machine (VM). You are able to "pause" the VM, and when you take it out of suspension, all the processes go on like nothing happened. An interesting use of VMware, and other virtualization software, is the ease and speed of bringing up VMs. Once a honeynet is compromised and we have learned as much as we can from it, we want to start over. With a virtual honeynet, all we have to do is copy files or use the undoable disk or nonpersistent disk feature in VMware Workstation to discard any changes made. Another feature of VMware Workstation is the ability to run several networks behind the host operating system. So, if you only have one box, you can have your honeynet and personal computers all on the one box without worrying about data pollution on either side. If you would like to learn more about VMware and its capabilities for honeypot technology, check out Kurt Seifried's excellent papers, "Honeypotting with VMware—The Basics" [20], and "Monitoring VMware Honeypots," by Ryan Barnett [21].

• VMware GSX Server

The VMware GSX Server is a heavy-duty version of VMware Workstation. It is meant for running many higher-end servers. As we will see, this is perfect for use as a honeynet. GSX Server currently runs on Linux and Windows as a host operating system. If you would like to learn more about deploying virtual honeynets on GSX, check out "Know Your Enemy: Learning with VMware" [22].

The advantages of using GSX Server are as follows:

1. **Wide range of operating system support**: GSX Server supports Windows (including 95, 98, NT, 2000, XP, and .NET server), various Linux distributions, and potentially BSD and Solaris (not officially supported).
2. **Networking**: It includes all of the options that Workstation has.
3. **No X means more GuestOSs**: GSX Server does not need X running to have VMware running. This allows you to run many more GuestOSs at the same time. However, it does require that some of the X libraries be installed if the host is running Linux.
4. **Web interface**: GSX Server can be managed through a Web page interface. GuestOSs can be started, paused, stopped, and created via the Web page.
5. **Remote terminal**: This is one of the best features of GSX Server. Through the Web page and with some VMware software, you can remotely access the GuestOSs as if you were sitting at the console. You are able to do things like remote installs and checking out the system without generating traffic on the honeynet.
6. **Ability to mount**: GSX server has the ability to mount VMware virtual disk images, just as in Workstation.
7. **VMware GSX Server supports more host memory (up to 8 GigaByte (GB))**: There are more central processing units (CPUs) (up to eight) and more memory per VM (2 BG) than VMware Workstation.
8. It includes a Perl application programming interface (API) to manage GuestOSs.
9. **Similar to Workstation**: GSX Server is a supported product, including patches and upgrades.

Some disadvantages are the following:

1. **Cost**: A GSX Server license will run around $3500 (again, cost may vary over time; please check for the latest price).
2. **Limited types of GuestOSs**: Operating systems like Solaris X86 and FreeBSD are not officially supported (however, you may be able to install them). This can limit the diversity of your honeynet.

3. **Memory hog**: GSX Server recommends greater than 256 MB just to run the GSX Server software. Operating systems based on a graphical user interface (GUI), such as Windows XP, require another 256 MB for each instance.

4. **Closed source**: Just like Workstation, it is closed source.

5. **Fingerprinting**: It may be possible to fingerprint the VMware software on a honeypot, especially if the VMware tools are installed on the systems. This could give the honeypots away to the blackhat. However, like Workstation, there are configuration options that can reduce that risk.

VMware also makes a VMware ESX Server. Instead of being just a software solution, ESX Server runs in hardware of the interface. ESX Server provides its own VM operating system monitor that takes over the host hardware. This allows more granular control of resources allocated to VMs, such as CPU shares, network bandwidth shares, and disk bandwidth shares, and it allows those resources to be changed dynamically. This product is even higher end than GSX Server. Some of its features are as follows: It can support multiple processors, more concurrent VMs (up to 64 VMs), more host memory (up to 64 GB), and more memory per VM (up to 3.6 GB) than GSX Server.

- User Mode Linux

User Mode Linux (UML) is a special kernel module that allows you to run many virtual versions of Linux at the same time. Developed by Jeff Dike, UML gives you the ability to have multiple instances of Linux running on the same system at the same time. It is a relatively new tool with great potential. You can learn in detail how to deploy your own UML honeynet in the paper, "Know Your Enemy: Learning with User-Mode Linux" [23]. Some advantages to using User Mode Linux are as follows:

1. UML is free and open source: You have access to the source code.

2. UML has a small footprint and fewer resource requirements. UML does not need to use X. It can also run an extensive number of systems with little memory.

3. UML has the ability to create several virtual networks and even create virtual routers, all inside the original virtual network.

4. UML supports both bridging and networking, similar to VMware.

5. UML has the ability to log keystrokes through the GuestOS kernel. The keystrokes are logged right on the host operating system, so there are no issues with how to get the keystrokes off the honeypot in a stealth manner.

6. UML comes with preconfigured and downloadable file systems, making it fast and easy to populate your honeynet with honeypots. Like VMware, these file system images are mountable.

7. You can access UML consoles in a wide variety of ways, including through pseudoterminals, xterms, and portals on the host to which you can telnet. And, there is always screen—the terminal or interface via which a communication can be made by the user. Run UML inside screen, detach it, and you can log in to the host from anywhere and attach it back.

Some disadvantages are the following:

1. Currently, UML only supports Linux VMs; however, a port to Windows is under development.

2. As a new tool, there are some bugs, documentation, and security issues.

3. There is no GUI; currently, all configurations and implementations are done at the command line. There is a steeper learning curve.

4. As an open source tool, there is no official or commercial support.

5. Similar to VMware, it may be possible to fingerprint a UML honeynet due to the virtualization software.

4.6 Conclusion

Before concluding this chapter, it should be clarified that honeypots do not perform the same functions as an IDS. Yes, they have some similarities, but from an operational point of view, they are fairly different. For example, if we would like to devise a good IDS for a network, we must collect valuable data about attacks, then analyze these attacks to generate signatures for them; then, we have to use these signatures in the IDS. Honeypots, on the other hand, are good tools to collect valuable data, but they are set up for being attacked by the potential attackers. A honeypot is not a usual defense mechanism meant for protecting a system, but an IDS is a core part of the defense system or strategy. Honeypots are often deployed for collecting valuable information about the attackers that could be analyzed and used for developing appropriate countermeasures; an IDS simply implements a set of rules, based on which it detects whether there is any rogue entity that enters into the network and then it asks to purge it.

References

1. Spitzner, L. *Honeypots: Tracking Hackers.* Reading, MA: Addison-Wesley Professional, September 20, 2002.
2. Stoll, C. *The Cuckoo's Egg: Tracking a Spy through the Maze of Computer Espionage.* New York: Pocket Books, October 1, 2000.
3. Cheswick, B. An evening with Berferd in which a cracker is lured, endured, and studied. In *Proceedings of the Winter 1992 USENIX Technical Conference.* San Francisco: USENIX Association, January 20–24, 1992.
4. NetFacade honeypot. Available at http://www22.verizon.com/fns/solutions/netsec/netsec_netfacade.html (accessed August 11, 2012).
5. The Honeynet Project. 2001. *Know Your Enemy.* Boston: Addison-Wesley. Available at http://project.honeynet.org/book/ (accessed August 11, 2012).
6. Deception Toolkit. Available at http://www.all.net/dtk/index.html (accessed August 11, 2012).
7. Nmap, port scanning tool developed by Fyodor. Available at http://www.insecure.org/nmap (accessed August 11, 2012).
8. Specter Honeypot. Available at http://www.specter.com (accessed August 11, 2012).
9. Mantrap Honeypot. Available at http://www.mantrap.com (accessed August 11, 2012).
10. Snort, OpenSource Intrusion Detection System. Available at http://www.snort.org (accessed August 11, 2012).
11. The Honeynet Project. Available at http://project.honeynet.org (accessed August 11, 2012).
12. CERT. *Multiple Vulnerabilities in Several Implementations of the Lightweight Directory Access Protocol (LDAP).* CERT Advisory CA-2001-18. Available at http://www.cert.org/advisories/CA-2001-18.html (accessed August 11, 2012).
13. CERT. *Buffer Overflow in CDE Subprocess Control Service.* CERT Advisory CA-2001-31. Available at http://www.cert.org/advisories/CA-2001-31.html (accessed August 11, 2012).

14. CERT. *Exploitation of Vulnerability in CDE Subprocess Control Service.* CERT Advisory CA-2002-01. Available at http://www.cert.org/advisories/CA-2002-01.html (accessed August 11, 2012).

15. DDoS and Security Reports. Available at http://ddos.arbornetworks. com/ (accessed August 11, 2012).

16. Tan, K.Y. Phishing and spamming via IM (SPIM). Available at http:// isc.sans.org/diary.php?storyid = 1905. (accessed August 11, 2012).

17. Schneier, B. *Secrets and Lies: Digital Security in a Networked World.* New York: Wiley, August 14, 2000.

18. Pasman, D.N. Catching hackers using a virtual honeynet: A case study. Presented at the Sixth Twente Conference on IT, Enschede, University of Twente, February 2, 2007.

19. Wicherski, G. Medium interaction honeypots. April 2006. Available at http://citeseerx.ist.psu.edu/viewdoc/summary?doi = 10.1.1.133.9431 (accessed August 11, 2012).

20. Seifried, K., "Honeypotting with VMware - basics", available at: http:// www.seifried.org/security/ids/20020107-honeypot-vmware-basics.html (last accessed December 06, 2012)

21. Barnett, R.C., "Monitoring VMware Honeypots", available at: http:// honeypots.sourceforge.net/monitoring_vmware_honeypots.html

22. "Know Your Enemy: Learning with VMware", 27 January, 2003, available at: http://old.honeynet.org/papers/vmware/ (last accessed December 06, 2012)

23. "Know Your Enemy: Learning with User-Mode Linux", 20 December, 2002, available at: http://old.honeynet.org/papers/uml/ (last accessed December 06, 2012)

5

INTERNET WORMS

5.1 Introduction

A computer worm is a stand-alone malware computer program that replicates itself in order to spread to other computers without requiring any human intervention by sending copies of its code in network packets and ensuring the code is executed by the computers that receive it. Often, worms use a computer network to spread themselves. This is due to security shortcomings on the target computer. Unlike a computer virus, a worm does not need to attach itself to an existing program. Worms almost always cause at least some harm to the network, even if only by consuming bandwidth, whereas viruses almost always corrupt or modify files on a targeted computer. When computers become infected, they spread further copies of the worm and possibly perform other malicious activities [1, 2].

The first experiments with programs similar to modern worms were reported in 1982 [1]. However, computer worms were not considered a major security threat until the advent of the Internet, which connects a huge number of computers around the globe. So, in some sense, with the beginning of the Internet, the worm epidemics began. The first recorded Internet worm outbreak happened in 1988 [3, 4]; since then, several major incidents have been reported [5–8]. Therefore, Internet worms pose a major threat to Internet infrastructure security, and they may cause the loss of millions of dollars. As our goal is to have secure networking infrastructure, our networks must be protected as much as possible to avoid possible loss of any kind.

5.2 Infection

Remotely infecting a computer requires coercing the computer into running the worm code. To achieve this, worms exploit low-level software defects, also known as vulnerabilities. Vulnerabilities are common in current software because often they are large, complex, and mostly written in unsafe programming languages. Several different classes of vulnerabilities have been discovered over the years. The following vulnerabilities are considered the most common types of vulnerabilities exploitable by worms: buffer overflows [9], arithmetic overflows [10], memory management errors [11], and incorrect handling of format strings [12]. These are among the most common types of vulnerabilities exploitable by worms.

While we should expect new types of vulnerabilities to be discovered in the future, the mechanisms used by worms to gain control of a program's execution should change less frequently. Currently, worms gain control of the execution of a remote program using one of three mechanisms [1]:

- injecting new code into the program,
- injecting new control-flow edges into the program (e.g., forcing the program to call functions that should not be called), or
- corrupting data used by the program.

These three infection mechanisms are discussed in the next few sections in detail. To facilitate the discussion, we use a program with simple stack-based buffer overflow vulnerability [1], shown in Figure 5.1, but it is important to note that all the other types of vulnerabilities enable the same types of successful infection. The program in Figure 5.1 processes a message received from the network. The *ProcessRequest* function checks if the first byte in the message is within an allowed range and then copies the two subsequent fields in the message to a stack-based buffer called *request* and to a buffer supplied in the parameter *userid*, respectively. The code assumes fields in the message are separated by the newline character. The defect in the program is that it does not check that the first field of the message will fit in the *request* stack-based buffer. Consequently, the worm can send a message with a large first field and overwrite the stack frame. This defect can be exploited to infect the program in many ways.

5.2.1 Code Injection

The simplest means of infection requires injecting new code into a running process and coercing the process into executing the new

```
-------------------
void ProcessRequest(char *message, char *user_id)

{
char request[8];
char message_id = *message - ID_BASE;
if(message_id > LOW_ID && message_id < HIGH_ID)

{
int len = CopyField(request,message + 1);
CopyField(user_id,message + len + 2);
ExecuteRequest(request,user_id);

        }

        system(log_activity_command);

}


int CopyField(char *destination, char *source)

{
int len = 0;
while(*source != '\n')
{
len++;
*destination++ = *source++;
        }

*destination = '\0';
return len;
}
```

Figure 5.1 Vulnerable code in the C++ programming language. The code has a buffer overflow vulnerability, enabling code injection, edge injection, and data injection attacks.

code. To use this type of attack on the program in Figure 5.1, the worm could craft a packet including its code at the end of the message and using a first field large enough to overwrite the return address on the stack frame. Inside the first field, at the position that would overwrite the return address, the worm would supply the address of its code in the virtual address space of the program under attack (the code would be there as part of the message just received). This would ensure that on executing the *ret* instruction at the end of the function the process would start to run worm code.

By analyzing the vulnerable program in assembly language, as shown in Figure 5.2, the details of the attack can be understood well. When the *ProcessRequest* function starts to execute, the *esp* register points to the return address saved by the call instruction that transferred control to the function. The function starts by saving the *ebp* register on the stack, decrementing *esp* by 4 in the process (the stack grows toward lower addresses). Instruction 3 moves the first byte of the message into the *al* register (the first parameter for the function is passed in the *ebx* register). The function then executes the range check on the first byte of the message. Instruction 7 subtracts 8 from *esp*, thus allocating 8 bytes on the stack, to hold the request variable. Therefore, the return address is stored at a 12-byte offset from the start of the request. This means that the worm should place the value to be used as the return address at offset 13 in the attack message (since the first byte is not copied). Instruction 16 makes *eax* point to the start of the request buffer. The function then enters a loop (lines 21 to 26) that copies the first field of the message and eventually overwrites the stored return address. To decide which value to supply as the return address, the worm only needs to know the virtual address range where the network message is stored and use a value that points to the start of the worm code within that range. (If the message is not stored at a predictable address, the worm can find code sequences that transfer control to the attack payload elsewhere in memory.)

5.2.2 *Edge Injection*

Infecting a remote computer does not require directly injecting new code into a running process. Another way for infection is to inject a new control-flow edge into the vulnerable program by forcing a control-flow transition that should not happen [1, 13]. To use this type of attack on the program in Figure 5.1, the worm could again craft a message including a first field large enough to overwrite the return address on the stack frame. This can allow the worm to supply as a return address the address of a function already loaded by the program. For example, the attacker could supply the address of

```
1:  push ebp                              //on entry, ebx points to the message parameter
2:  mov ebp,esp
3:  mov al,byte ptr [ebx]                 //move first byte of message into al
4:  mov ecx,dword ptr [ebp+8]
5:  sub al,10h
6:  sub al,31h
7:  sub esp,8                             //allocate stack space for request buffer
8:  cmp al,0Eh ;perform range check on first byte
9:  ja 45
10: mov dl,byte ptr [ebx+1]               //move second byte of message into dl
11: push esi
12: push edi
13: lea edi, [ebx+1]                      //move address of second byte into edi
14: xor esi,esi
15: cmp dl,0Ah
16: lea eax, [ebp-8]                      //move address of request buffer into eax
17: je 28
18: mov ecx,eax
19: sub edi,ecx
20: lea esp, [esp+0h]
21: mov byte ptr [eax],dl                 //loop to copy the first
22: mov dl,byte ptr [edi+eax+1]           //field of the message
23: add eax,1                             //into the request buffer,
24: add esi,1                             //while searching for
25: cmp dl,0Ah                            //the character 0A.
26: jne 21
```

Figure 5.2 Vulnerable program in IA-32 assembly language (compiled from the source code in Figure 5.1). The code is vulnerable to code injection, edge injection, and data injection attacks.

```
27: mov ecx,dword ptr [ebp+8]        //move userid parameter into ecx
28: lea esi,[esi+ebx+2]
29: mov byte ptr [eax],0
30: mov al,byte ptr [esi]            //move first byte of second field into al
31: cmp al,0Ah
32: mov edx,ecx                      //move userid parameter into edx
33: je 40
34: sub esi,ecx                      //loop to copy the second
35: mov byte ptr [edx],al            //field of the message into
36: mov al,byte ptr [esi+edx+1]      //the userid parameter, while
37: add edx,1                        //searching for the character 0A.
38: cmp al,0Ah
39: jne 35
40: lea eax,[ebp-8]
41: mov byte ptr [edx],0
42: call ExecuteRequest               //call ExecuteRequest(request,user_id)
43: pop edi
44: pop esi
45: push 403018h                      //push address of log_activity_command
46: call system                       //call system(log_activity_command)
47: add esp,4
48: mov esp,ebp
49: pop ebp
50: ret                               //load value pointed to by esp into eip
```

Figure 5.2 (Continued) Vulnerable program in IA-32 assembly language (compiled from the source code in Figure 5.1). The code is vulnerable to code injection, edge injection, and data injection attacks.

the system function from the C runtime library and an appropriate argument to that function. This can eventually allow the worm to run arbitrary programs. It could, for example, use a file transfer program to download its code and subsequently run it. We should mention that this attack can evade algorithms that only detect code injection because no new code is loaded by the process running the vulnerable program.

The detailed steps of this attack are similar to the ones described in the previous section, with the added complication that the worm needs to fabricate a correct stack frame for the system function. This can easily be accomplished by noting that this function takes a single parameter: a pointer to a string. Thus, the code for the function expects to find this pointer at the address 4 bytes above the value of the *esp* register when the function is invoked (at this point, *esp* points to the return address, and the parameter is above that). Consequently, besides supplying the address of the system function as in the previous section, the worm will insert in the message a string with the name of the program it wishes to run, and 8 bytes after the start of the address of system (i.e., at offset 21, in the attack message), it will supply the address where the string will be stored in the virtual address space of the target program. Therefore, the worm can easily extend this technique to fabricate several stack frames and force the program to issue a series of function calls.

5.2.3 Data Injection

Finally, to infect a remote computer does not even require forcing any control-flow error in a running process: Attacks can succeed just by corrupting data. One general form of this type of attack requires corrupting the arguments of functions called by the program. By changing the values of the arguments, the worm changes the behavior of the program without injecting any code or forcing any control-flow transfers.

By using the example in Figure 5.1, we can see that after processing the message, the function *ProcessRequest* calls the system to run an external program that maintains an activity log for the program. The call to the system takes as a parameter a pointer (log-activity-command) to a string with the appropriate logging command. The worm can successfully attack the program by corrupting this string, thus forcing the program to run other commands (e.g., commands that download the worm code). Corrupting this string is a slightly more elaborate process than corrupting the function's return address because neither the string nor the pointer to the string is stored in the stack frame for the function (the region that can easily be overwritten by overflowing the request buffer). However, the worm can still manipulate the code in the function to do the appropriate overwrite. It indicates that the code copies the second field in the message to the *userid* parameter. This parameter is in the function's stack frame and can be easily overwritten. Therefore, all the worm needs to do is to overwrite *userid* to make it point to the *log-activity-command* string and supply, as the second field in the attack message, a string with the command it wishes to run.

The detailed steps of this attack can again be understood by analyzing the code in Figure 5.2. The code reveals that the *userid* argument is passed to the function on the stack, immediately above the return address. To see this, note that instruction 27 loads the *userid* pointer into the *ecx* register, and instructions 35 to 39 copy the second field of the message into *userid*. As in the attacks discussed, the worm can supply a large first field in the attack message, overflowing the request buffer. This allows the worm to supply a value that will overwrite *userid* at offset 17 in the attack message. Examining the call to the system at lines 45 and 46, we can see that the log-activity-command is stored at address 0x00403018. Therefore, the worm supplies this value at offset 17 in the attack message and whatever command it wants to run as a string in the second field in the message. Thus, the loop at lines 35 to 39, which should copy the second field in the message into *userid*, is in fact copying the second field into the log-activity-command string. The worm command is executed when the program calls the system on line 46.

5.3 Spreading

The general operational method of the computer worm is first to infect a computer, then infect other computers, giving rise to a propagation process that has many similarities with the spread of human diseases. Empirical evidence [7] showed that the spread of real worms, such as Code Red and Slammer, can be described using the epidemic model

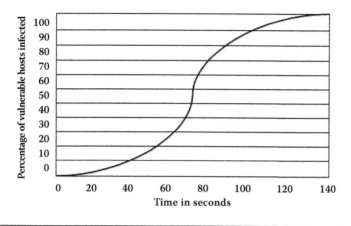

Figure 5.3 Example of propagation of a Slammer-like worm.

for infectious diseases described in Hethcote [14]. Assuming a population of S susceptible hosts and an average infection rate of β and using I_t as the total number of infected hosts at time t, the worm infection is modeled by the following equation:

$$\frac{dI_t}{dt} = \beta I_t \left(1 - \frac{I_t}{S} \right)$$

Figure 5.3 shows the propagation of a Slammer-like worm as predicted by the model. It shows that initially the number of infected hosts grows exponentially until a majority of hosts are infected. The model matches accurately with the initial stages of the Code Red and Slammer outbreaks [7], but later stages tend to deviate from the model due to network congestion effects or human intervention.

We can determine the speed of worm propagation by how fast infected computers can find new victims to infect, and worms can find new victims in many ways [1, 15, 16]. Scanning worms send attack messages to Internet Protocol (IP) addresses that they generate locally, trying to scan the complete IP address space. The address space may be scanned randomly or linearly or could attempt to give preference to address regions that are more likely to be populated with victims.

Topological worms find new victims by finding their addresses in the infected computers. Thus, they spread along a topology maintained by the computers that they infect. There are many examples of such topologies; for example, peer-to-peer networks [1, 17–19] form well-connected topologies that can be exploited in this way. Game server farms, where many computers connect to a few servers, can also facilitate this type of spreading.

Hit-list worms use lists of vulnerable hosts collected in stealth before launching the attack, thus avoiding the need to discover victims during the attack. Hit-list worms have the following properties:

- A high success rate (compared to scanning) allows such worms to infect millions of hosts in seconds.
- Propagation speed is likely to be too fast for any reactive defense proposal.
- Their behavior is different from scanning worms, making them relatively harder to detect.

There are various methods for building hit lists:

- Web search (e.g., find Web servers)
- Gnutella crawling: find active normal hosts
- Random scanning: ping/nmap random addresses

During the attack, these worms possibly partition the list of victims among all the infected machines to speed up the attack.

All of these strategies for finding new victims have been observed in one form or another on the Internet. Worms can also combine several strategies. For instance, the Witty [8] worm used a hit list to ramp up the initial phase of its spread and then switched to scanning the Internet for subsequent victims.

5.4 Hiding

There are several techniques that can be used by worms to disguise their spread on the Internet. In this section, we focus on three evasion techniques: traffic shaping, polymorphism, and fingerprinting detectors.

5.4.1 Traffic Shaping

We should mention that worms usually have complete control over the network traffic generated by the computers they infect. Therefore, they can blend attack traffic with normal traffic to evade detection by analyzing traffic patterns. For example, some detection and mitigation systems are based on the observation that scanning worms are likely to target many invalid addresses [20, 21]. Some of these systems use a limit on the ratio of failed to successful connections; traffic from computers that exceed this limit is blocked. These systems can easily be evaded if the worm establishes a successful connection to another worm instance for each address that it scans. In addition, other systems assume that worms must initiate connections to other computers at a high rate [22–24] to propagate rapidly. These systems detect worm traffic by monitoring the rate at which unique destination addresses are contacted and block the sender if the rate exceeds some limit. These systems can be evaded if worms initiate connections less than the rate limit in areas of the network where the limits are enforced.

Also, the traffic shaping is used to mount denial-of-service attacks on systems that analyze network traffic [25, 26]. For example, worms can generate suspicious traffic patterns using fake IP source addresses to block traffic from legitimate machines. This type of maliciously induced false positive is a serious concern for the deployment of containment systems based exclusively on analyzing network traffic.

5.4.2 Polymorphism

The most difficult technique that the worms can use to hide themselves is polymorphism. Polymorphic worms are considered the most dangerous threats to Internet security, and the danger lies in changing their payloads in every infection attempt to avoid security systems. Polymorphic worms change their payloads using techniques such as encryption and code obfuscation [1]. For instance, if the worm attack messages contain code, the worm can replace a sequence of code instructions with another completely different sequence of instructions that achieves the same purpose (i.e., a semantically equivalent sequence of instructions). These techniques and others are discussed in Section 5.7.4.

Polymorphic worms create a great problem both for detection and for protection. From the detection point of view, systems that try to detect worms by identifying common byte strings in suspicious network traffic will have difficulty detecting polymorphic worms since they may have little invariant content across different messages. For instance, a polymorphic worm exploiting the same vulnerability as Slammer could generate attack messages that differ in all bytes except one. On the other hand, if such systems are configured to detect very short repeated byte strings, they are likely to generate false positives.

From the protection point of view, polymorphic worms make it difficult to block attacks using byte string signatures because such signatures will likely be either too long or too short. Signatures that are too long cannot match worm traffic mutations. A shorter signature increases the chance of appearing in normal traffic. Consequently, the false-negative ratio decreases, but the false-positive ratio increases dramatically.

5.4.3 Fingerprinting

There is another technique that can be used by the worms to avoid detection, which is to try to identify if they are interacting with a detector, before fully revealing their attack. We refer to this type of activity as fingerprinting the detector [1, 24, 27, 28].

Worms can try to fingerprint detectors remotely, that is, try to infer if a remote machine is a detector from its responses to network messages. Some honeypot systems [29] mimic responses to commonly used protocols without fully implementing the corresponding network services. These systems are more vulnerable to fingerprinting because they cannot generate the full spectrum of responses expected from a real network service. Detectors in Vigilante run full operating system and applications software, thereby minimizing their exposure to this type of attack.

Another form of remote fingerprinting requires analyzing the timing of message exchanges. For example, if responses take more time than normal, the remote system may be a detector. It is unclear if this type of attack can be mounted across wide-area networks, where the central processing unit (CPU) speeds, load, and latency to remote machines are unknown.

In addition, worms can fingerprint detectors locally, after they start to run on an infected machine. For example, if a detector is trying to identify a certain type of behavior (e.g., a malicious pattern of usage of operating system services), the worm can first check if it is running inside the detection environment, and if so, it can take evasive actions. This type of fingerprinting has been observed on the Internet. Holz and Raynal [30] reported that Agobot uses an input/output (I/O) back door [31] to detect if it is running inside a virtual machine. Agobot also detects the presence of debuggers and breakpoints.

5.5 Worm Components

At the core of any worm system are five components [32]. A worm may contain any or all of these components, usually in some combination. These components are integrated with each other to compromise a machine and then use the compromised machine to compromise another one and so on. These components are

- Reconnaissance
- Attack components
- Communication components
- Command components
- Intelligence components

We give the definitions of these components next.

5.5.1 Reconnaissance

The worm network has to hunt out (perform reconnaissance) other network nodes to infect. This component is responsible for discovering hosts on the network that are capable of being compromised by the worm's known methods.

5.5.2 Attack Components

The tasks of these components are to launch attacks against an identified target system. Attacks can include the traditional buffer or heap overflow, string-formatting attacks, Unicode misinterpretations (in the case of IIS attacks), and misconfigurations.

5.5.3 Communication Components

Nodes in the worm network can talk to each other; the communication between these nodes helps a worm to do its task easily. The communication components give the worms the interface to send messages between nodes or some other central location.

5.5.4 Command Components

Once worms compromise a machine, the nodes in the worm network can be issued operation commands using this component. The command element provides the interface to the worm node to issue and act based on given commands.

5.5.5 Intelligence Capabilities

The worm nodes need to communicate effectively. Therefore, the worm network needs to know the location of the nodes as well as characteristics of them. The intelligence portion of the worm network provides the information needed to be able to contact other worm nodes, which can be accomplished in a variety of ways.

To have an operational worm, not all of these components are required. Only basic reconnaissance and attack components are needed to build an effective worm that can spread over a great distance. However, this minimal worm will be somewhat limited in that it lacks additional capabilities, such as DDoS (distributed denial-of-service) capabilities or a system-level interface to the compromised host.

5.6 Worm Life

It is most important to know the worm's life because understanding this life will help us to make a good defense mechanism against Internet worms. The life of a worm consists of the following stages, which it continues to cycle through until it is tackled or eliminated [33]:

- Target selection
- Exploitation
- Infection
- Propagation

Figure 5.4 shows a computer worm's usual life cycle.

In the following paragraphs, we give the details of different stages.

1. Target selection. The target selection stage is the phase when an uninfected host is chosen to be attacked. In this phase, the worm performs reconnaissance to determine other potential victims.

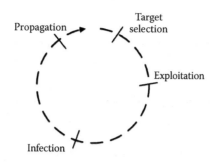

Figure 5.4 Computer worm's life cycle.

2. Exploitation. The exploitation phase is when the worm compromises the target by exploiting a particular vulnerability. Often, worms use well-known vulnerabilities and published exploits to compromise their targets.

3. Infection. The infection stage is the broadest in the life cycle, as the worm copies itself on the victim machine and then performs any number of different actions.

4. Propagation. In the propagation stage, the worm attempts to spread by choosing new targets. The difference between this stage and target selection is simply the point of view from which the actions take place. In target selection, a remotely infected host chooses the local host as a target, often in the form of a probe coming in through inbound network traffic. In the propagation stage, the infected local host is the one choosing a new target, using probes going out in outbound network traffic. This is an important distinction and allows new techniques to be used in worm detection.

There are many propagation methods used by the worms [32]: random scanning, random scanning using lists, island hopping, directed attacking, and hit-list scanning.

5.6.1 Random Scanning

Random network scanning is the simplest method for a worm to spread. In this method, the worm node randomly generates a network to scan. This worm node then begins to search for potential victims in that network space and attacks vulnerable hosts. This random walk is the classic spread model for network-based worms.

5.6.2 Random Scanning Using Lists

In random scanning using lists, the worm carries a list of numbers used to assist in the generation of the networks to probe and attack. This list is built from assigned and used address space from the Internet. By using this method, the worm will be able to focus on locations where hosts are likely to be present, which improves the worm's efficiency.

5.6.3 Island Hopping

Island hopping is so named because it treats network blocks as islands on which it focuses attention before hopping away to a new, random destination. First discussed as a theoretical spread model after the release of Code Red 1, this spread pattern has proven to be highly effective in the long term.

The use of these island-hopping methods also facilitates the spread of the worm behind firewalls and NAT (network address translator) devices. As the worm is biased toward attacking hosts in the same network block, this would typically be behind the firewall and therefore would be exposed to the worm's attacks. For example, the island-hopping techniques employed by Nimda and Code Red 1 [33] appeared to strike an effective balance between random and directed scanning. The worm is likely to stay in a host-rich environment, one that is likely to have similar security policies. This means that the worm has a high probability of finding another vulnerable host in the same network, increasing its productivity and growth.

The Slapper worm generates lists of hosts to probe and attack by using a pseudorandom list of octets. The list, built into the worm, contains the first octet of the network address. The addresses are chosen because they represent address space, which is assigned and in use.

5.6.4 Directed Attacking

Another method that can be used by a worm is to direct its attack at a particular network. In this method, a worm carries a target network to penetrate and focuses its efforts on that network. This type of worm attack would be used in information warfare.

5.6.5 Hit-List Scanning

Finally, a hit list contains the addresses and information of nodes vulnerable to the worm's attacks. This list is generated from scans made before unleashing the worm. For example, an attacker would scan the Internet to find 50,000 hosts vulnerable to a particular Web server exploit. This list is carried by the worm as it progresses and is used to direct its attack. When a node is attacked and compromised, the hit list splits into halves; one of the halves remains with the parent node, and the other half goes to the child node. This mechanism continues, and the worm's efficiency improves with every permutation.

5.7 Polymorphic Worms: Definition and Anatomy

5.7.1 Polymorphic Worm Definition

A polymorphic worm is a computer worm that changes its appearance in every infection attempt [34].

5.7.2 Polymorphic Worm Structure

As stated in Fogla et al. [34], we can identify the following components in a sample of polymorphic worm:

Protocol framework. Worms have to exploit a given vulnerability to infect new hosts and continue their spread. This vulnerability, in many cases, is associated with a particular application code and execution path in this code. This execution path can be activated by few or, often, one type of particular protocol request.

Exploit bytes. These bytes are used by the worm to exploit the vulnerability. They are necessary for the correct execution of the attack.

Worm body. These bytes contain instructions executed by the worm instances on new infected victims. These bytes can assume different values in each instance because the polymorphic worms change their payloads in every infection attempt.

Polymorphic decryptor. The polymorphic decryptor decodes the worm body and starts its execution. Since the shellcode of a polymorphic worm is encrypted when it is sent to a victim, a polymorphic worm should decrypt the shellcode during or before execution.

Other bytes. These bytes do not affect the successful execution of both the worm body and exploit bytes.

5.7.3 Invariant Bytes

In a polymorphic worm sample, we can classify three kinds of bytes: invariant, code, and wildcard [35].

Invariant bytes: As mentioned, polymorphic worms have a feature that is changing their payloads in every infection attempt to evade security systems, but there are some invariant substrings that are fixed in a polymorphic worm (i.e., that means a polymorphic worm cannot change its payload completely). These have a fixed value in every possible instance. If the values of the invariant substrings of a polymorphic worm are changed, the exploit no longer can work. They can be part of the protocol framework and exploit bytes, but in some cases, they are also of the worm body or the polymorphic decryptor. Such bytes are useful in signature generation because they are absolutely necessary for the exploit to work, and their content is replicated across worm instances.

Code bytes: Code bytes come from components like the worm body or decryption routine, in which there are instructions to be executed. Although the code section of worm samples can be subjected to polymorphism and encryption techniques, and thus they can assume different shapes in each instance, polymorphic engines are not perfect; some of these bytes can present invariant values.

Wildcard bytes: These are the bytes that can take any value without affecting worms' spreading capabilities.

5.7.4 Polymorphic Worm Techniques

One of the most important goals of the attackers is to try every possible way to extend the lifetime of Internet worms. To evade the

```
        mov edi, 00403045h  ; Set EDI to Start
        add edi, ebp        ; Adjust according to base
        mov ecx, 0A6Bh      ; length of encrypted virus body
        mov al, [key]       ; pick the key
Decrypt:
        xor [edi], al       ; decrypt body
        inc edi             ; increment counter position
        loop Decrypt        ; until all bytes are decrypted
        jmp Start           ; Jump to Start (jump over some data)
DB      key 86              ; variable one byte key
Start:                      ; encrypted/decrypted virus body
```

Figure 5.5 A decryptor example of a worm.

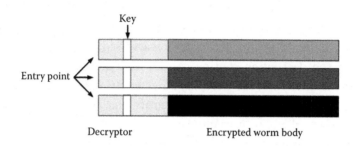

Figure 5.6 Different variants of a polymorphic worm using the same decryptor.

signature-based system, a polymorphic worm appears differently each time it replicates itself. In this section, we show some techniques that the polymorphic worms can use to change their payloads.

There are many techniques to make polymorphic worms [36].

- One technique relies on self-encryption with a variable key. First, it encrypts the body of a worm, which erases both signatures and statistical characteristics of the worm byte string. Then, a copy of the worm, the decryption routine, and the key are sent to a victim machine, where the encrypted text is turned into a regular worm program by the decryption routine (e.g., the code presented in Figure 5.5). The program is then executed to infect other victims and possibly damage the local system. Figure 5.6 explains a simple polymorphic worm using the same decryptor. The worm body attached after the descriptor part appears differently based on different keys. While different copies of a worm look different if different keys are used, the encrypted text tends to follow a

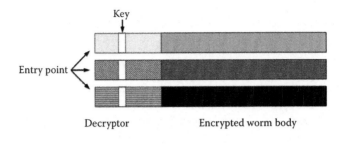

Key

Entry point

Decryptor   Encrypted worm body

Figure 5.7 Different variants of a polymorphic worm using different decryptors.

uniform byte frequency distribution, which itself is a statistical feature that can be captured by anomaly detection based on its deviation from normal traffic distributions. In fact, if the same decryption routine is always used, the byte sequence in the decryption routine can be used as the worm signature. Therefore, the best way to generate a signature to such a worm is to find a way to identify the decryption routine region, which is invariant over different instances of the same Internet worm.

• Another method of polymorphism is to change the decryption routine each time a copy of the worm is sent to another victim host, which is considered a more sophisticated method than the first-mentioned technique. This can be achieved by keeping several decryption routines in a worm. When the worm tries to make a copy, one routine is randomly selected, and other routines are encrypted together with the worm body. Figure 5.7 is an example of such a worm. To further complicate the problem, the attacker can change the entry point of the program such that the decryption routine will appear at different locations of the traffic payload, as shown in Figure 5.8. The number of different decryption routines is limited by the total length of the worm. For example, consider a buffer-overflow attack that attempts to copy malicious data to an unprotected buffer. Oversize malicious data may cause severe memory corruption outside the buffer, leading to a system crash and spoiling the compromise. Given a limited number of decryption routines, it is possible to identify all of them as attack signatures after enough samples of the worm have been obtained.

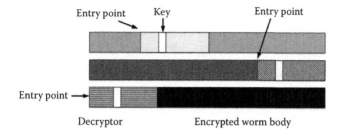

Entry point   Key   Entry point

Entry point →

Decryptor   Encrypted worm body

Figure 5.8 Different variants of a polymorphic worm with different decryptors and different entry points.

```
Original code

55          push       ebp
8BEC        mov        ebp, esp
8B7608      mov        esi, dwoed ptr [ebp + 08]
85F6        test       esi, esi
743B        je         401045
8B7E0C      mov        edi, dword ptr [ebp + 0C]
09FF        or         edi, edi
7434        je         401045
31D2        xor        edx, edx


With garbage code

55          push       ebp
8BEC        mov        ebp, esp
8B7608      mov        esi, dword ptr [ebp + 08]
85F6        test       esi, esi
90          nop
90          nop
90          nop
743B        je         401045
8B7E0C      mov        edi, dword ptr [ebp + 0C]
09FF        or         edi, edi
7434        je         401045
31D2        xor        edx, edx
```

Figure 5.9 Different variants of a polymorphic worm with garbage-code insertion.

- Garbage-code insertion is another polymorphism technique that inserts garbage instructions into the copies of a worm. For example, a number of nop (i.e., no operation) instructions can be inserted into different places in the worm body, thus making it more difficult to compare with the byte sequences of two instances of the same worm. Figure 5.9 is an example of this technique.

The level of polymorphism in this type of worm is decided by the ratio of the length of the garbage instruction region to the total length of the worm. For those worms with a moderate ratio, it is quite conceivable that there will be a good chance that regions sharing the same byte sequence exist in different instances of the worms, which in turn can be served as the signature of the worm. With an increased length, the overlapped regions will be shortened, and it is problematic to identify them.

However, the frequencies of the garbage instructions in a worm can differ greatly from those in normal traffic; this is from the statistics point of view. If that is the case, anomaly detection systems can be used to detect the worm. Furthermore, some garbage instructions such as nop can be easily identified and removed. For better obfuscated garbage, techniques of executable analysis can be used to identify and remove those instructions that will never be executed.

- Another technique is called instruction-substitution, in which it replaces one instruction sequence with a different but equivalent sequence. Unless the substitution is done over the entire code without compromising the code integrity (which is a great challenge by itself), it is likely that shorter signatures can be identified from the stationary portion of the worm.

- Code transposition is a polymorphism technique that changes the order of the instructions with the help of jumps. The excess jump instructions provide a statistical clue, and executable analysis techniques can help remove the unnecessary jump instructions.

- Finally, the register-reassignment technique swaps the usage of the registers, which causes extensive "minor" changes in the code sequence. These techniques are best illustrated in Figure 5.10.

5.7.5 Signature Classes for Polymorphic Worms

Signatures for polymorphic worms can be classified into two broad categories: content-based signatures, which aim at using similarity in different instances of byte sequences to characterize a given worm, and behavior-based signatures, which aim at characterizing worms through understanding the semantics of their byte sequences [37].

Original code

```
55          push ebp
8BEC        mov ebp, esp
8B7608      mov esi, dwoed ptr [ebp + 08]
85F6        test esi, esi
743B        je 401045
8B7E0C      mov edi, dword ptr [ebp + 0C]
09FF        or edi, edi
7434        je 401045
31D2        xor edx, edx
```

Obfuscated code

```
55 push     ebp
54 push     esp
5D pop      ebp
8B7608      mov esi, dword ptr [ebp + 08]
09F6        or esi, esi
743B        je 401045
8B7E0C      mov edi, dword ptr [ebp + 0C]
85FF        test edi, edi
7434        je 401045
28D2        sub edx, edx
```

```
558BEC8B760885F6743B8B7E0C09FF743431D2
55545D8B760809F6743B8B7E0C85FF743428D2
```

Figure 5.10 Different variants of a polymorphic worm with different polymorphic techniques.

5.8 Internet Worm Prevention Methods

There are two different methods to prevent worm attacks [38]:

- The first one is to prevent vulnerabilities.
- The second one is to prevent exploitation of vulnerabilities. Such prevention guards against not only worm attacks but also intrusions of any kind.

5.8.1 Prevention of Vulnerabilities

Secure programming languages and practices: Most of the vulnerabilities can be avoided by good programming practices and secure design of protocols and software architectures. No matter how good software systems are, untenable assumptions and betrayed trusts will make them vulnerable. Protocols and software architectures can be proved or verified

by theorem provers such as HOL [39], but there is always
a chance for human error and carelessness even in the most
careful of programmers. In addition, C [40], the most common programming language with which critical applications
are programmed due to the efficiency and low-level control
of data structures and memory that it offers, does not inher-
ently offer safe and secure constructs. Vulnerabilities such as
buffer overflows in C programs are possible, although caused
by human errors, because it is legitimate to write beyond
the array and string boundaries in C. Thus, there is a need
for more secure programming and execution environments.
Fortunately, help is available for securing programs in the
form of the following:

1. *Static analysis* tools, which identify programming constructs in general that can lead to vulnerabilities. Lint is
   one of the most popular tools of this kind. LCLint [41, 42]
   is another one. MOPS [43, 44] is a model-checking tool
   to examine source code for conformity to certain security
   properties. These properties are expressed as predicates,
   and the tool uses model checking to verify conformation.
   Metal [45, 46] and SLAM [47, 48] are two more examples
   of such types of tools.

2. *Runtime checking* of program status by the use of assert
   statements in C, but they are usually turned off in the
   production versions of the software to avoid performance
   degradation [49].

3. A combination of both of these. Systems such as CCured
   [50] perform static analysis and automatically insert runtime checks where safety cannot be guaranteed statically.
   These systems can also be used to retort legacy C code to
   prevent vulnerabilities.

4. Safe languages offer the best promise. These languages,
   such as Java and Cyclone [49], offer almost no scope for
   vulnerabilities. Cyclone, a dialect of C, ensures this by
   enforcing safe programming practices—it refuses to com-
   pile unsafe programs such as those that use uninitialized
   pointers; it revokes some of the privileges, such as unsafe
   casts, setjmp, longjmp, implicit returns, and so on that

were available to C programmers; and it follows the third technique mentioned—a combination of static analysis and inserting runtime checkers or assertions.

However, Java's type-checking system can itself be attacked, exposing Java programs and Java virtual machines to danger [51]. Moreover, high-level languages such as Java do not provide the low-level control that C provides, whereas Cyclone provides a safer programming environment by a combination of static analysis and inserting runtime checks, yet maintaining the low level of control that C offers to the programmers.

Secure execution environments: To make sure that there are no vulnerabilities, we should provide a secure execution environment. A good method to provide a secure execution environment is to instrument each memory access with assertions for memory integrity.

Purify [52] is a tool that adopts this method for C programs. However, it has a high-performance penalty that prevents it from being used in the production environment. It can, however, be used as a debugger.

5.8.2 Prevention of Exploits

Although there are many mechanisms available for prevention of vulnerabilities, no single tool's (or mechanism's) coverage is complete. Moreover, some of the tools are hard to use or have severe performance penalties and hence are not used in production environments. Therefore, software continues to be shipped with vulnerabilities, and attackers continue to write exploits. Even if all future systems ship without any vulnerability, there is a huge legacy of systems with vulnerabilities. Preventing exploits of those vulnerabilities, both known and unknown, is thus convenient and required. There are several perspectives from which this is achieved:

1. *Access Control Matrix and Lists (OS Perspective)*: Traditionally, the responsibility for preventing mischief, data theft, accidents, and deliberate vandalism and maintaining the integrity of computer systems has been taken up by the operating system.

This responsibility is satisfied by controlling access to resources as dictated by the Access Control Matrix [53, 54]. Each entry in this matrix specifies the set of access rights to a resource that a process gets when executing in a certain protection domain. On time-sharing multiuser systems such as UNIX, protection domains are defined to be users, and the Access Control Matrix is implemented as an Access Control List. This is in addition to the regular UNIX file permissions based on user groups, thus allowing arbitrary subsets of users and groups [55].

2. *Firewalls and Intrusion Prevention Systems (IPSs) (Network Perspectives)*: Another method to prevent exploits is to filter exploit traffic at the network level based on certain rules and policies. Such traffic filtering is implemented mostly at the border gateways of networks and sometimes at the network layer of the network protocol stack on individual machines. An example policy is never to accept any Transmission Control Protocol (TCP) connection from a particular IP address. Another example may be to drop connections whose packet contents match a certain pattern. The former is usually enforced by some kind of software called a firewall, for example, netfilters' iptables [56]. The latter is enforced by IPSs based on signatures, such as Snort-inline [57].

3. *Deterrents (Legal Perspective)*: There are several technical and legal measures that have been undertaken to deter mischief mongers from tampering with computer systems. Enactment and enforcement of laws in combination with building up audit trails [58] on computers (to serve as incriminating evidence) have contributed, to a great extent, to securing computers.

5.9 Conclusion

The intent of this chapter was to present critical information regarding Internet worms, their life cycle, various types, and techniques with practical sample codes and details. By this time, many researchers have worked on relevant topics and discovered how to contain the kind of worm that scans the Internet randomly, looking for vulnerable hosts to infect. We have mentioned some of the remedies, but as an evolutionary topic with continuous sophistication from the attacking side, the information presented here should be considered incomplete. Upgrading knowledge with the latest trends and issues is suggested; the basic information provided here we hope will be useful for understanding more complex details about various kinds of Internet worms.

References

1. Costa, M. End-to-End Containment of Internet Worm Epidemics. PhD thesis, Churchill College, University of Cambridge, October 2006.
2. Sellke, S.H., Shroff, N.B., and Bagchi, S. Modeling and automated containment of worms. *IEEE Transactions on Dependable and Secure Computing*, 2008, Volume 5, Issue 2, pp. 71–86.
3. Spafford, E.H. The Internet worm: Crisis and aftermath. *Communications of the ACM*, 1989, Volume 32, Issue 6, pp. 678–687.
4. Eichin, M.W., and Rochlis, J.A. With microscope and tweezers: An analysis of the Internet virus of November 1988. *Proceedings of 1989 IEEE Symposium on Security and Privacy*, MIT, Cambridge, MA, May 1989, pp. 326–343.
5. Moore, D., Shannon, C., and Brown, J. Code-Red: A case study on the spread and victims of an Internet worm. *Proceedings of the 2nd ACM SIGCOMM Workshop on Internet Measurement*, November 2002, pp. 273–284.
6. Bailey, M., Cooke, E., Jahanian, F., Watson, D., and Nazario, J. The blaster worm: Then and now. *IEEE Security and Privacy*, 2005, Volume 3, Issue 4, pp. 26–31.
7. Moore, D., Paxson, V., Savage, S., Shannon, C., Staniford, S., and Weaver, N. Inside the Slammer worm. *IEEE Security and Privacy*, 2003, Volume 1, Issue 4, 2003, pp. 33–39.
8. Shannon, C., and Moore, D. The spread of the Witty worm. *IEEE Security and Privacy*, 2004, Volume 2, Issue 4, pp. 46–50.
9. One, A., Smashing the stack for fun and profit. *Phrack*, 1995, Volume 7, Issue 49. Available at http://www.phrack.com/issues.html?issue = 49&id = 14 (accessed August 12, 2012).
10. blexim. Basic integer overflows. *Phrack*, December 2002, Volume 60. Available at http://www.phrack.org/issues.html?issue=60&id=10 (accessed August 12, 2012).
11. jp. Advanced Doug Lea's malloc exploits. *Phrack*, September 2003, Volume 61. Available at http://www.phrack.org/issues.html?issue=61&id=6 (accessed August 12, 2012).
12. gera and riq. Advances in format string exploitation. *Phrack*, July 2002, Volume 59. Available at http://www.phrack.org/issues.html?issue=59&id=7 (accessed August 12, 2012).
13. Nergal01. The advanced return-into-lib(c) exploits: Pax case study. *Phrack*, 2001, Volume 58. Available at http://www.phrack.org/issues.html?issue=58&id=4 (accessed August 12, 2012).

14. Hethcote, H.W. The mathematics of infectious diseases. *SIAM Review*, 2000, Volume 42, Issue 4, pp. 599–653.

15. Staniford, S., Paxson, V., and Weaver, N. How to own the Internet in your spare time. *Proceedings of the 11th USENIX Security Symposium*, August 5–9, 2002, San Francisco, CA, pp. 149–167.

16. Weaver, N., Paxson, V., Staniford, S., and Cunningham, R. A taxonomy of computer worms. *Proceedings of the 2003 ACM Workshop on Rapid Malcode*, October 27, 2003, Washington, DC, pp. 11–18.

17. Rowstron, A., and Druschel, P. Pastry: Scalable, distributed object location and routing for large-scale peer-to-peer systems. *Proceedings of the 18th IFIP/ACM International Conference on Distributed Systems Platforms (Middleware 2001)*. Heidelberg, Germany, November 2001.

18. Stoica, I., Morris, R., Karger, D., Kaashoek, M.F., and Balakrishnan, H. Chord: A scalable peer-to-peer lookup service for Internet applications. *Proceedings of the 2001 Conference on Applications, Technologies, Architectures, and Protocols for Computer Communications (ACM SIGCOMM '01)*, August 2001, pp. 149–160.

19. Ratnasamy, S., Francis, P., Handley, M., Karp, R., and Shenker, S. A scalable content-addressable network. *Proceedings of the 2001 Conference on Applications, Technologies, Architectures, and Protocols for Computer Communications (ACM SIGCOMM '01)*, August 2001, pp. 161–172.

20. Paxson, V., Bro: A system for detecting network intruders in real time. *Computer Networks: The International Journal of Computer and Telecommunications Networking*, 1999, Volume 31, Issue 23–24, pp. 2435–2463.

21. Weaver, N., Staniford, S., and Paxson, V., Very fast containment of scanning worms. *Proceedings of the 13th Conference on USENIX Security Symposium (SSYM'04)*, August 2004, Volume 13, p. 3.

22. Roesch, M. Snort: Lightweight intrusion detection for networks. *Proceedings of the 13th USENIX Conference on System Administration (LISA '99)*, November 1999, pp. 229–238.

23. Heberlein, L.T., Dias, G.V., Levitt, K.N., Mukerjeeand, B., Wood, J., and Wolber, D. A network security monitor. *1990 IEEE Computer Society Symposium on Research in Security and Privacy*, May 1990, pp. 296–304.

24. Williamson, M.M. Throttling viruses: Restricting propagation to defeat mobile malicious code. In *Proceedings of 18th Annual Computer Security Applications Conference*. HP Labs Bristol, Stoke Gifford, UK: HP Labs Bristol, December 2002, pp. 61–68.

25. Abawajy, J., Pathan, M., Rahman, M., Pathan, A.-S.K., and Deris, M.M. *Network and Traffic Engineering in Emerging Distributed Computing Applications*. Hershey, PA: IGI Global, July 2012.

26. Perdisci, R., Dagon, D., Lee, W., Fogla, P., and Sharif, M. Misleading worm signature generators using deliberate noise injection. *Proceedings of the 2006 IEEE Symposium on Security and Privacy (SP '06)* May 21–24, 2006, Oakland, CA, pp. 17–31.

27. Lin, W.S., Zhao, H.V., and Liu, K.J.R. Behavior forensics with side information for multimedia fingerprinting social networks. *IEEE Transactions on Information Forensics and Security*, 2009, Volume 4, Issue 4, Part 2, pp. 911–927.

28. Bethencourt, J., Franklin, J., and Vernon, M. Mapping Internet sensors with probe response attacks. *Proceedings of the 14th Conference on USENIX Security Symposium (SSYM'05)*, 2005, Volume 14, pp. 193–208.

29. Provos, N. A virtual honeypot framework. *Proceedings of the 13th Conference on USENIX Security Symposium (SSYM'04)*, August 2004, Volume 13, pp. 1–14.

30. Holz, T., and Raynal, F. Detecting honeypots and other suspicious environments. *Proceedings from the Sixth Annual IEEE SMC Information Assurance Workshop, 2005. (IAW '05)*, June 15–17, 2005, pp. 29–36.

31. VMware backdoor I/O port. Available at https://sites.google.com/site/chitchatvmback/backdoor (accessed August 12, 2012).

32. Nazario, J. *Defense and Detection Strategies against Internet Worms*. Norwood, MA: Artech House, October 2003.

33. Buchholz, F., Daniels, T., Early, J., Gopalakrishna, R., Gorman, R., Kuperman, B., Nystrom, S., Schroll, A., and Smith, A., Digging for worms, fishing for answers. In *Proceedings of the 18th Annual Computer Security Applications Conference (ACSAC 2002)*. New York: ACM, 2002, p. 219.

34. Fogla, P., Sharif, M., Perdisci, R., Kolesnikov, O., and Lee, W. Polymorphic blending attacks. *Proceedings of the 15th Conference on USENIX Security Symposium (USENIX-SS'06)*, 2006, Volume 15, Article No. 17.

35. Newsome, J., Karp, B., and Song, D. Polygraph: Automatically generating signatures for polymorphic worms. *2005 IEEE Symposium on Security and Privacy*, May 2005, pp. 226–241.

36. Tang, Y., and Chen, S. An automated signature-based approach against polymorphic Internet worms. *IEEE Transactions on Parallel and Distributed Systems*, 2007, Volume 18, Issue 7, pp. 879–892.

37. Cavallaro, L., Lanzi, A., Mayer, L., and Monga, M. LISABETH: Automated content-based signature generator for zero-day polymorphic worms. *Proceedings of the Fourth International Workshop on Software Engineering for Secure Systems (SESS '08), Leipzig, Germany*, May 2008, pp. 41–48.

38. Cheetancheri, S.G. Collaborative Defense against Zero-Day and Polymorphic Worms: Detection, Response and an Evaluation Framework. PhD thesis, University of California at Davis, 2007.

39. Automated Reasoning Group. The HOL system. Available at http://www.cl.cam.ac.uk/research/hvg/HOL/ (accessed August 12, 2012).

40. Ritchie, D.M. The development of the C language. *ACM SIGPLAN Notices*, 1993, Volume 28, Issue 3, pp. 201–208.

41. Evans, D. Static detection of dynamic memory errors. *Proceedings of the ACM SIGPLAN 1996 Conference on Programming Language Design and Implementation (PLDI '96), Philadelphia, PA*, May 1996, pp. 44–53.

42. Larochelle, D., and Evans, D. Statically detecting likely buffer overflow vulnerabilities. *Proceedings of the 10th Conference on USENIX Security Symposium (SSYM'01)*, August 2001, Volume 10, pp. 177–190.

43. Chen, H., Dean, D., and Wagner, D. Model checking one million lines of C code. In *Proceedings of the 11th Annual Network and Distributed System Security Symposium (NDSS)*, February 4–6, 2004, San Diego, CA.

44. Chen, H., and Wagner, D. Mops: An infrastructure for examining security properties of software. *Proceedings of the 9th ACM Conference on Computer and Communications Security (CCS), Washington, DC,* November 2002, pp. 235–244.

45. Engler, D., Chelf, B., Chou, A., and Hallem, S. Checking system rules using system-specific, programmer-written compiler extensions. *Proceedings of the 4th Conference on Symposium on Operating System Design & Implementation (OSDI'00), San Diego, CA,* October 2000, Volume 4, p. 1.

46. Engler, D., Chen, D.Y., Hallem, S., Chou, A., and Chelf, B. Bugs as deviant behavior: A general approach to inferring errors in systems code. In *Proceedings of the Eighteenth ACM Symposium on Operating Systems Principles (SOSP '01),* October 21–24, 2001, Banff, Canada, pp. 57–72.

47. Ball, T., Majumdar, R., Millstein, T.D., and Rajamani, S.K. Automatic predicate abstraction of c programs. *Proceedings of the ACM SIGPLAN 2001 Conference on Programming Language Design and Implementation (PLDI '01),* June 20–22, 2001, Snowbird, UT, pp. 203–213.

48. Ball, T., and Rajamani, S.K. Automatically validating temporal safety properties of interfaces. In *Proceedings of the Eighth International SPIN Workshop (SPIN 01), Lecture Notes in Computer Science 2057,* M. Dwyer, ed. New York: Springer, 2001, pp. 103–122.

49. Jim, T., Morrisett, J.G., Grossman, D., Hicks, M.W., Cheney, J., and Wang Y. Cyclone: A safe dialect of C. In *Proceedings of the General Track of the annual conference on USENIX Annual Technical Conference (ATEC '02).* Berkeley, CA: USENIX Association, 2002, pp. 275–288.

50. Necula, G.C., McPeak, S., and Weimer, W. Ccured: type-safe retrofitting of legacy code. *Proceedings of the Principles of Programming Languages,* January 16–18, 2002, Portland, OR, pp. 128–139.

51. Dean, D., Felten, E.W., and Wallach, D.S. Java security: From HotJava to Netscape and beyond. *Proceedings of the 1996 IEEE Symposium on Security and Privacy (SP '96),* May 6–8, 1996, Oakland, CA, pp. 190–200.

52. Hastings, R., and Joyce, B. Purify: Fast detection of memory leaks and access errors. *Proceedings of the Winter 1992 USENIX Conference,* January 1992, San Francisco, CA, pp. 125–138.

53. Lampson, B.W. Dynamic protection structures. *Proceedings of AFIPS '69 (Fall),* 1969, pp. 27–38.

54. Lampson, B.W. Protection. *ACM SIGOPS Operating Systems Review,* 1974, Volume 8, Issue 1, pp. 18–24.

55. Garfinkel, S., and Spafford, G. *Practical Unix and Internet Security,* 2nd ed. Sebastopol, CA: O'Reilly Media, April 8, 1996.

56. The netfilter.org project. Available at http://www.netfilter.org/(accessed August 12, 2012).

57. SNORT IDS. Available at http://www.snort.org (accessed August 12, 2012).
58. Lunt, T.F. Automated audit trail analysis and intrusion detection: A survey. *Proceedings of the 11th National Computer Security Conference,* Baltimore, MD, 1988.

6

READING RESOURCES ON AUTOMATED SIGNATURE GENERATION SYSTEMS

6.1 Introduction

This is a short chapter that precedes in-depth discussions about zero-day polymorphic worms and their tackling methods in the following chapters. The reason for placing this chapter in this position is so that various reading resources on the topic may be consulted to be able to understand the specialized terms that will be used. Although we have tried to make various issues easily accessible, some special or technical terms may need further reading and investigation.

This chapter points to the significant relevant works done so far in the area of automated signature generation (ASG) for zero-day polymorphic worms. The objective is that readers could obtain these additional reading resources to investigate the technical details and positions of various researchers. To be able to generate signatures for zero-day polymorphic worms, we suggest you follow these steps:

1. First, read all the materials and techniques presented throughout all the chapters in this book. This could give you extensive information about automated signature generation for zero-day polymorphic worms.
2. Then, you should read this chapter, which can give you a glimpse of the most important works that have been done so far on this topic. You should work on fixing the weaknesses of these works, which could allow you to devise new mechanisms on this topic.

3. You should propose new thoughts, findings, and techniques for automated signature generation for zero-day polymorphic worms.

All the significant proposed techniques that were available while writing this book can be divided into network-based, host-based, and hybrid system mechanisms. Network-based mechanisms exclusively analyze network traffic; host-based systems use information available at the end hosts. Hybrid systems are combinations of both network-based and host-based mechanisms. This chapter discusses previous proposals in each of these areas.

6.1.1 Hybrid System (Network Based and Host Based)

Mohssen Mohammed, Neco Ventura, H. Anthony Chan, Mohsin Hashim, and Eihab Bashier [1–3] proposed a double-honeynet system to collect all polymorphic worm instances automatically without human interaction and to generate a signature based on the collected worm patterns. The double-honeynet system is a hybrid system (network based and host based). The system operates at the network level by filtering unwanted traffic using a local router and operates at the host level by allowing polymorphic worms to interact with honeynet 1 and honeynet 2 hosts. Interaction between the two honeynets works by forming a loop, which allows us to collect all polymorphic worm instances. This mechanism reduces the false positives and false negatives dramatically, which is generally limited with the current worm detection systems.

To generate signatures for zero-day polymorphic worms, the work consists of two parts. In the first part, polymorphic worm instances are collected by designing a novel double-honeynet system able to detect new worms that have not been seen previously. Unlimited honeynet outbound connections are introduced to collect all polymorphic worm instances. Therefore, this system produces accurate worm signatures.

In the second part, signatures are generated for the polymorphic worms that are collected by the double-honeynet system. Both a modified Knuth-Morris-Pratt (MKMP) algorithm, which is string-matching based, and a modified principal component analysis (MPCA), which is statistics based, are used. The MKMP algorithm compares the polymorphic worm substrings to find the multiple invariant substrings that are shared between all polymorphic worm instances and uses them as signatures. The MPCA determines the most significant substrings that are shared between polymorphic worm instances and uses them as signatures.

The major contributions of this work are as follows:

- It provided a design of a novel double-honeynet system able to detect worms that have not been seen previously.
- It introduced unlimited honeynet outbound connections that allow collecting all polymorphic worm instances, which enables the system to produce accurate worm signatures.
- It provided the ability of the system to generate signatures to match all polymorphic worm instances.
- The double-honeynet system is a hybrid system that is both network based and host based. This allows collecting polymorphic worm instances on the network level and host level, which reduces the false positives and false negatives dramatically.

6.1.2 Network-Based Mechanisms

One of the first systems proposed was Honeycomb, developed by Kreibich and Crowcroft. More recently, Honeycomb [4] proposed generating byte string signatures from the traffic observed at honeypots. Honeycomb assumes all traffic received by honeypots is suspicious. Signatures are generated by finding the longest common substring in two network connections. The system can generate false positives if legitimate traffic reaches the honeypot. Malicious false positives are also a problem since an attacker can send traffic to the honeypot to generate a signature. Honeycomb can also have false negatives. It uses a configurable minimum length for its signatures to avoid false positives, but this will allow polymorphic worms to spread undetected. Polymorphic worms can have little invariant content across attack messages, thereby making it difficult to match them with byte strings.

Kim and Karp [5] described the Autograph system for automated generation of signatures to detect worms. Autograph also generates byte string signatures automatically. Rather than relying on honeypots, Autograph identifies suspicious network flows at the firewall boundary. It stores the address of each unsuccessful inbound Transmission Control Protocol (TCP) connection, assuming the computer generating such connection requests is scanning for vulnerable machines. When a configurable number of such attempts is recorded, Autograph marks the source Internet Protocol (IP) address as infected. All subsequent connections involving IP addresses marked as infected are inserted into a pool of suspicious network flows. Periodically, Autograph selects the most common byte strings in the suspicious flows as worm signatures. To limit the amount of false positives, Autograph can be configured with a list of disallowed signatures; the authors suggested a training period during which an administrator runs the system and gradually accumulates the list of disallowed signatures. The system is also configured with a minimum signature size, which can result in false negatives, especially with polymorphic worms.

The work of Singh, Estan, Varghese, and Savage [6] described the Earlybird system for generating signatures to detect worms. Earlybird is based on the observation that it is rare to see the same byte strings within packets sent from many sources to many destinations. Unlike Autograph, Earlybird does not require an initial step that identifies suspicious network flows based on scanning activity. Earlybird generates a worm signature when a byte string is seen in more than a threshold number of packets and it is sent/received to/from more than a threshold number of different IP addresses. Earlybird uses efficient algorithms to approximate content prevalence and address dispersion; therefore, it scales to high-speed network links. To avoid false positives, Earlybird uses white lists and minimum signature sizes. As with Honeycomb and Autograph, malicious false positives are a concern, and polymorphic worms are likely to escape containment.

We should mention that all the systems [4–6] generate a single signature to match all worm instances based on the assumption that there exists a single payload substring that will remain invariant across worm connections. A single signature is not qualified enough to match all worm instances with low false positives and low false negatives. To obtain more accurate signatures for polymorphic worms, signatures should be based on the idea that there is more than one substring shared between all polymorphic worm instances.

James Newsome, Brad Karp, and Dawn Song described the Polygraph system for generating signatures for polymorphic worms. Polygraph [7] argues that single byte string signatures cannot block polymorphic worms. In an effort to generate signatures that match polymorphic worms, Polygraph generates signatures that are multiple disjoint byte strings instead of a single byte string. Polygraph relies on a preliminary step that classifies network flows as suspicious or innocuous. Tokens are identified as repeated byte strings across the suspicious network flows. A subsequent step groups tokens into signatures. Polygraph proposes three types of matching with these signatures: matching all the byte strings in a signature, matching the byte strings in order, or assigning a numeric score to each byte string and base matching in an overall numeric threshold. Their evaluation showed that none of these types of signature is superior to the others for every worm. All of them can have false positives and false negatives.

Zhichun Li, Manan Sanghi, Yan Chen, Ming-Yang Kao, and Brian Chavez, described the Hamsa system for generating signatures for polymorphic worms [8]. Hamsa generates content-based signatures. The protocol frame part ε, exploit data γ, and worm content π are used to generate the signatures. Given a suspicious flow, token extraction is performed by using a suffix array-based algorithm to find all byte sequences that occur in at least λ fraction of the suspicious flow pool. Hamsa defines a worm signature that is constrained to include a multiset of tokens in any order in each of the suspicious flows. The first token to appear in the worm signature is selected as the one with the smallest false-positive value. The token that has the least false-positive value in conjunction with the first token is selected as the second token. The rest of the tokens are evaluated similarly, and the final worm signature is produced. Appropriately choosing the values for the model proposed, this greedy approach is claimed to find a good signature with the assumption that the exploit data γ and the protocol frame part ε together forming the invariant parts of the worm are not under the control of the worm author since the worm author has to exploit a software vulnerability over a static protocol structure to finally execute the worm content.

LISABETH [9] is an automated content-based signature generator for zero-day polymorphic worms. The authors claimed that

LISABETH is an improved version of Hamsa [8] in terms of resilience to flow pool poisoning attacks and signature generation performance.

We should mention that Polygraph [7], LISABETH [9], and Hamsa [8] generate automated signatures for polymorphic worms based on the following fact: There are multiple invariant substrings that must often be present in all variants of polymorphic worm payloads, even if the payload changes in every infection. All these systems capture the packet payloads at the network level. A polymorphic worm does not change its payload until it reaches the host level, so these systems cannot capture the remaining instances of the polymorphic worm. However, the systems may capture different types of polymorphic worms where each of them exploits a different vulnerability from each other. So, in this case, it may be difficult for these systems to find invariant contents shared between these polymorphic worms because they exploit different vulnerabilities.

"An Architecture for Generating Semantics-Aware Signatures" by Yegneswaran, Giffin, Barford, and Jha [10] described Nemean. Nemean uses protocol-specific information to generate signatures that are regular expressions and may include session-level context, but it requires some manual steps and also cannot cope with pollution of the network data that are used as inputs to the signature generation process.

"An Automated Signature-Based Approach against Polymorphic Internet Worms" by Yong Tang and Shigang Chen [11] described a system to detect new worms and generate signatures automatically. This system implemented double honeypots (inbound honeypot and outbound honeypot) to capture worm payloads. The inbound honeypot is implemented as a high-interaction honeypot, whereas the outbound honeypot is implemented as a low-interaction honeypot. This system has some limitations. The outbound honeypot is not able to make outbound connections because it is implemented as a low-interaction honeypot that is not able to capture the remaining instances of the polymorphic worm.

6.1.3 Host-Based Mechanisms

Vigilante [12] and TaintCheck [13] benefit from knowledge about the state of the host during an attack. They perform dynamic data flow analysis to track program activity, including buffer overflows and control transfers. They identify worm signatures in terms of program behavior rather than packet payload.

Buttercup [14] proposes identifying the return address range used in worm attack messages and filtering messages that include such addresses. To reduce false positives, their system searches for the return address value starting at a predetermined offset in messages and stops after a configurable number of bytes have been checked. While Buttercup requires these addresses to be externally specified, TaintCheck [13] proposes to obtain them automatically by using the exact return address observed in attack messages. These systems can have false positives because the 4-byte sequences used as a return address can appear in normal messages. The system can also have false negatives since attackers can use a wide range of values of return addresses by searching the address space of vulnerable applications for sequences of bytes that correspond to instructions that transfer control to the worm code.

ARBOR [15] generates signatures based on the size of network messages and the fraction of non-ASCII characters in them. Its signatures also include host context: Messages are dropped at specific code locations and when specific call sequences are observed. ARBOR can still have false positives and false negatives.

COVERS [16] also generates signatures based on length of inputs and fraction of non-ASCII characters in them, but includes an input correlation mechanism to identify attack packets and the specific bytes in those packets that were involved in an observed security fault. COVERS does not provide guarantees on the rate of false positives or false negatives.

References

1. Mohammed, M.M.Z.E., Chan, H.A., and Ventura, N. Honeycyber: Automated signature generation for zero-day polymorphic worms, in *IEEE Military Communications Conference, 2008 (IEEE MILCOM 2008)*. San Diego, CA: November 16–19, 2008, pp. 1–6.
2. Mohammed, M.M.Z.E., Chan, H.A., Ventura, N., Hashim, M., and Amin, I. A modified Knuth-Morris-Pratt algorithm for zero-day polymorphic worms detection. *Proceedings of the 2009 International Conference on Security and Management (SAM'09)*, July 13–16, 2009, Las Vegas, NV.

3. Mohammed, M.M.Z.E., Chan, H.A., Ventura, N., Hashim, M., Amin, I., and Bashier, E. Accurate signature generation for polymorphic worms using principal component analysis. In *2010 IEEE GLOBECOM Workshops (GC Workshops)*. Miami, FL: December 6–10, 2010, pp. 1555–1560.

4. Kreibich, C., and Crowcroft, J. Honeycomb: creating intrusion detection signatures using honeypots. *ACM SIGCOMM Computer Communication Review*, 2004, Volume 34, Issue 1, pp. 51–56.

5. Kim, H.-A., and Karp, B. Autograph: Toward automated, distributed worm signature detection. *Proceedings of the 13th Conference on USENIX Security Symposium (SSYM'04)*, 2004, Volume 13, p. 19.

6. Singh, S., Estan, C., Varghese, G., and Savage, S. Automated worm fingerprinting. *Proceedings of the 6th Conference on Symposium on Operating Systems Design and Implementation (OSDI'04)*, 2004, Volume 6, p. 4.

7. Newsome, J., Karp, B., and Song, D. Polygraph: Automatically generating signatures for polymorphic worms. *Proceedings of the 2005 IEEE Symposium on Security and Privacy*, May 2005, pp. 226–241.

8. Li, Z., Sanghi, M., Chen, Y., Kao, M.-Y., and Chavez, B. Hamsa: Fast signature generation for zero-day polymorphic worms with provable attack resilience. In *2006 IEEE Symposium on Security and Privacy*. Oakland, CA: May 21–24, 2006, pp. 15–47.

9. Cavallaro, L., Lanzi, A., Mayer, L., and Monga, M. LISABETH: Automated content-based signature generator for zero-day polymorphic worms. In *Proceedings of the Fourth International Workshop on Software Engineering for Secure Systems (SESS '08)*. Leipzig, Germany: May 2008, pp. 41–48.

10. Yegneswaran, V., Giffin, J., Barford, P., and Jha, S. An architecture for generating semantics-aware signatures. *Proceedings of the 14th Conference on USENIX Security Symposium (SSYM'05)*, 2005, Volume 14, p. 7.

11. Tang, Y., and Chen, S. An automated signature-based approach against polymorphic internet worms. *IEEE Transaction on Parallel and Distributed Systems*, 2007, Volume 18, Issue 7, pp. 879–892.

12. Costa, M., Crowcroft, J., Castro, M., Rowstron, A., Zhou, L., Zhang, L., and Barham, P. Vigilante: End-to-end containment of internet worms. In *Proceedings of the Twentieth ACM Symposium on Operating Systems Principles (SOSP '05)*. New York: ACM Press, 2005, pp. 133–147.

13. Newsome, J., and Song, D. Dynamic taint analysis for automatic detection, analysis and signature generation of exploits on commodity software. In *Proceedings of the Network and Distributed System Security Symposium (NDSS 2005)*, San Diego, CA, February 2005.

14. Pasupulati, A., Coit, J., Levitt, K., Wu, S.F., Li, S.H., Kuo, J.C., and Fan, K.P. Buttercup: On network-based detection of polymorphic buffer overflow vulnerabilities. *IEEE/IFIP Network Operations and Management Symposium, 2004 (NOMS 2004)*, 2004, Volume 1, pp. 235–248.

15. Liang, Z., and Sekar, R. Automatic generation of buffer overflow signatures: An approach based on program behavior models. In *21st Annual Computer Security Applications Conference*, IEEE Computer Society, Tucson, AZ, December 5–9, 2005, 10 pp., 224.

16. Liang, Z., and Sekar, R. Fast and automated generation of attack signatures: A basis for building self-protecting servers. *Proceedings of the 12th ACM Conference on Computer and Communications Security (CCS '05)*, November 2005, pp. 213–222.

7

SIGNATURE GENERATION ALGORITHMS FOR POLYMORPHIC WORMS

7.1 String Matching

String matching [1] is an important subject in the wider domain of text processing. String-matching algorithms are the basic components used for implementations of practical software used in most available operating systems. Moreover, they emphasize programming methods that serve as paradigms in other fields of computer science (system or software design). They also play an important role in theoretical computer science by providing challenging problems.

String matching generally consists of finding a substring (called a pattern) within another string (called the text). The pattern is generally denoted as

$$x = x[0...m-1]$$

whose length is m and the text is generally denoted as

$$y = y[0...n-1]$$

whose length is n. Both the string patterns and text are built over a finite set of characters, which is called the alphabet and denoted by Σ, whose size is denoted by σ.

The string-matching algorithm plays an important role in network intrusion detection systems (IDSs), which can detect malicious attacks and protect network systems. In fact, at the core of almost every modern IDS, there is a string-matching algorithm. This is a crucial technique because it allows detection systems to base their actions on the content that is actually flowing to a machine. From a vast number of packets, the string identifies those packets that contain data, matching the fingerprint of a known attack. Essentially, the string-matching algorithm compares the set of strings in the rule set with the data seen in the packets, which flow across the network. In the next section, we discuss exact string-matching algorithms and approximate string-matching algorithms.

7.1.1 Exact String-Matching Algorithms

In this section we will discuss different types of exact string-matching algorithms such as the brute force algorithm, Aho–Corasick algorithm, Boyer–Moore algorithm, Karp–Rabin algorithm, and Knuth–Morris–Pratt (KMP) algorithm.

7.1.1.1 Brute Force Algorithm

The brute force algorithm is a step-by-step recipe for solving a problem. A brute force algorithm is one that proceeds in a simple and obvious way but will require a huge number of steps (perhaps an unfeasibly large number of steps) to complete. A brute force algorithm is often the least-desirable choice because of the number of steps that will be involved; often, looking for underlying patterns, regularities, or organizational tricks will help you discover algorithms that are cleverer, subtler, and more efficient [1].

The main features for the brute force algorithm are as follows:

- no preprocessing phase;
- constant extra space needed;
- always shifts the window by exactly one position to the right;
- comparisons can be done in any order;
- searching phase in $O(mn)$ time complexity;
- the expected number of text character comparisons is $2n$.

Next, we present the brute force algorithm [2]. We need to find a pattern P with size m in a text T with size n.

```
Algorithm BruteForceMatch(T,P)
        Input text T of size n and pattern P of size m
        Output starting index of a substring of T equal
        to P or -1 if no such substring exists
        For i := 0 to n-m
                {test shift i of the pattern}
```

```
j := 0
While j < m ∧ T [i + j] = P[j]
        j := j + 1
if j = m
        return i {match at i}
else
        break while loop  {mismatch}
return -1 {no match anywhere}
```

7.1.1.2 Aho–Corasick Algorithm   The Aho–Corasick [3] string-matching algorithm is a string-searching algorithm invented by Alfred V. Aho and Margaret J. Corasick. It is a kind of dictionary-matching algorithm that locates elements of a finite set of strings (the "dictionary") within an input text. It matches all patterns simultaneously. The complexity of the algorithm is linear in the length of the patterns plus the length of the searched text plus the number of output matches. Note that as all matches are found, there can be a quadratic number of matches if every substring matches (e.g., dictionary = *a, aa, aaa, aaaa* and input string is *aaaa*).

Informally, the algorithm constructs a finite-state machine that resembles a trie with additional links between the various internal nodes. These extra internal links allow fast transitions between failed pattern matches (e.g., a search for **cat** in a trie that does not contain **cat**, but contains **cart**, and thus would fail at the node prefixed by **ca**) and other branches of the trie that share a common prefix (e.g., in the previous case, a branch for **attribute** might be the best lateral transition). This allows the automaton to transition between pattern matches without the need for backtracking.

When the pattern dictionary is known in advance (e.g., a computer virus database), the construction of the automaton can be performed once offline and the compiled automaton stored for later use. In this case, its runtime is linear in the length of the input plus the number of matched entries.

Figure 7.1 is the Aho–Corasick data structure constructed from the specified dictionary, with each row in the table representing a node in the trie, with the column path indicating the (unique) sequence of characters from the root to the node. The data structure has one node for every prefix of every string in the dictionary. So, if (bca) is in the dictionary, then there will be nodes for (bca), (bc), (b), and (). There is a

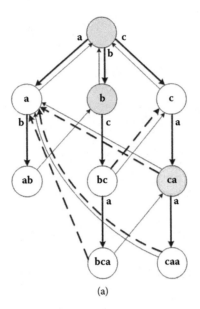

(a)

Dictionary {a, ab, bc, bca, c, caa}

Path	In Dictionary	Suffix Link	Dict Suffix Link
()	−		
(a)	+	()	
(ab)	+	(b)	
(b)	−	()	
(bc)	+	(c)	(c)
(bca)	+	(ca)	(a)
(c)	+	()	
(ca)	−	(a)	(a)
(caa)	+	(a)	(a)

Figure 7.1 Aho–Corasick concept.

black directed "child" arc from each node to a node whose name is found by appending one character. So, there is a black arc from (bc) to (bca). There is a thin directed "suffix" arc from each node to the node that is the longest possible strict suffix of it in the graph. For example, for node (caa), its strict suffixes are (aa), (a), and (). The longest of these that exists in the graph is (a). So, there is a thin arc from (caa) to (a). There is a dashed "dictionary suffix" arc from each node to the next node in the dictionary that can be reached by following thin arcs. For example, there is a dashed arc from (bca) to (a) because (a) is the first node in the dictionary (i.e., a white node) that is reached when following the thin arcs to (ca) and then on to (a). At each step, the current node is extended by finding its child, and if that does not exist, finding its suffix's child, and if that does not work, finding its suffix's suffix's child, and so on, finally ending in the root node if nothing is seen before.

When the algorithm reaches a node, it outputs all the dictionary entries that end at the current character position in the input text. This is done by printing every node reached by following the dictionary suffix links, starting from that node, and continuing until it reaches a node with no dictionary suffix link. In addition, the node itself is printed if it is a dictionary entry.

Execution on input string **abccab** yields the steps shown in Table 7.1.

7.1.1.3 Boyer–Moore Algorithm The Boyer–Moore [4] algorithm is considered the most efficient string-matching algorithm for usual applications. The algorithm scans the characters of the pattern from right to left beginning with the rightmost one. Figure 7.2 shows the Boyer–Moore algorithm's concept.

Table 7.1   Analysis of Input String *abccab*

NODE	REMAINING STRING	OUTPUT: END POSITION	TRANSITION	OUTPUT
()	abccab		start at root	
(a)	bccab	a:1	() to child (a)	Current node
(ab)	ccab	ab:2	(a) to child (ab)	Current node
(bc)	cab	bc:3, c:3	(ab) to suffix (b) to child (bc)	Current node, Dict suffix node
(c)	ab	c:4	(bc) to suffix (c) to suffix () to child (c)	Current node
(ca)	b	a:5	(c) to child (ca)	Dict suffix node
(ab)		ab:6	(ca) to suffix (a) to child (ab)	Current node

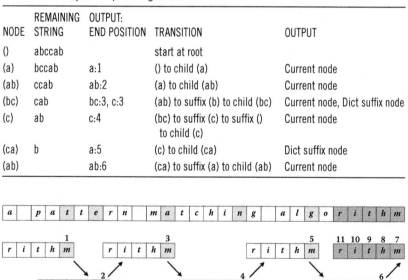

Figure 7.2   Boyer–Moore concept.

The Boyer–Moore's pattern-matching algorithm is based on two heuristics:

- **Looking glass heuristic**: Compare P with a subsequence of T moving backward.
- **Character-jump heuristic**: When a mismatch occurs at $T[i]$ = c:
  - If P contains c, shift P to align the last occurrence of c in P with $T[i]$.
  - Else, shift P to align $P[0]$ with $T[i + 1]$.

Boyer–Moore's algorithm preprocesses the pattern P and the alphabet Σ to build the last-occurrence function L mapping Σ to integers, where $L(c)$ is defined as

- The largest index i such that $P[i] = c$ or
- −1 if no such index exists

Figure 7.3 shows an example:

- $\Sigma = \{a, b, c, d\}$
- P = abacab

The last-occurrence function can be represented by an array indexed by the numeric codes of the characters.

The Boyer–Moore Algorithm is shown in Figure 7.4.

7.1.1.4 Rabin–Karp Algorithm   Michael O. Rabin and Richard M. Karp came up with the idea of hashing the pattern and checking it against a hashed substring from the text in 1987 [1]. In general, the idea seems to be quite simple; the only thing is that we need a hash function that gives different hashes for different substrings. Such a hash function, for instance, may use the ASCII codes for every character, but we must be careful about multilingual support.

The hash function may vary depending on many things, so it may consist of ASCII char-to-number converting, but it can also be anything

c	a	b	c	d
$L(c)$	4	5	3	−1

Figure 7.3   Example of last-occurrence function's output.

Case 1: $j \leq 1 + l$

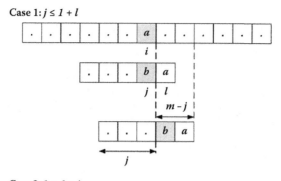

Case 2: $1 + l \leq j$

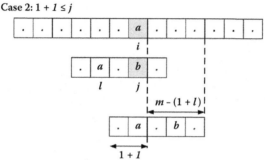

Figure 7.4 Boyer–Moore algorithm.

---

else. The only thing we need is to convert a string (pattern) into some hash that is faster to compare. Let us say we have the string "*hello world*" and let us assume that its hash is hash("*hello world*") = 12345. So, if hash('*he*') = 1 we can say that the pattern "he" is contained in the text "*hello world.*" Thus, in every step, we take from the text a substring with length m, where m is the pattern length. Thus, we hash this substring, and we can directly compare it to the hashed pattern, as shown in Figure 7.5.

7.1.1.4.1 Multiple Pattern Match The Rabin–Karp algorithm is great for a multiple pattern match. Indeed, its nature is supposed to support such functionality, which is its advantage in comparison to other string-searching algorithms.

7.1.1.4.2 Complexity The Rabin–Karp algorithm has the complexity of O(nm) where n is the length of the text, and m is the length of the pattern. So, how is it compared to brute-force matching? Brute-force matching complexity is O(nm), so it seems there is not much gain in performance. However, it is considered that the complexity of

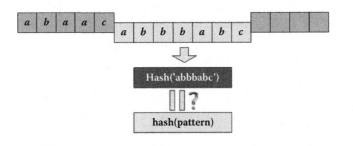

Figure 7.5   Rabin–Karp algorithm.

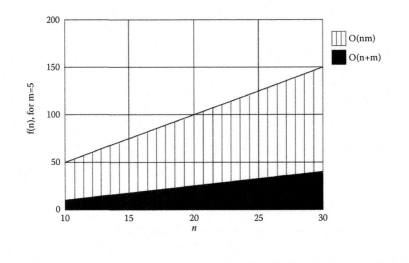

Figure 7.6   Rabin–Karp algorithm complexity.

the Rabin–Karp algorithm is O($n+m$) in practice, which makes it a bit faster, as shown in Figure 7.6.

It should be noted that the Rabin–Karp algorithm also needs O(m) preprocessing time.

7.1.1.5 Knuth–Morris–Pratt Algorithm   The KMP algorithm and its practical use case are discussed in Chapter 9 again, but here we present the basic idea. The KMP string-searching algorithm (or KMP algorithm) [5, 6] searches for occurrences of a "word" W within a main "text string" S by employing the observation that when a mismatch occurs, the word itself embodies sufficient information to determine where the next match could begin, thus bypassing reexamination of previously matched characters.

Let us use an example to illustrate how the algorithm works. To illustrate the algorithm's working method, we go through a sample run (relatively artificial) of the algorithm. At any given time, the algorithm is in a state determined by two integers m and i. Here, m denotes the position within S that is the beginning of a prospective match for W, and i denotes the index in W denoting the character currently under consideration. This is depicted at the start of the run, like the following:

```
m:  0123456789012345678901 2
S:  ABC ABCDAB ABCDABCDABDE
W:  ABCDABD
i:  0123456
```

We proceed by comparing successive characters of W to "parallel" positional characters of S, moving from one to the next if they match. However, in the fourth step in our noted case, we get that $S[3]$ is a space, and $W[3]$ is equal to the character D (i.e., $W[3]$ = 'D'), which is a mismatch. Rather than beginning to search again at the position $S[1]$, we note that no 'A' occurs between positions 0 and 3 in S except at 0. Hence, having checked all those characters previously, we know that there is no chance of finding the beginning of a match if we check them again. Therefore, we simply move on to the next character, setting m = 4 and i = 0.

```
m:  0123456789012345678901 2
S:  ABC ABCDAB ABCDABCDABDE
W:      ABCDABD
i:      0123456
```

We quickly obtain a near-complete match "ABCDAB," but when at W[6] (S[10]), we again have a discrepancy. However, just prior to the end of the current partial match, we passed an "AB," which could be the beginning of a new match, so we must take this into consideration. As we already know that these characters match the two characters prior to the current position, we need not check them again; we simply reset m = 8, i = 2 and continue matching the current character. Thus, not only do we omit previously matched characters of S but also previously matched characters of W.

```
m:  01234567890123456789012
S:  ABC ABCDAB ABCDABCDABDE
W:          ABCDABD
i:          0123456
```

This search fails immediately, however, as the pattern still does not contain a space; as in the first trial, we return to the beginning of *W* and begin searching at the next character of *S*: *m* = 11, reset *i* = 0. (Here, *m* will first become 10 since $m + i - T[i] = 8 + 2 - 0 = 10$ and then become 11 since $T[0] = -1$).

```
m:  01234567890123456789012
S:  ABC ABCDAB ABCDABCDABDE
W:          ABCDABD
i:          0123456
```

Again, we immediately hit on a match "ABCDAB," but the next character 'C' does not match the final character 'D' of the word *W*. By reasoning as before, we set *m* = 15 to start at the two-character string "AB" leading up to the current position, set *i* = 2, and continue matching from the current position.

```
m:  01234567890123456789012
S:  ABC ABCDAB ABCDABCDABDE
W:              ABCDABD
i:              0123456
```

This time, we are able to complete the match, whose first character is $S[15]$.

7.1.1.5.1 Description and Pseudocode for the Search Algorithm The example contains all the elements of the algorithm. For the moment, we assume the existence of a "partial match" table *T*, described in the following material, which indicates where we need to look for the start of a new match in the event that the current one ends in a mismatch. The entries of *T* are constructed so that if we have a match starting at $S[m]$ that fails when comparing $S[m + i]$ to $W[i]$, then the next possible match will start at index $m + i - T[i]$ in *S* (that is, $T[i]$ is the amount of "backtracking" we need to do after a mismatch). This has two implications: First, $T[0] = -1$, which indicates that if $W[0]$ is a mismatch, we cannot backtrack and must simply check the next character; second, although the next possible match will begin at index $m + i - T[i]$, as in the example, we need not actually check any of the $T[i]$ characters after that, so that we continue searching from $W[T[i]]$. The following is a sample pseudocode implementation of the KMP search algorithm.

```
algorithm kmp_search:
    input:
        an array of characters, S (the text to be
        searched)
        an array of characters, W (the word sought)
    output:
        an integer (the zero-based position in S at
        which W is found)

    define variables:
        an integer, m ← 0 (the beginning of the
        current match in S)
        an integer, i ← 0 (the position of the current
        character in W)
        an array of integers, T (the table, computed
        elsewhere)

    while m+i is less than the length of S, do:
        if W[i] = S[m + i],
            if i equals the (length of W)-1,
                return m
            let i ← i + 1
        otherwise,
            let m ← m + i - T[i],
            if T[i] is greater than -1,
                let i ← T[i]
            else
                let i ← 0

    (if we reach here, we have searched all of S
    unsuccessfully)
    return the length of S
```

7.1.2 *Approximate String-Matching Algorithms*

In this section, we give an overview of the approximate string-matching algorithms; then we present some example approximate string-matching algorithms, such as longest common subsequence (LCS), longest increasing subsequence, and longest common substring.

7.1.2.1 Preliminaries   The problem of string matching is simply stated in Harris [7]. Given a body of text $T[1 \ldots n]$, we try to find a pattern $P[1 \ldots m]$, where $m \leq n$. This can be used to search bodies of texts for specific patterns or, for example, in biology can be used to search strands of DNA (deoxyribonucleic acid) for specific sequences of genes. The issue of exact string matching has been extensively studied. However, approximate string matching is a much more complicated problem to solve that has many more real-world applications. The truth is that in real-world applications, the issue is not so systematic. This is where approximate string matching is needed. Instead of searching for the exact string, approximate string matching searches for patterns that are close to P. In other words, approximate string matching allows for a certain amount of error between the two strings being compared. One of the earliest applications of approximate string matching was in text searching. The approximate string-matching algorithms can be applied to account for errors in typing. Internet searching is particularly difficult because there is so much information, and much of it has errors in it. Also, since the Internet spans many different languages, errors frequently arise in comparing words across language barriers. Also, text editors have to use approximate string matching when performing spell-checks. In addition, spell-checkers have to generate a list of "suggested words" that are close in spelling to the misspelled word. Exact string matching is efficient to generate signatures for polymorphic worms.

7.1.2.2 Dynamic Programming   Approximate string-matching algorithms use a dynamic programming method. In mathematics and computer science, dynamic programming is a method for solving complex problems by breaking them down into simpler subproblems [8]. It is applicable to problems exhibiting the properties of overlapping subproblems, which are only slightly smaller, and optimal substructure (which is described in the following material). When applicable, the method takes far less time than naive methods.

The key idea behind dynamic programming is quite simple. In general, to solve a given problem, we need to solve different parts of the problem (subproblems), then combine the solutions of the subproblems to reach an overall solution. Often, many of these subproblems are really the same. The dynamic programming approach seeks to solve each subproblem only once, thus reducing the number of computations. This is especially useful when the number of repeating subproblems grows exponentially as a function of the size of the input.

Top-down dynamic programming simply means storing the results of certain calculations, which are later used again since the completed calculation is a subproblem of a larger calculation. Bottom-up dynamic programming involves formulating a complex calculation as a recursive series of simpler calculations.

7.1.2.2.1 History of Dynamic Programming Richard Bellman first used the term *dynamic programming* in the 1940s for describing the process of solving problems when one needs to find the best decisions one after another. By 1953, he refined this to the modern meaning, referring specifically to nesting smaller decision problems inside larger decisions, and the field was thereafter recognized by the IEEE (Institute of Electrical and Electronics Engineers) as a systems analysis and engineering topic. Bellman's contribution is remembered in the name of the Bellman equation, which is a central result of dynamic programming that restates an optimization problem in recursive form.

The term *dynamic* was chosen by Bellman to capture the time-varying aspect of the problems. The word *programming* refers to the use of the method to find an optimal program, in the sense of a military schedule for training or logistics.

7.1.2.2.2 Overview of Dynamic Programming Dynamic programming is both a mathematical optimization method and a computer programming method. In both contexts, it refers to simplifying a complicated problem by breaking it down into simpler subproblems in a recursive manner. Although some decision problems cannot be taken apart this way, decisions that span several points in time do often break apart recursively; Bellman called this the "principle of optimality." Likewise, in computer science, a problem that can be broken down recursively is said to have optimal substructure.

If subproblems can be nested recursively inside larger problems so that dynamic programming methods are applicable, then there is a relation between the value of the larger problem and the values of the subproblems. In the optimization literature, this relationship is called the *Bellman equation*.

7.1.2.3 Dynamic Programming in Mathematical Optimization   When we talk about mathematical optimization, dynamic programming usually refers to simplifying a decision by breaking it down into a sequence of decision steps over time. This is done by defining a sequence of *value functions* $V_1, V_2, \ldots, V_n$, with an argument y representing the state of the system at times i from 1 to n. The definition of $V_n(y)$ is the value obtained in state y at the last time n. The values V_i at earlier times $i = n - 1, n - 2, \ldots, 2, 1$ can be found by working backward, using a recursive relationship called the Bellman equation. For $i = 2, \ldots, n$, V_{i-1} at any state y is calculated from V_i by maximizing a simple function (usually the sum) of the gain from decision $i - 1$ and the function V_i at the new state of the system if this decision is made. Since V_i has already been calculated for the needed states, the operation yields V_{i-1} for those states. Finally, V_1 at the initial state of the system is the value of the optimal solution. The optimal values of the decision variables can be recovered one by one by tracking back the calculations already performed.

7.1.2.4 Dynamic Programming in Computer Programming   To apply dynamic programming for solving any problem, the problem must possess two critical attributes: (1) optimal substructure and (2) overlapping subproblems. However, when the overlapping problems are much smaller than the original problem, the strategy is called *divide and conquer* rather than dynamic programming. This is why merge-sort, quick-sort, and finding all matches of a regular expression are not classified as dynamic programming problems.

Optimal substructure means that the solution to a given optimization problem can be obtained by the combination of optimal solutions to its subproblems. The preliminary step toward devising a dynamic programming solution is to check whether the problem exhibits such optimal substructure, which is usually described by means of recursion. For example, given a graph $G = (V, E)$, the shortest path p from a vertex u to a vertex v exhibits optimal substructure: Take any intermediate vertex w on this shortest path p. If p is truly the shortest path, then the path p_1 from u to w and p_2 from w to v are indeed the shortest paths between the corresponding vertices.

Overlapping subproblems mean that the space of subproblems must be small; that is, any recursive algorithm solving the problem should solve the same subproblems repeatedly, rather than generating new subproblems. For example, let us consider the recursive formulation for generating the Fibonacci series: $F_i = F_{i-1} + F_{i-2}$, with base case $F_1 = F_2 = 1$. Then, $F_{43} = F_{42} + F_{41}$, and $F_{42} = F_{41} + F_{40}$. Now, F_{41} is being solved in the recursive subtrees of both F_{43} and F_{42}. Even though the total number of subproblems is actually small (only 43 of them), we end up solving the same problems repeatedly if we adopt a naive recursive solution such as this. Dynamic programming takes account of this fact and solves each subproblem only once. It should be noted here that the subproblems must be only *slightly* smaller (typically taken to mean a constant additive factor) than the larger problem; when they are a multiplicative factor smaller, the problem is no longer classified as dynamic programming.

7.1.2.5 Longest Common Subsequence The LCS [9] problem is to find the longest subsequence common to all sequences in a set of sequences (often just two).

For two sequences $X = x_1 \cdots x_m$ and $Y = y_1 \cdots y_n$ ($n \geq m$), we say that X is a subsequence of Y, and equivalently, Y is a supersequence of X, if for some $i_1 < \cdots < i_p$, $x_j = y_{i_j}$.

Given a finite set of sequences S, an LCS of S is a longest possible sequence s such that each sequence in S is a supersequence of s [1, 9].

EXAMPLE 7.1
Y = "longest", X = "large."

$$\text{String } y: \text{l o n g e s t}$$
$$| \quad | \; |$$
$$\text{String } x: \text{l a r g e}$$

LCS(Y,X) = "lge"

7.1.2.6 Longest Increasing Subsequence The longest increasing subsequence problem is to find a subsequence of a given sequence in which the subsequence elements are in sorted order, lowest to highest, and in which the subsequence is as long as possible. This subsequence is not necessarily contiguous, or unique. Longest increasing subsequences are studied in the context of various disciplines related to mathematics, including algorithmics, random matrix theory, representation theory, and physics. The longest increasing subsequence problem is solvable in time $O(n \log n)$, where n denotes the length of the input sequence [10].

EXAMPLE 7.2
In the binary Van der Corput sequence [11]:

0, 8, 4, 12, 2, 10, 6, 14, 1, 9, 5, 13, 3, 11, 7, 15, ...

a longest increasing subsequence is

0, 2, 6, 9, 13, 15.

This subsequence has length six; the input sequence has no seven-member increasing subsequences. The longest increasing subsequence in this example is not unique; for instance,

0, 4, 6, 9, 11, 15

is another increasing subsequence of equal length in the same input sequence.

Note: A Van der Corput sequence is a low-discrepancy sequence over the unit interval first published in 1935 by the Dutch mathematician J. G. Van der Corput. It is constructed by reversing the base n representation of the sequence of natural numbers (1, 2, 3, ...).

7.1.2.7 Longest Common Substring The longest common substring problem is to find the longest string (or strings) that is a substring (or are substrings) of two or more strings [1].

EXAMPLE 7.3
The longest common substring of the strings "ABABC", "BABCA" and "ABCBA" is string "ABC" of length 3. Other common substrings are "AB," "BC," and "BA."

ABABC

| | |

BABCA

| |

ABCBA

PROBLEM DEFINITION

Given two strings S of length m and T of length n, find the longest strings that are substrings of both S and T.

A generalization is the *k-common substring problem*. Given the set of strings $= \{S_1, \ldots, S_K\}$, where $|S_i| = n_i$ and $\sum n_i = N$, find for each $2 \le k \le K$ the longest strings that occur as substrings of at least k strings.

7.2 Machine Learning

Machine learning (ML), a branch of artificial intelligence, is a scientific discipline concerned with the design and development of algorithms that take as input empirical data, such as that from sensors or databases, and yield patterns or predictions thought to be features of the underlying mechanism that generated the data. A learner can take advantage of examples (data) to capture characteristics of interest of their unknown underlying probability distribution. Data can be seen as instances of the possible relations between observed variables. A major focus of ML research is the design of algorithms that recognize complex patterns and make intelligent decisions based on input data. One fundamental difficulty is that the set of all possible behaviors given all possible inputs is too large to be included in the set of observed examples (training data). Hence, the learner must generalize from the given examples to produce a useful output in new cases. In this section, we discuss supervised learning and in the next section unsupervised learning.

7.2.1 Supervised Learning

Supervised ML explores algorithms that reason from the externally supplied instances to produce general hypotheses, which will make predictions about future instances [12]. The main goal of supervised learning is to build a concise model of the distribution of class labels in terms of predictor features. The resulting classifier is then used to assign class labels to the testing instances where the values of the predictor features are known but the value of the class label is unknown. Here, we discuss various supervised ML classification techniques.

7.2.1.1 The Basics As noted, the ML field basically stems from the broad field of artificial intelligence, which aims to mimic intelligent abilities of humans by machines. In the field of ML, one considers the important question of how to make machines able to "learn." Learning in this context is understood as inductive inference, where one observes examples that represent incomplete information about some "statistical phenomenon." In unsupervised learning, one typically tries to uncover hidden regularities (e.g., clusters) or to detect anomalies in the data (for instance, some unusual machine function or a network intrusion). In supervised learning, there is a label associated with each example. It is supposed to be the answer to a question about the example. If the label is discrete, then the task is called a classification problem; otherwise, for real valued labels, we speak of a regression problem. Based on these examples (including the labels), one is particularly interested in predicting the answer for other cases before they are explicitly observed. Hence, learning is not only a question of remembering but also of generalization to unseen cases [13].

There are several applications for ML, but data mining is considered the most significant. Any system developed by human beings has some flaws, so people have made mistakes when trying to establish relationships among multiple features. This makes it difficult for them to find solutions to certain problems. ML can often be successfully applied to these problems, improving the efficiency of systems and the designs of machines.

In ML algorithms, every instance in any dataset used is represented using the same set of features. The features may be continuous, categorical, or binary. The learning is called supervised if instances are given with known labels (the corresponding correct outputs) (see Table 7.2). In contrast, for unsupervised learning, instances are unlabeled. By applying these unsupervised (clustering) algorithms, researchers hope to discover unknown, but useful, classes of items. Another kind of ML is reinforcement learning. The training information provided to the learning system by the environment (external trainer) is in the form of a scalar reinforcement signal that constitutes a measure of how well the system operates. The learner is not told which actions to take but rather must discover which actions yield the best reward by trying each action in turn [14].

Table 7.2   Instances with Known Labels (the Corresponding Correct Outputs)

DATA IN STANDARD FORMAT					
CASE	FEATURE 1	FEATURE 2	...	FEATURE N	CLASS
1	XXX	X		XX	Good
2	XXX	X		XX	Good
3	XXX	X		XX	Bad
...					

Numerous ML applications involve tasks that can be set up as supervised. In the present section, we concentrate on the techniques necessary to do this. In particular, this work is concerned with classification problems in which the output of instances admits only discrete, unordered values.

7.2.1.2 Supervised Learning Algorithms Overview   Inductive ML is the process of learning a set of rules from instances (examples in a training set) or, more generally, creating a classifier that can be used to generalize from new instances [14]. The process of applying supervised ML to a real-world problem is described in Figure 7.7.

As we see in Figure 7.7, the first step is collecting the dataset. If a requisite expert is available, then the expert could suggest which fields (attributes, features) are the most informative. If not, then the simplest method is that of brute force, which means measuring everything available in the hope that the right (informative, relevant) features can be isolated. However, a dataset collected by the brute-force method is not directly suitable for induction. It contains in most cases noise and missing feature values and therefore requires significant preprocessing [14].

After collecting the dataset, the second step is the data preparation and data preprocessing. Depending on the circumstances, researchers can choose from a number of methods to handle missing data [15]. Hodge and Austin [16] have introduced a survey of contemporary techniques for outlier (noise) detection. These researchers have identified the techniques' advantages and disadvantages. Instance selection is used not only to handle noise but also to cope with the infeasibility of learning from very large datasets. Instance selection in these datasets is an optimization problem that attempts to maintain the mining quality while minimizing the sample size [17]. It reduces data

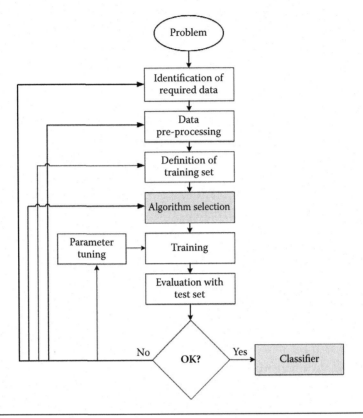

Figure 7.7   The process of supervised ML.

and enables a data-mining algorithm to function and work effectively with very large datasets. There is a variety of procedures for sampling instances from a large dataset [18].

Feature subset selection is the process of identifying and removing as many irrelevant and redundant features as possible. This reduces the dimensionality of the data, which enables data-mining algorithms to operate faster and more effectively. The fact that there are many features that depend on one another often unduly influences the accuracy of supervised ML classification models. This problem can be addressed by constructing new features from the basic feature set. This technique is called feature construction/transformation. These newly generated features may lead to the creation of more concise and accurate classifiers. In addition, the discovery of meaningful features contributes to better comprehensibility of the produced classifier and a better understanding of the learned concept [14].

7.2.2 *Algorithm Selection*

To obtain a perfect result using supervised ML techniques, we should use a suitable technique for a problem. So, the choice of which specific learning algorithm we should use is a critical step. Once preliminary testing is judged to be satisfactory, the classifier (mapping from unlabeled instances to classes) is available for routine use. The classifier's evaluation is most often based on prediction accuracy (the percentage of correct prediction divided by the total number of predictions). There are many techniques that are used to calculate a classifier's accuracy; the following are three kinds of techniques:

- One technique is to split the training set by using two-thirds for training and the other third for estimating performance.
- Cross validation is a technique in which the training set is divided into mutually exclusive and equal-size subsets; for each subset, the classifier is trained on the union of all the other subsets. The average of the error rate of each subset is therefore an estimate of the error rate of the classifier.
- Leave-one-out validation is a special case of cross validation. All test subsets consist of a single instance. This type of validation is, of course, more expensive computationally but is useful when the most accurate estimate of a classifier's error rate is required. If the error rate evaluation is unsatisfactory, we must return to a previous stage of the supervised ML process (as detailed in Figure 7.7). A variety of factors must be examined: Perhaps relevant features for the problem are not being used, a larger training set is needed, the dimensionality of the problem is too high, the selected algorithm is inappropriate, or parameter tuning is needed. Another problem could be that the dataset is unbalanced [14].

There is a common method for comparing supervised ML algorithms, which is to perform statistical comparisons of the accuracies of trained classifiers on specific datasets. If we have sufficient supply of data, we can sample a number of training sets of size N, run the two learning algorithms on each of them, and estimate the difference in accuracy for each pair of classifiers on a large test set. The average of these differences is an estimate of the expected difference in generalization error across all possible training sets of size N, and their variance is an estimate of the variance of the classifier in the total set. The next step is to perform a paired t test to check the null hypothesis, which is the mean difference between the classifiers is zero. This test can produce two types of errors:

- Type I error is the probability that the test rejects the null hypothesis incorrectly (i.e., it finds a "significant" difference although there is none). Type II error is the probability that the null hypothesis is not rejected when there actually is a difference. The test's type I error will be close to the chosen significance level.

- In practice, however, we often have only one dataset of size N, and all estimates must be obtained from this sole dataset. Different training sets are obtained by subsampling, and the instances not sampled for training are used for testing. Unfortunately, this violates the independence assumption necessary for proper significance testing. The consequence of this is that type I errors exceed the significance level. This is problematic because it is important for the researcher to be able to control type I errors and know the probability of incorrectly rejecting the null hypothesis. Several heuristic versions of the t test have been developed to alleviate this problem [14].

In practice, however, we often have only one dataset of size N, and all estimates must be obtained from this sole dataset. Different training sets are obtained by subsampling, and the instances not sampled for training are used for testing. Unfortunately, this violates the independence assumption necessary for proper significance testing. The consequence of this is that type I errors exceed the significance level. This is problematic because it is important for the researchers to be able to control type I errors and know the probability of incorrectly rejecting the null hypothesis. Several heuristic versions of the t test have been developed to alleviate this problem [19, 20].

The test's outcome should be independent of the particular partitioning resulting from the randomization process because this would make it much easier to replicate experimental results published in the literature. However, in practice, there is always certain sensitivity to the partitioning used. To measure replicability, we need to repeat the same test several times on the same data with different random partitioning—usually 10 repetitions—and count how often the outcome is the same.

Supervised classification is one of the tasks most frequently carried out by so-called intelligent systems. Thus, large numbers of techniques have been developed based on artificial intelligence (logical/symbolic techniques), perceptron-based techniques, and statistics (Bayesian networks [BNs], instance-based techniques). In the next section, we focus on the most important ML techniques.

7.2.3 Logic-Based Algorithms

In this section, we focus on two groups of logical (symbolic) learning methods: decision trees and rule-based classifiers.

7.2.3.1 Decision Trees

Decision trees classify instances by sorting them from the root to some leaf node, where

- Each internal node specifies a test of some attribute.
- Each branch corresponds to a value for the tested attribute.
- Each leaf node provides a classification for the instance.

Figure 7.8 is an example of a decision tree for the training set of Table 7.3.

Here, we give some explanation for Figure 7.8. The instance $\langle at1 = a1, at2 = b2, at3 = a3, at4 = b4 \rangle$ would sort to the nodes at1, at2, and

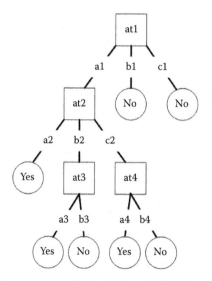

Figure 7.8 A decision tree.

Table 7.3 Training Set

at1	at2	at3	at4	Class
a1	a2	a3	a4	Yes
a1	a2	a3	b4	Yes
a1	b2	a3	a4	Yes
a1	b2	b3	b4	No
a1	c2	a3	a4	Yes
a1	c2	a3	b4	No
b1	b2	b3	b4	No
c1	b2	b3	b4	No

finally at3, which would classify the instance as positive (represented by the values "Yes"). The problem of constructing optimal binary decision trees is an NP-complete problem; thus, theoreticians have searched for efficient heuristics for constructing near-optimal decision trees [14].

The feature that best divides the training data would be the root node of the tree. There are numerous methods for finding the feature that best divides the training data, such as information gain [21] and gini index [22]. While myopic measures estimate each attribute independently, the ReliefF algorithm [23] estimates them in the context of other attributes. However, a majority of studies have concluded that there is no single best method. Comparison of individual methods may still be important when deciding which metric should be used in a particular dataset. The same procedure is then repeated on each partition of the divided data, creating subtrees until the training data are divided into subsets of the same class.

In the following, we present a general pseudocode for building decision trees:

```
Check for base cases
  For each attribute a
    Find the feature that best
    divides the training data such as
    information gain from splitting on a
Let a_best be the attribute with the
highest normalized information gain
    Create a decision node node that
    Splits on a_best
Recurse on the sub-lists obtained by
splitting on a_best and add those
nodes as children of node
```

A decision tree, or any learned hypothesis h, is said to overfit training data if another hypothesis h' exists that has a larger error than h when tested on the training data but a smaller error than h when tested on the entire dataset. There are two common approaches that decision tree induction algorithms can use to avoid overfitting training data:

- Stop the training algorithm before it reaches a point at which it perfectly fits the training data, or
- Prune the induced decision tree. If the two trees employ the same kind of tests and have the same prediction accuracy, the one with fewer leaves is usually preferred.

The most straightforward way of tackling overfitting is to pre-prune the decision tree by not allowing it to grow to its full size. Establishing a nontrivial termination criterion such as a threshold test for the feature quality metric can do that. Decision tree classifiers usually employ postpruning techniques that evaluate the performance of decision trees, as they are pruned by using a validation set. Any node can be removed and assigned the most common class of the training instances that are sorted to it. A comparative study of well-known pruning methods was presented in Elomaa and Rousu [24], concluding that there is no single best pruning method.

Even though the divide-and-conquer algorithm is quick, efficiency can become important in tasks with hundreds of thousands of instances. The most time-consuming aspect is sorting the instances on a numeric feature to find the best threshold t. This can be expedited if possible thresholds for a numeric feature are determined just once, effectively converting the feature to discrete intervals, or if the threshold is determined from a subset of the instances. Elomaa and Rousu [24] stated that the use of binary discretization with C4.5 [25] needed about half the training time of using C4.5 multisplitting. In addition, according to their experiments, multisplitting of numerical features did not carry any advantage in prediction accuracy over binary splitting.

Decision trees use splits based on a single feature at each internal node, so they are usually univariate. In fact, most decision tree algorithms cannot perform well with problems that require diagonal partitioning. The division of the instance space is orthogonal to the axis of one variable and parallel to all other axes. Therefore, the resulting regions after partitioning are all hyperrectangles. However, there are a few methods that construct multivariate trees. One example is Zheng's [26], who improved the classification accuracy of the decision trees by constructing new binary features with logical operators such as conjunction, negation, and disjunction. In addition, Zheng [26] created at-least M-of-N features. For a given instance, the value of an at least M-of-N representation is true if at least M of its conditions is true of the instance, otherwise it is false. Gama and Brazdil [27] combined a decision tree with a linear discriminant for constructing multivariate decision trees. In this model, new features are computed as linear combinations of the previous ones.

In fact, decision trees can be a significantly more complex representation for some concepts due to the replication problem. A solution to this problem is using an algorithm to implement complex features at nodes in order to avoid replication. Markovitch and Rosenstein [28] presented the FICUS construction algorithm, which receives the standard input of supervised learning as well as a feature representation specification and uses them to produce a set of generated features. While FICUS is similar in some aspects to other feature construction algorithms, its main strength is its generality and flexibility. FICUS was designed to perform feature generation given any feature representation specification complying with its general-purpose grammar [14].

7.2.3.2 C4.5 Algorithm   The most well-known algorithm for building decision trees is the C4.5 [25]. C4.5 is an algorithm used to generate a decision tree developed by Ross Quinlan. This is an extension of Quinlan's earlier ID3 algorithm. The decision trees generated by C4.5 can be used for classification, and for this reason, C4.5 is often referred to as a statistical classifier.

C4.5 builds decision trees from a set of training data in the same way that ID3 does, using the concept of information entropy. The training data are a set $S = s_1, s_2, \ldots$ of already classified samples. Each sample, $s_i = x_1, x_2, \ldots$, is a vector where $x_1, x_2, \ldots$ represent attributes or features of the sample. The training data are augmented with a vector $C = c_1, c_2, \ldots$ where $c_1, c_2, \ldots$ represent the class to which each sample belongs.

At each node of the tree, C4.5 chooses one attribute of the data that most effectively splits its set of samples into subsets enriched in one class or the other. Its criterion is the normalized information gain (difference in entropy) that results from choosing an attribute for splitting the data. The attribute with the highest normalized information gain is chosen to make the decision. The C4.5 algorithm then recurses on the smaller sublists.

This algorithm has a few base cases:

- All the samples in the list belong to the same class. When this happens, it simply creates a leaf node for the decision tree indicating to choose that class.
- None of the features provides any information gain. In this case, C4.5 creates a decision node higher up the tree using the expected value of the class.
- An instance of previously unseen class is encountered. Again, C4.5 creates a decision node higher up the tree using the expected value.

In pseudocode, the general algorithm for building decision trees is as follows:

```
1- Check for base cases
2- For each attribute a
    1-Find the normalized information gain from
    splitting on a
3-Let a_best be the attribute with the highest
normalized information gain
4- Create a decision node that splits on a_best
5- Recurse on the sublists obtained by splitting on
a_best, and add those nodes as children of node
```

7.2.4 Learning Set of Rules

Decision trees can be translated into a set of rules by creating a separate rule for each path from the root to a leaf in the tree. However, rules can also be directly induced from training data using a variety of rule-based algorithms.

Classification rules represent each class by disjunctive normal form (DNF). A k-DNF expression is of the form: $(X_1 \wedge X_2 \wedge \ldots \wedge X_n) \vee (X_n + 1 \wedge X_n + 2 \wedge \ldots X_{2n}) \vee \ldots \vee (X_{(k-1)n+1} \wedge X_{(k-1)n+2} \wedge \ldots \wedge X_{kn})$, where k is the number of disjunctions, n is the number of conjunctions in each disjunction, and X_n is defined over the alphabet $X_1, X_2, \dots, X_j \cup \sim X_1,$ $\sim X_2, \dots, \sim X_j.$ The goal is to construct the smallest rule set that is consistent with the training data. A large number of learned rules is usually a sign that the learning algorithm is attempting to "remember" the training set, instead of discovering the assumptions that govern it. A separate-and-conquer algorithm (covering algorithms) search for a rule that explains a part of its training instances separates these instances and recursively conquers the remaining instances by learning more rules until no instances remain. A general pseudocode for rule learners is as follows [16]:

```
On presentation of training examples:
    1. Initialize rule set to a default
(usually empty, or a rule assigning all
objects to the most common class).
    2. Initialize examples to either all
available examples or all examples not
correctly handled by rule set.
    3. Repeat
        (a) Find best, the best rule with
    respect to examples.
        (b) If such a rule can be found
            i. Add best to rule set.
            ii. Set examples to all
            examples not handled
            correctly by rule set.
        until no rule best can be found
        (for instance, because no
        examples remain).
```

There are many differences between heuristics for rule learning and heuristics for decision trees, but the main difference between them is that the latter evaluates the average quality of a number of disjointed sets (one for each value of the feature that is tested), and rule learners only evaluate the quality of the set of instances that is covered by the candidate rule. More advanced rule learners differ from this simple pseudocode mostly by adding additional mechanisms to prevent overfitting of the training data, for instance, by stopping the specialization process with the use of a quality measure or by generalizing overly specialized rules in a separate pruning phase [14].

7.2.4.1 RIPPER Algorithm   RIPPER is a well-known rule-based algorithm [29]. RIPPER is elaborated as repeated incremental pruning to produce error reduction. This algorithm was designed by Cohen in 1995. RIPPER is especially more efficient on large noisy datasets. There are two kinds of loops in the RIPPER algorithm: outer and inner. The outer loop adds one rule at a time to the rule base, and the inner loop adds one condition at a time to the current rule. The information gain measure is maximized by adding the conditions to the rule. This process is continued until it covers no negative example.

7.2.4.2 Perceptron-Based Techniques   The perceptron is another well-known rule-based algorithm of an input into one of two possible outputs. It is a type of linear classifier, that is, a classification algorithm that makes its predictions based on a linear predictor function combining a set of weights with the feature vector describing a given input. The learning algorithm for perceptrons is an online algorithm in that it processes elements in the training set one at a time.

The perceptron algorithm was invented in 1957 at the Cornell Aeronautical Laboratory by Frank Rosenblatt.

In the context of artificial neural networks (ANNs), the perceptron algorithm is also termed the single-layer perceptron to distinguish it from the case of a multilayer perceptron, which is a more complicated neural network. As a linear classifier, the (single-layer) perceptron is the simplest kind of feed-forward neural network [30].

7.2.4.2.1 Single-Layer Perceptrons   A single-layer perceptron can be briefly described as follows: If x_1 through x_n are input feature values and w_1 through w_n are connection weights/prediction vector (typically real numbers in the interval [-1, 1]), then the perceptron computes the sum of weighted inputs $\Sigma_i x_i w_i$, and output goes through an adjustable threshold. If the sum is above threshold, the output is 1; otherwise it is 0. The most common way that the perceptron algorithm is used for learning from a batch of training instances is to run the algorithm repeatedly through the training set until it finds a prediction vector that is correct on all of the training set. This prediction rule is then used for predicting the labels on the test set [14].

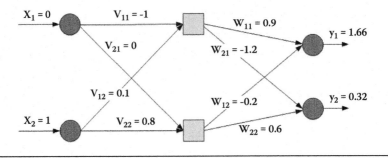

Figure 7.9 Feed-forward ANN.

7.2.4.2.2 Multilayer Perceptrons A single-layer perceptron can only classify linearly separable sets of instances. If a straight line or plane can be drawn to separate the input instances into their correct categories, input instances are linearly separable, and the perceptron will find the solution. If the instances are not linearly separable, learning will never reach a point at which all instances are classified properly. So, multilayer perceptrons have been created to address this problem. A multilayer neural network consists of a large number of units (neurons) joined together in a pattern of connections (Figure 7.9). Units in a net are usually segregated into three classes: input units, which receive information to be processed; output units, where the results of the processing are found; and units in between known as "hidden units." Feed-forward ANNs (Figure 7.9) allow signals to travel one way only, from input to output.

In the first step, the network is trained on a set of paired data to determine input-output mapping. The weights of the connections between neurons are then fixed, and the network is used to determine the classifications of a new set of data.

During the classification phase, the signal at the input units propagates all the way through the net to determine the activation values at all the output units. Each input unit has an activation value that represents some features external to the net. Then, every input unit sends its activation value to each of the hidden units to which it is connected. Each of these hidden units calculates its own activation value, and this signal is then passed on to output units. The activation value for each receiving unit is calculated according to a simple activation function. The function sums together the contributions of all sending units, where the contribution of a unit is defined as the weight of the connection between the send-ing and receiving units multiplied by the sending unit's activation value. This sum is usually then further modified, for example, by adjusting the activation sum to a value between 0 and 1 or by set-ting the activation value to zero unless a threshold level for that sum is reached.

Properly determining the size of the hidden layer is considered the main problem because an underestimate of the number of neurons can lead to poor approximation and generalization capabilities; excessive nodes can result in overfitting and eventually make the search for the global optimum more difficult. Finding the minimum amount of neu-rons and the number of instances necessary to program a given task into feed-forward neural networks is a challenging study to perform.

In fact, an ANN depends on three fundamental aspects:

- Input and activation functions of the unit
- Network architecture
- The weight of each input connection

Given that the first two aspects are fixed, the behavior of the ANN is defined by the current values of the weights. The weights of the net to be trained are initially set to random values, and then instances of the training set are repeatedly exposed to the net. The values for the input of an instance are placed on the input units, and the output of the net is compared with the desired output for this instance. Then, all the weights in the net are adjusted slightly in the direction that would bring the out-put values of the net closer to the values for the desired output. There are many algorithms with which a network can be trained. However, the most well known and widely used learning algorithm to estimate the values of the weights is the backpropagation algorithm. Generally, the backpropagation algorithm includes the following six steps:

1. Present a training sample to the neural network.
2. Compare the network's output to the desired output from that sample. Calculate the error in each output neuron.
3. For each neuron, calculate what the output should have been and a scaling factor, how much lower or higher the output must be adjusted to match the desired output. This is the local error.
4. Adjust the weights of each neuron to lower the local error.

5. Assign "blame" for the local error to neurons at the previous level, giving greater responsibility to neurons connected by stronger weights.

6. Repeat the previous steps on the neurons at the previous level, using each one's blame as its error. With more details, the general rule for updating weights is

$$\Delta W_{ji} = \eta \delta_j O_i$$

where

η = a positive number (called the learning rate) that determines the step size in the gradient descent search. A large value enables backpropagation to move faster to the target weight configuration, but it also increases the chance of its never reaching this target.

O_i = the output computed by neuron i.

$\delta_j = O_j(1 - O_j)(T_j - O_j)$, for the output neurons, where, T_j is the wanted output for neuron j.

$\delta_j = O_j(1 - O_j)\Sigma_k \delta_k W_{kj}$ is for the internal (hidden) neurons.

The backpropagation algorithm will have to perform a number of weight modifications before it reaches a good weight configuration. For n training instances and W weights, each repetition/epoch in the learning process takes $O(nW)$ time, but in the worst case, the number of epochs can be exponential to the number of inputs. For this reason, neural nets use a number of different stopping rules to control when training ends. The four most common stopping rules are as follows:

- stop after a specified number of epochs,
- stop when an error measure reaches a threshold,
- stop when the error measure has seen no improvement over a certain number of epochs, and
- stop when the error measure on some of the data that has been sampled from the training data (hold-out set, validation set) is more than a certain amount of the error measure on the training set (overfitting).

Feed-forward neural networks are usually trained by the original backpropagation algorithm or by some variant. Their greatest problem is that they are too slow for most applications. One of the approaches to speed up the training rate is to estimate optimal initial weights. Another method for training multilayer feed-forward ANNs is the weight-elimination algorithm, which automatically derives the appropriate topology and therefore avoids the problems with overfitting. Genetic algorithms have been used to train the weights of neural networks and to find the architecture of neural networks. There are also Bayesian methods in existence that attempt to train neural networks. A number of other techniques have emerged recently that attempt to improve ANN training algorithms by changing the architecture of the networks as training proceeds. These techniques include pruning useless nodes or weights and constructive algorithms, for which extra nodes are added as required [14].

7.2.4.2.3 Radial Basis Function Networks ANN learning can be achieved, among others, through

- synaptic weight modification,
- network structure modifications (creating or deleting neurons or synaptic connections),
- use of suitable attractors or other suitable stable state points, and
- appropriate choice of activation functions. Since backpropagation training is a gradient descending process, it may become stuck in local minima in this weight space. It is because of this possibility that neural network models are characterized by high variance and unsteadiness.

Radial basis function (RBF) networks have also been widely applied in many science and engineering fields. An RBF network is a three-layer feedback network in which each hidden unit implements a radial activation function, and each output unit implements a weighted sum of hidden unit outputs. Its training procedure is usually divided into two stages:

- The centers and widths of the hidden layer are determined by clustering algorithms.
- The weights connecting the hidden layer with the output layer are determined by singular value decomposition (SVD) or least mean squared (LMS) algorithms.

The problem of selecting the appropriate number of basis functions remains a critical issue for RBF networks. The number of basis functions controls the complexity and the generalization ability of RBF networks. RBF networks with too few basis functions cannot fit the training data adequately due to limited flexibility. On the other hand, those with too many basis functions yield poor generalization abilities since they are too flexible and erroneously fit the noise in the training data [14].

7.2.5 Statistical Learning Algorithms

Rather than simply a classification, statistical approaches are characterized by having an explicit underlying probability model that provides a probability that an instance belongs in each class. Linear discriminant analysis (LDA) and the related Fisher's linear discriminant are simple methods used in statistics and ML to find the linear combination of features that best separate two or more classes of object. LDA works when the measurements made on each observation are continuous quantities. When dealing with categorical variables, the equivalent technique is discriminant correspondence analysis [14].

There is another general technique for estimating probability distributions from data: maximum entropy. The main principle in maximum entropy is that when nothing is known, the distribution should be as uniform as possible, that is, have maximal entropy. Labeled training data are used to derive a set of constraints for the model that characterize the class-specific expectations for the distribution.

The most well-known representative of statistical learning algorithms are BNs.

7.2.5.1 Naive Bayes Classifiers

A naive Bayes classifier is a simple probabilistic classifier based on applying Bayes' theorem, which is composed of directed acyclic graphs (DAGs) with only one parent (representing the unobserved node) and several children (corresponding to observed nodes) with a strong assumption of independence among child nodes in the context of their parent. Thus, the independence model (naive Bayes) is based on estimating [14]

$$R = \frac{P(i\,|\,X)}{P(j\,|\,X)} = \frac{P(i)P(X\,|\,i)}{P(j)P(X\,|\,j)} = \frac{P(i)\prod P(X_r\,|\,i)}{P(j)\prod P(X_r\,|\,j)}$$

By comparing these two probabilities, the larger probability indicates that the class label value that is more likely to be the actual label (if $R > 1$: predict i; else predict j). Cestnik et al. [31] first used the naive Bayes in the ML community. Since the Bayes classification algorithm uses a product operation to compute the probabilities $P(X, i)$, it is especially prone to being unduly impacted by probabilities of 0. This can be avoided by using a Laplace estimator or m-estimate, by adding one to all numerators and adding the number of added ones to the denominator [32].

The major advantage of the naive Bayes classifier is its short computational time for training. In addition, since the model has the form of a product, it can be converted into a sum through the use of logarithms—with significant consequent computational advantages. If a feature is numerical, the usual procedure is to discretize it during data preprocessing, although a researcher can use the normal distribution to calculate probabilities [14].

7.2.5.2 Bayesian Networks   A Bayesian network (BN) is a graphical model for probability relationships among a set of variables (features); Figure 7.10 explains the BN structure. The BN structure S is a DAG, and the nodes in S are in one-to-one correspondence with the features X. The arcs represent casual influences among the features; the lack of possible arcs in S encodes conditional independencies. Moreover, a feature (node) is conditionally independent from its nondescendants

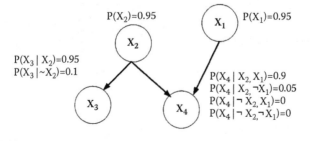

Figure 7.10   The structure of a Bayes network.

given its parents [X_1 is conditionally independent from X_2, given X_3 if $P(X_1|X_2, X_3) = P(X_1|X_3)$ for all possible values of X_1, X_2, X_3].

The BN can be divided into two subtasks in terms of the task of learning:

- initially, the learning of the DAG structure of the network,
- and then the determination of its parameters.

Probabilistic parameters are encoded into a set of tables, one for each variable, in the form of local conditional distributions of a variable given its parents. Given the independences encoded into the network, the joint distribution can be reconstructed by simply multiplying these tables. Within the general framework of inducing BNs, there are two scenarios: known structure and unknown structure.

In the first scenario, the structure of the network is given (e.g., by an expert) and assumed to be correct. Once the network structure is fixed, learning the parameters in the conditional probability tables (CPTs) is usually solved by estimating a locally exponential number of parameters from the data provided. Each node in the network has an associated CPT that describes the conditional probability distribution of that node given the different values of its parents [14].

In spite of the remarkable power of BNs, they have an inherent limitation. This is the computational difficulty of exploring a previously unknown network. Given a problem described by n features, the number of possible structure hypotheses is more than exponential in n. If the structure is unknown, one approach is to introduce a scoring function (or a score) that evaluates the "fitness" of networks with respect to the training data and then to search for the best network according to this score. Several researchers have shown experimentally that the selection of a single good hypothesis using greedy search often yields accurate predictions [33]. The following is a pseudocode for training BNs:

```
Initialize an empty Bayesian network
G containing n nodes (i.e., a BN with n
Nodes but no edges)
    1.   Evaluate the score of G: Score (G)
    2.   G' =G
    3.   for i = 1 to n do
    4.   for j = 1 to n do
```

```
 5.  if i • j then
 6.  if there is no edge between the
     nodes i and j in G• then
 7.  Modify G'by adding an edge between
     The nodes i and j in G• such that i
     is a parent of j: (i • j)
 8.  if the resulting G'is a DAG then
 9.  if (Score(G') > Score(G)) then
10.  G = G'
11.  end if
12.  end if
13.  end if
14.  end if
15.  G'= G
16.  end for
17.  end for
```

A BN structure can also be found by learning the conditional independence relationships among the features of a dataset. Using a few statistical tests (such as the chi-squared and mutual information test), one can find the conditional independence (CI) relationships among the features and use these relationships as constraints to construct a BN. These algorithms are called CI-based algorithms or constraint-based algorithms. Cowell [34] has shown that for any structure search procedure based on CI tests, an equivalent procedure based on maximizing a score can be specified.

The most interesting feature of BNs, compared to decision trees or neural networks, is the possibility of taking into account prior information about a given problem in terms of structural relationships among its features. This prior expertise, or domain knowledge, about the structure of a BN can take the following forms:

1. Declaring that a node is a root node (i.e., it has no parents).
2. Declaring that a node is a leaf node (i.e., it has no children).
3. Declaring that a node is a direct cause or direct effect of another node.
4. Declaring that a node is not directly connected to another node.
5. Declaring that two nodes are independent, given a condition set.
6. Providing partial node ordering, that is, declaring that a node appears earlier than another node in the ordering.
7. Providing a complete node ordering.

There is a problem in BN classifiers; they are not suitable for datasets with many features. The reason for this is that trying to construct a very large network is simply not feasible in terms of time and space. A final problem is that before the induction, the numerical features need to be discretized in most cases [14].

7.2.5.3 Instance-Based Learning Instance-based learning is considered another category under the header of statistical methods. Instance-based learning algorithms are lazy-learning algorithms as they delay the induction or generalization process until classification is performed. Lazy-learning algorithms require less computation time during the training phase than eager-learning algorithms (such as decision trees, neural and Bayes nets) but more computation time during the classification process. One of the most straightforward instance-based learning algorithms is the nearest neighbor algorithm.

The *k* nearest neighbor (kNN) is based on the principle that the instances within a dataset will generally exist in close proximity to other instances that have similar properties. If the instances are tagged with a classification label, then the value of the label of an unclassified instance can be determined by observing the class of its nearest neighbors. The kNN locates the *k* nearest instances to the query instance and determines its class by identifying the single most frequent class label. The following is a pseudocode example of the instance-based learning method.

```
Procedure InstanceBasedLearner (Testing Instances)
    for each testing instance
    {
    find the k most nearest instances of
    the training set according to a
    distance metric
    Resulting Class= most frequent class
    label of the k nearest instances
    }
```

In general, instances can be considered as points within an *n*-dimensional instance space where each of the *n* dimensions corresponds to one of the *n* features that are used to describe an instance.

Table 7.4 Approaches to Define the Distance between Instances (x and y)

$$\text{Minkowsky}: D(x,y)=\left(\sum_{i=1}^{m}|x_i-y_i|^r\right)^{1/r}$$

$$\text{Manhattan}: D(x,y)=\sum_{i=1}^{m}|x_i-y_i|$$

$$\text{Chebychev}: D(x,y)=\max_{i=1}^{m}|x_i-y_i|$$

$$\text{Euclidean}: D(x,y)=\left(\sum_{i=1}^{m}|x_i-y_i|^2\right)^{1/2}$$

$$\text{Camberra}: D(x,y)=\sum_{i=1}^{m}\frac{|x_i-y_i|}{|x_i+y_i|}$$

$$\text{Kendall's Rank Correlation}: D(x,y)=1-\frac{2}{m(m-1)}\sum_{i=j}^{m}\sum_{j=1}^{i-1}\text{sign}(x_i-x_j)\text{sign}(y_i-y_j)$$

The absolute position of the instances within this space is not as significant as the relative distance between instances. This relative distance is determined using a distance metric. Ideally, the distance metric must minimize the distance between two similarly classified instances while maximizing the distance between instances of different classes. Many different metrics have been presented. The most significant ones are presented in Table 7.4.

The choice of k affects the performance of the kNN algorithm. Presented next are some reasons why a kNN classifier might incorrectly classify a query instance:

- When noise is present in the locality of the query instance, the noisy instances win the majority vote, resulting in the incorrect class being predicted. A larger k could solve this problem.
- When the region defining the class, or fragment of the class, is so small that instances belonging to the class that surrounds the fragment win the majority vote. A smaller k could solve this problem.

As mentioned, the major disadvantage of instance-based classifiers is their large computational time for classification. A key issue in many applications is to determine which of the available input features should be used in modeling via feature selection because it could improve the classification accuracy and scale down the required classification time. Furthermore, choosing a more suitable distance metric for the specific dataset can improve the accuracy of instance-based classifiers.

7.2.6 Support Vector Machines

Support vector machines (SVMs) are supervised learning models with associated learning algorithms that analyze data and recognize patterns; they are used for classification and regression analysis. The basic SVM takes a set of input data and predicts, for each given input, which of two possible classes forms the input, making it a nonprobabilistic binary linear classifier. Given a set of training examples, each marked as belonging to one of two categories, an SVM training algorithm builds a model that assigns new examples into one category or the other. An SVM model is a representation of the examples as points in space, mapped so that the examples of the separate categories are divided by a clear gap that is as wide as possible. New examples are then mapped into that same space and predicted to belong to a category based on which side of the gap they fall.

More formally, an SVM constructs a hyperplane or set of hyperplanes in a high- or infinite-dimensional space, which can be used for classification, regression, or other tasks. Intuitively, a good separation is achieved by the hyperplane that has the largest distance to the nearest training data point of any class (so-called functional margin) since, in general, the larger the margin the lower the generalization error of the classifier.

If the training data are linearly separable, then a pair (w, b) exists such that

$$\mathbf{W}^\mathrm{T}\, \mathbf{X}_i + b \geq 1, \text{ for all } \mathbf{X}_i \in P$$

$$\mathbf{W}^\mathrm{T}\, \mathbf{X}_i + b \leq -1, \text{ for all } \mathbf{X}_i \in N$$

With the decision rule given by $f_{w,b}(\mathbf{X})$ sgn$(\mathbf{W}^\mathrm{T}\mathbf{X}+ b)$, where w is termed the weight vector, and b is the bias (or –b is termed the threshold).

It is easy to show that, when it is possible to linearly separate two classes, an optimum separating hyperplane can be found by minimizing

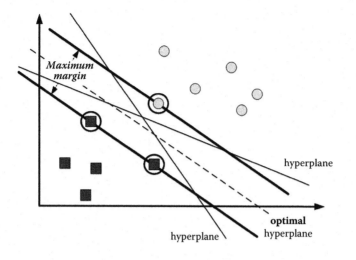

Figure 7.11 Maximum margin.

the squared norm of the separating hyperplane. The minimization can be set up as a convex quadratic programming (QP) problem:

$$\textbf{Minimize}_{w,b}\,\Phi\,(\textbf{w}) = \tfrac{1}{2}\,||\,\textbf{w}\,||^2 \qquad (7.1)$$

$$\text{Subject to } \textbf{y}_i(\textbf{W}^T\,\textbf{X}_i + b) \geq 1, i = 1, \ldots, l.$$

In case of linearly separable data, once the optimum separating hyperplane is found, data points that lie on its margin are known as support vector points, and the solution is represented as a linear combination of only these points (see Figure 7.11). Other data points are ignored.

Therefore, the model complexity of an SVM is unaffected by the number of features encountered in the training data (the number of support vectors selected by the SVM learning algorithm is usually small). For this reason, SVMs are well suited to deal with learning tasks for which the number of features is large with respect to the number of training instances.

A general pseudocode for SVM is as follows:

```
1)  Introduce positive Lagrange multipliers, one for
each of the inequality constraints (1). This gives
Lagrangian:
```

$$L_P \equiv \frac{1}{2}\,w^2 - \sum_{i=1}^{N} \propto_i\, y_i\!\left(x_i \cdot w - b\right) + \sum_{i=1}^{N} \propto_i$$

2) Minimize L_p with respect to w,b.
This is a convex quadratic programming problem.

3) In the solution, those points for which $\propto_i > 0$ are called "support vectors"

Even though the maximum margin allows the SVM to select among multiple candidate hyperplanes, for many datasets, the SVM may not be able to find any separating hyperplane at all because the data contains misclassified instances. The problem can be addressed by using a soft margin that accepts some misclassifications of the training instances. This can be done by introducing positive slack variables ξ_i, $i = 1, \ldots, N$ in the constraints, which then become [14]

$$w \cdot x_i - b \geq +1 - \xi \text{ for } y_i = +1$$

$$w \cdot x_i - b \leq -1 + \xi \text{ for } y_i = -1$$

$$\xi \geq 0.$$

Thus, for an error to occur, the corresponding ξ_i must exceed unity, so $\Sigma_i \xi_i$ is an upper bound on the number of training errors. In this case, the Lagrangian is

$$L_P \equiv \frac{1}{2} w^2 + C \sum_i \xi_i - \sum_i \propto_i \left\{ y_i \left(x_i . w - b \right) - 1 + \xi_i \right\} - \sum_i \mu_i \xi_i$$

where the μ_i is the Lagrange multiplier introduced to enforce positivity of the ξ_i.

Nevertheless, most real-world problems involve nonseparable data for which no hyperplane exists that successfully separates the positive from negative instances in the training set. One solution to the inseparability problem is to map the data onto a higher-dimensional space and define a separating hyperplane there. This higher-dimensional space is called the transformed feature space, as opposed to the input space occupied by the training instances.

With an appropriately chosen transformed feature space of sufficient dimensionality, any consistent training set can be made separable. A linear separation in transformed feature space corresponds to a nonlinear separation in the original input space. Mapping the data to some other (possibly infinite-dimensional) Hilbert space H is denoted by Φ : $R^d \rightarrow H$. Then, the training algorithm would only depend on the data through dot products in H, that is, on functions of the form $\Phi(x_i).\Phi(x_j)$.

If there were a "kernel function" K such that $K(x_i, x_j) = \Phi(x_i).(x_j)$, we would only need to use K in the training algorithm and would never need to explicitly determine Φ. Thus, kernels are a special class of functions that allow inner products to be calculated directly in feature space without performing the mapping described. Once a hyperplane has been created, the kernel function is used to map new points into the feature space for classification.

The selection of an appropriate kernel function is important since the kernel function defines the transformed feature space in which the training set instances will be classified.

Some popular kernels are the following:

$$(1) \quad K(x, y) = (x \cdot y + 1)^P$$

$$(2) \quad K(x, y) = e^{-x - y^2/2\sigma^2}$$

$$(3) \quad K(x, y) = \tanh(\kappa \ x \cdot y - \delta)^P$$

Training the SVM is done by solving an Nth-dimensional QP problem, where N is the number of samples in the training dataset. Solving this problem in standard QP methods involves large matrix operations, as well as time-consuming numerical computations, and is mostly slow and impractical for large problems. Sequential minimal optimization (SMO) is a simple algorithm that can, relatively quickly, solve the SVM QP problem without any extra matrix storage and without using numerical QP optimization steps. SMO decomposes the overall QP problem into QP subproblems.

Finally, the training optimization problem of the SVM necessarily reaches a global minimum and avoids ending in a local minimum, which may happen in other search algorithms, such as neural networks. However, the SVM methods are binary; thus, in the case of a multiclass problem, one must reduce the problem to a set of multiple binary classification problems. Discrete data present another problem, although with suitable rescaling good results can be obtained.

7.3 Unsupervised Learning

7.3.1 A Brief Introduction to Unsupervised Learning

In the previous section, we discussed the supervised ML techniques. In this section, we give an overview of unsupervised learning from the perspective of statistical modeling. Unsupervised learning can be motivated from information theoretic and Bayesian principles. We briefly review basic models in unsupervised learning, including factor analysis (FA), principal components analysis (PCA), mixtures of Gaussian models, independent component analysis (ICA), hidden Markov models (HMMs) [35], state-space models (SSMs), and many variants and extensions. We derive the expectation-maximization (EM) algorithm and give an overview of fundamental concepts in graphical models and inference algorithms on graphs. Then, we present a quick review of approximate Bayesian inference, including Markov chain Monte Carlo (MCMC), Laplace approximation, Bayesian information Criterion (BIC), variational approximations, and expectation propagation (EP). We assume that the reader is familiar with elementary linear algebra, probability theory, and calculus but not much else. Before starting the discussion of unsupervised learning models, we present a brief introduction about the following:

- Unsupervised learning
- Machine learning, statistics, and information theory
- Bayes rule

These points are necessarily incomplete given the enormous range of topics under the rubric of unsupervised learning. It should be noted that many of the technical descriptions were taken from Ghahramani [36] or based on that work. As the technical details are of standard level, we have often kept the information almost the same and provided explanations whenever needed to relate the issues to this book's subject matter.

7.3.1.1 What Is Unsupervised Learning? Machine learning is the field of research devoted to the formal study of learning systems. This is a highly interdisciplinary field that borrows and builds on ideas from statistics, computer science, engineering, cognitive science, optimization theory, and many other disciplines of science and mathematics [36].

In ML, unsupervised learning refers to the problem of trying to find hidden structure in unlabeled data. Since the examples given to the learner are unlabeled, there is no error or reward signal to evaluate a potential solution. This distinguishes unsupervised learning from supervised learning and reinforcement learning [37].

Consider a machine (or living organism) that receives some sequence of inputs x_1, x_2, x_3, ... , where x_t is the sensory input at time t. This input, which we often call the data, could correspond to an image on the retina, the pixels in a camera, or a sound waveform. It could also correspond to less obviously sensory data, for example, the words in a news story or the list of items in a supermarket shopping basket.

Before reading further, let us remember what we have learned so far and some extra information. There are basically four different kinds of ML:

1. Supervised ML
2. Reinforcement learning
3. Game theory and generalized reinforcement learning
4. Unsupervised learning

We discuss each of these types in the following material so that the difference among them can be better understood.

In supervised learning, the machine is given a sequence of desired outputs: y_1, y_2, ... , and the goal of the machine is to learn to produce the correct output given a new input. This output could be a class label (in classification) or a real number (in regression).

In reinforcement learning, the machine interacts with its environment by producing actions: a_1, a_2, ... These actions affect the state of the environment, which in turn results in the machine receiving some scalar rewards (or punishments), r_1, r_2, ... The goal of the machine is to learn to act in a way that maximizes the future rewards that it receives (or minimizes the punishments) over its lifetime. Reinforcement learning is closely related to the fields of decision theory (in statistics and management science) and control theory (in engineering). The fundamental problems studied in these fields are often formally equivalent, and the solutions are the same, although different aspects of problem and solution are usually emphasized.

A third kind of ML is closely related to game theory and generalized reinforcement learning. Here again, the machine receives inputs, produces actions, and receives rewards. However, the environment the machine interacts with is not some static world, but rather it can contain other machines that can also sense, act, receive rewards, and learn. Thus, the goal of the machine is to act to maximize rewards in light of the other machines' current and future actions. Although there is a great deal of work in game theory for simple systems, the dynamic case with multiple adapting machines remains an active and challenging area of research.

Finally, in unsupervised learning, the machine simply receives inputs, $x_1, x_2, \ldots$, but obtains neither supervised target outputs nor rewards from its environment. It may seem somewhat mysterious to imagine what the machine could possibly learn given that it does not receive any feedback from its environment. However, it is possible to develop a formal framework for unsupervised learning based on the notion that the machine's goal is to build representations of the input that can be used for decision making, predicting future inputs, efficiently communicating the inputs to another machine, and so on. In a sense, unsupervised learning can be thought of as finding patterns in the data above and beyond what would be considered pure unstructured noise. There are two simple classic examples of unsupervised learning:

- Clustering
- Dimensionality reduction

We discuss these in the next section along with some information on how unsupervised learning relates to statistics and information theory.

7.3.1.2 Machine Learning, Statistics, and Information Theory   Machine learning has received tremendous attention in recent years from both statistics and computer science communities. It derives information automatically from data, and such information can be used to predict information for future data. ML gives birth to a wide variety of exciting technologies, such as search engines, various recommendation systems, and IBM Watson and hence has a profound impact on our daily life. As we know that information theory has many interesting interactions with statistical theory, it is not surprising that information theory also plays an important role in many ML algorithms. For example, entropy is employed in popular classification models, including decision tree and max-entropy regression models [38].

In fact, almost all works in unsupervised learning can be viewed in terms of learning a probabilistic model of the data. Even when the machine is given no supervision or reward, it may make sense for the machine to estimate a model that represents the probability distribution for a new input x_t given previous inputs $x_1, \ldots x_{t-1}$ (consider the obviously useful examples of stock prices or the weather). That is the learner models $P(x_t \mid x_1, \ldots, x_{t-1})$. In simpler cases for which the order in which the inputs arrive is irrelevant or unknown, the machine can build a model of the data that assumes the data points: x_1, x_2, ... are independently and identically drawn from some distribution $P(x)^2$.

Such a model can be used for outlier detection or monitoring. Let x represent patterns of sensor readings from a nuclear power plant and assume that $P(x)$ is learned from data collected from a normally functioning plant. This model can be used to evaluate the probability of a new sensor reading; if this probability is abnormally low, then either the model is poor or the plant is behaving abnormally, in which case one may want to shut it down.

Also, a probabilistic model can be used for classification. Assume $P1(x)$ is a model of the attributes of credit card holders who paid on time, and $P2(x)$ is a model learned from credit card holders who defaulted on their payments. By evaluating the relative probabilities $P1(x')$ and $P2(x')$ on a new applicant x', the machine can decide to classify the new applicant into one of these two categories.

With a probabilistic model, one can also achieve efficient communication and data compression. Imagine that we want to transmit, over a digital communication line, symbols x randomly drawn from $P(x)$. For example, x may be letters of the alphabet or images, and the communication line may be the Internet. Intuitively, we should encode our data so that symbols that occur more frequently have code words with fewer bits in them; otherwise, we are wasting bandwidth. Shannon's source-coding theorem quantifies this by telling us that the optimal number of bits to use to encode a symbol with probability $P(x)$ is $-\log_2 P(x)$. Using these numbers of bits for each symbol, the expected coding cost is the entropy of the distribution P.

$$H(P) \stackrel{\text{def}}{=} -\sum_{x} P(x) \log_2 P(x) \qquad (7.2)$$

In general, the true distribution of the data is unknown, but we can learn a model of this distribution. Let us call this model $Q(x)$. The optimal code with respect to this model would use $-\log_2 Q(x)$ bits for each symbol x. The expected coding cost, taking expectations with respect to the true distribution, is

$$-\sum_{x} P(x) \log_2 Q(x) \qquad (7.3)$$

The difference between these two coding costs is called the Kullback–Leibler (KL) divergence:

$$KL(P \| Q) \stackrel{\text{def}}{=} \sum_{x} P(x) \log \frac{P(x)}{Q(x)} \qquad (7.4)$$

The KL divergence is nonnegative and zero if and only if $P = Q$. It measures the coding inefficiency in bits from using a model Q to compress data when the true data distribution is P. Therefore, the better our model of the data, the more efficiently we can compress and communicate new data. This is an important link between ML, statistics, and information theory [36].

7.3.1.3 Bayes Rule The Bayes rule is stated as

$$P(y|x) = \frac{P(x|y)P(y)}{P(x)} \qquad (7.5)$$

which follows from the equality, $P(x, y) = P(x)P(y|x) = P(y)P(x|y)$, can be used to motivate a coherent statistical framework for ML. In the following, the basic idea is explained. Imagine that we wish to design a machine that has beliefs about the world, and it updates these beliefs based on observed data. The machine must somehow represent the strengths of its beliefs numerically. It has been shown that if you accept certain axioms of coherent inference, known as the Cox axioms, then a remarkable result follows: If the machine is to represent the strength of its beliefs by real numbers, then the only reasonable and coherent way of manipulating these beliefs is to have them satisfy the rules of probability, such as Bayes rule. Therefore, $P(X = x)$ can be used not only to represent the frequency with which the variable X takes on the value x (as in so-called frequentist statistics) but also to represent the degree of belief that $X = x$. Similarly, $P(X = x|Y = y)$ can be used to represent the degree of belief that $X = x$ given that one knows $Y = y$.

We derive the following simple framework for ML from the Bayes rule. Assume a universe of models Ω; let $\Omega = \{1, \dots , M\}$, although it need not be finite or even countable. The machine starts with some prior beliefs over models $\in \Omega$, such that

$$\sum_{m=1}^{M} P(m) = 1$$

A model is simply some probability distribution over data points, that is, $P(x|m)$. For simplicity, let us further assume that in all the models, the data are taken to be independently and identically distributed (iid). After observing a dataset $D = \{x_1 , \dots , x_N\}$, the beliefs over models is given by

$$p(m|D) = \frac{P(m)P(D|m)}{P(D)} \propto P(m) \prod_{n=1}^{N} P(x_n | m) \qquad (7.6)$$

which we read as the *posterior over models* is the *prior* multiplied by the *likelihood*, normalized.

The predictive distribution over new data, which would be used to encode new data efficiently, is

$$P(x|D) = \sum_{m=1}^{M} P(x|m)P(m | D) \qquad (7.7)$$

Again, this follows from the rules of probability theory and the fact that the models are assumed to produce iid data.

Often, models are defined by writing down a parametric probability distribution. Thus, the model m might have parameters θ, which are assumed to be unknown (this could in general be a vector of parameters). To be a well-defined model from the perspective of Bayesian learning, one has to define a prior over these model parameters, $P(\theta|m)$, which naturally has to satisfy the following equality:

$$P(x|m) = \int P(x|\theta,m) P(\theta \mid m) d\theta \qquad (7.8)$$

Given the model m, it is also possible to infer the posterior over the parameters of the model, that is, $P(\theta|D, m)$, and to compute the predictive distribution $P(x|D, m)$. These quantities are derived in exact analogy to Equations 7.6 and 7.7, except that instead of summing over possible models, we integrate over parameters of a particular model. All the key quantities in Bayesian ML follow directly from the basic rules of probability theory.

Certain approximate forms of Bayesian learning are worth mentioning. Let us focus on a particular model m with parameters θ and an observed dataset D. The predictive distribution averages over all possible parameters weighted by the posterior:

$$P(x|D,m) = \int P(x|\theta) P(\theta \mid D,m) d\theta \qquad (7.9)$$

In certain cases, it may be cumbersome to represent the entire posterior distribution over parameters, so instead we choose to find a *point estimate* of the parameters $\hat{\theta}$. A natural choice is to pick the most probable parameter value given the data, which is known as the *maximum a posteriori* or MAP parameter estimate:

$$\hat{\theta}_{MAP} = \arg\max_{\theta} P(\theta|D,m)$$

$$= \arg\max_{\theta} \left[\log P(\theta|m) + \sum_{n} \log P(x_n \mid \theta,m) \right] \qquad (7.10)$$

Another natural choice is the maximum likelihood or ML parameter estimate:

$$\hat{\theta}_{ML} = \arg\max_{\theta} P(D|\theta,m) = \arg\max_{\theta} \sum_{n} \log P(x_n \mid \theta,m) \qquad (7.11)$$

Many learning algorithms [39] can be seen as finding ML parameter estimates. The ML parameter estimate is also acceptable from a frequentist statistical modeling perspective since it does not require deciding on a prior over parameters. However, ML estimation does not protect against overfitting—more complex models will generally have higher maxima of the likelihood. In order to avoid problems with overfitting, frequentist procedures often maximize a penalized or regularized log likelihood. If the penalty or regularization term is interpreted as a log prior, then maximizing penalized likelihood appears identical to maximizing a posterior. However, there are subtle issues that make a Bayesian MAP procedure and maximum penalized likelihood different. One difference is that the MAP estimate is not invariant to *reparameterization*, while the maximum of the penalized likelihood is invariant. The penalized likelihood is a function, not a density, and therefore does not increase or decrease depending on the Jacobian of the reparameterization [36].

7.3.2 Dimensionality Reduction and Clustering Models

There are many problems in the computer science field that need first dimensional reduction for their size so that the most important data can appear. In this section, we consider probabilistic models that are defined in terms of some latent or hidden variables. These models can be used to do dimensionality reduction and clustering, the two cornerstones of unsupervised learning.

7.3.2.1 Factor Analysis   Factor analysis (FA) is a statistical method used to describe variability among observed, correlated variables in terms of a potentially lower number of unobserved variables called factors. In other words, it is possible, for example, that variations in three or four observed variables mainly reflect the variations in fewer unobserved variables. FA searches for such joint variations in response to unobserved latent variables. The observed variables are modeled as linear combinations of the potential factors plus "error" terms. The information gained about the interdependencies between observed variables can be used later to reduce the set of variables in a dataset. FA originated in psychometrics and is used in behavioral sciences, social sciences, marketing, product management, operations research,

and other applied sciences that deal with large quantities of data [40]. In the following, we give more details about FA.

Let the data set D consist of D-dimensional real valued vectors, $D = \{y_1, \ldots y_N\}$. In FA, the data are assumed to be generated from the following model:

$$y = \Lambda x + \epsilon \tag{7.12}$$

where x is a K-dimensional, zero-mean, unit-variance multivariate Gaussian vector with elements corresponding to hidden (or latent) factors; Λ is a $D \times K$ matrix of parameters, known as the factor loading matrix, and is a D-dimensional, zero-mean, multivariate Gaussian noise vector with diagonal covariance matrix Ψ. Defining the parameters of the model to be $\theta = (\Psi, \Lambda)$, by integrating out the factors, one can readily derive that

$$p\left(y|\theta\right) = \int p\left(x|\theta\right) p\left(y|x,\theta\right) dx = \mathcal{N}(0, \Lambda\Lambda^T + \Psi) \tag{7.13}$$

where $N(\mu, \Sigma)$ refers to a multivariate Gaussian density with mean μ and covariance matrix Σ.

FA is an interesting model for several reasons. If the data are very high dimensional (i.e., D is large), then even a simple model like the full-covariance multivariate Gaussian will have too many parameters to reliably estimate or infer from the data. By choosing $K < D$, FA makes it possible to model a Gaussian density for high-dimensional data without requiring $O(D^2)$ parameters. Moreover, given a new data point, one can compute the posterior over the hidden factors, $p(x|y, \theta)$; since x is lower dimensional than y, this provides a low-dimensional representation of the data (for example, one could pick the mean of $p(x|y, \theta)$ as the representation for y) [36].

7.3.2.2 Principal Components Analysis As mentioned, when presented with the need to analyze a high-dimensional structure, a commonly employed and powerful approach is to seek an alternative lower-dimensional approximation to the structure that preserves its important properties. A structure that can often appear complex because of its high dimension may be largely governed by a small set of independent variables and so can be well approximated by a lower-dimensional representation. Dimension analysis and dimension reduction techniques attempt to find these simple variables and can therefore be a useful tool to understand the original structures. The most commonly used technique to analyze high-dimensional structures is the method of PCA. Given a high-dimensional object and its associated coordinate space, PCA finds a new coordinate space that is the best one to use for dimension reduction of the given object. Once the object is placed into this new coordinate space, projecting the object onto a subset of the axes can be done in a way that minimizes error. When a high-dimensional object can be well approximated in this way in a smaller number of dimensions, we refer to the smaller number of dimensions as the object's intrinsic dimensionality [41]. Next, we present some details about PCA.

PCA is an important limiting case of FA. One can derive PCA by making two modifications to FA. First, the noise is assumed to be isotropic; in other words, each element of $\in$ has equal variance: $\Psi = \sigma^2 I$, where I is a $D \times D$ identity matrix. This model is called probabilistic PCA. Second, if we take the limit of $\sigma \to 0$ in probabilistic PCA, we obtain standard PCA (which also goes by the names Karhunen-Loève expansion and SVD). Given a dataset with covariance matrix Σ, for maximum likelihood FA the goal is to find parameters Λ and Ψ for which the model $\Lambda\Lambda^T + \Psi$ has the highest likelihood. In PCA, the goal is to find Λ so that the likelihood is highest for $\Lambda\Lambda^T$. Note that this matrix is singular unless $K = D$, so the standard PCA model is not a sensible model. However, taking the limiting case, and further constraining the columns of Λ to be orthogonal, it can be derived that the principal components correspond to the K eigenvectors with the largest eigenvalue of Σ. PCA is thus attractive because the solution can be found immediately after *eigendecomposition* of the covariance. Taking the limit $\sigma \to 0$ of $p(x|y, \Lambda, \sigma)$, we find that it is a delta function at $x = \Lambda^T y$, which is the projection of y onto the principal components [36].

7.3.2.3 Independent Component Analysis Independent component analysis (ICA) is a statistical and computational technique for revealing hidden factors that underlie sets of random variables, measurements, or signals. ICA defines a generative model for the observed multivariate data, which is typically given as a large database of samples. In the model, the data variables are assumed to be linear or nonlinear mixtures of some unknown latent variables, and the mixing system is also unknown. The latent variables are assumed non-Gaussian and mutually independent, and they are called the independent components of the observed data. These independent components, also called sources or factors, can be found by ICA.

ICA can be seen as an extension to PCA and FA. ICA is a much more powerful technique; however, it is capable of finding the underlying factors or sources when these classic methods fail completely.

The data analyzed by ICA could originate from many different kinds of application fields, including digital images and document databases, as well as economic indicators and psychometric measurements. In many cases, the measurements are given as a set of parallel signals or time series; the term *blind source separation* is used to characterize this problem. Typical examples are mixtures of simultaneous speech signals that have been picked up by several microphones, brain waves recorded by multiple sensors, interfering radio signals arriving at a mobile phone, or parallel time series obtained from some industrial process.

Models like PCA, FA, and ICA can all be implemented using neural networks (multilayer perceptrons) trained using various cost functions. It is not clear what advantage this implementation/interpretation has from an ML perspective, although it provides interesting ties to biological information processing.

Rather than ML estimation, one can also do Bayesian inference for the parameters of probabilistic PCA, FA, and ICA [36].

7.3.2.4 Mixture of Gaussians   The densities modeled by PCA, FA, and ICA are all relatively simple in that they are unimodal and have fairly restricted parametric forms (Gaussian, in the case of PCA and FA). It is useful to consider mixture models when model data have more complex structure, such as clusters. Although it is straightforward to consider mixtures of arbitrary densities, we focus on Gaussians as a common special case. The density of each data point in a mixture model can be written as

$$p(y|\theta) = \sum_{k=1}^{K} \pi_k p(y|\theta_k) \qquad (7.14)$$

where each of the K components of the mixture is, for example, a Gaussian with differing means and covariances,

$$\theta_k = \left(\mu_k, \sum_k\right)$$

and π_k is the mixing proportion for component k, such that $\sum_{k=1}^{K}\pi_k = 1$ and $\pi_k > 0$, $\forall k$.

A different way to think about mixture models is to consider them as latent variable models, where associated with each data point is a K-ary discrete latent (i.e., hidden) variable s that has the interpretation that $s = k$ if the data point was generated by component k. This can be written as [36]

$$p(y|\theta) = \sum_{k=1}^{K} P(s = k|\pi)p(y|s = k,\theta) \qquad (7.15)$$

where $P(s = k | \pi) = \pi_k$ is the prior for the latent variable taking on value k, and $p(y|s = k, \theta) = p(y|\theta_k)$ is the density under component k, recovering Equation 7.14.

7.3.2.5 K-Means K-means [42] is one of the simplest unsupervised learning algorithms that solve the well-known clustering problem. The procedure follows a simple and easy way to classify a given dataset through a certain number of clusters (assume k clusters) fixed a priori. The main idea is to define k centroids, one for each cluster. These centroids should be placed in an intelligent way because of the fact that different locations cause different results. So, the better choice is to place them as far away as possible from each other. The next step is to take each point belonging to a given dataset and associate it to the nearest centroid. When no point is pending, the first step is completed, and an early groupage is done. At this point, we need to recalculate k new centroids as barycenters of the clusters resulting from the previous step. After we have these k new centroids, a new binding has to be done between the same dataset points and the nearest new centroid. A loop has been generated. As a result of this loop, we may notice that the k centroids change their locations step by step until no more changes are done. In other words, centroids do not move any more.

The mixture of Gaussian models is closely related to k-means as follows: Consider the special case in which all the Gaussians have a common covariance matrix proportional to the identity matrix, $\Sigma_k = \sigma^2 I$, $\forall k$, and let $\pi_k = 1/K$, $\forall k$. We can estimate the maximum likelihood parameters of this model using the iterative algorithm we are about to describe, known as EM. The resulting algorithm, as we take the limit $\sigma^2 \to 0$, becomes exactly the k-means algorithm. The model underlying k-means has only singular Gaussians and is therefore an unreasonable model of the data; however, k-means is usually justified from the point of view of clustering to minimize a distortion measure rather than fitting a probabilistic model [36].

7.3.3 Expectation–Maximization Algorithm

In statistics, an EM algorithm is an iterative method for finding maximum likelihood or MAP estimates of parameters in statistical models, where the model depends on unobserved latent variables. The EM iteration alternates between performing an expectation (E) step, which creates a function for the expectation of the log likelihood evaluated using the current estimate for the parameters, and maximization (M) step, which computes parameters maximizing the expected log likelihood found on the E step. These parameter estimates are then used to determine the distribution of the latent variables in the next E step.

The EM algorithm is used to find the maximum likelihood parameters of a statistical model when the equations cannot be solved directly. Typically, these models involve latent variables in addition to unknown parameters and known data observations. That is, either there are missing values among the data, or the model can be formulated more simply by assuming the existence of additional unobserved data points. (For example, a mixture model can be described more simply by assuming that each observed data point has a corresponding unobserved data point, or latent variable, specifying the mixture component to which each data point belongs.)

Finding a maximum likelihood solution requires taking the derivatives of the likelihood function with respect to all the unknown values (i.e., both the parameters and the latent variables) and simultaneously solving the resulting equations. In statistical models with latent variables, this usually is not possible. Instead, the result is typically a set of interlocking equations in which the solution to the parameters requires the values of the latent variables and vice versa, but substituting one set of equations into the other produces an unsolvable equation.

The EM algorithm proceeds from the observation that the following is a way to solve these two sets of equations numerically. One can simply pick arbitrary values for one of the two sets of unknowns, use them to estimate the second set, then use these new values to find a better estimate of the first set, and then keep alternating between the two until the resulting values both converge to fixed points. It is not obvious that this will work at all, but in fact it can be proven that in this particular context it does, and that the value is a local maximum of the likelihood function. In general, there may be multiple maxima and no guarantee that the global maximum will be found. Some likelihoods also have singularities in them (i.e., nonsensical maxima). For example, one of the "solutions" that may be found by EM in a mixture model involves setting one of the components to have zero variance and the mean parameter for the same component to be equal to one of the data points. A bit more detail about the EM algorithm is presented next.

We mentioned that the EM algorithm is an algorithm for estimating ML parameters of a model with latent variables. Consider a model with observed variables y, hidden/latent variables x, and parameters θ. We can lower bound the log likelihood for any data point as follows:

$$L(\theta) = \log p(y|\theta) = \log \int p(x, y|\theta) \, dx \qquad (7.16)$$

$$= \log \int q(x) \, \frac{p(x, y|\theta)}{q(x)} \, dx \qquad (7.17)$$

$$\geq \int q(x) \, \log \frac{p(x, y|\theta)}{q(x)} \, dx \stackrel{\text{def}}{=} F(q, \theta) \qquad (7.18)$$

where $q(x)$ is some arbitrary density over the hidden variables, and the lower bound holds due to the concavity of the log function (this inequality is known as Jensen's inequality). The lower bound F is a functional of both the density $q(x)$ and the model parameters θ. For a dataset of N data points $y^{(1)}, \ldots, y^{(N)}$, this lower bound is formed for the log likelihood term corresponding to each data point; thus, there is a separate density $q^{(n)}(x)$ for each point, and

$$F(q,\theta) = \sum_n F^{(n)}\left(q^{(n)}(\theta)\right)$$

The basic idea of the EM algorithm is to iterate between optimizing this lower bound as a function of q and as a function of θ. We can prove that this will never decrease the log likelihood. After initializing the parameters somehow, the kth iteration of the algorithm consists of the following two steps:

E step: *Optimize F with respect to the distribution q while holding the parameters fixed*

$$q_k(x) = \arg\max_{q(x)} \int q(x) \, \log \frac{p(x, y \mid \theta_{k-1})}{q(x)} \tag{7.19}$$

$$q_k(x) = p(x \mid y, \theta_{k-1}). \tag{7.20}$$

M step: *Optimize F with respect to the parameters while holding the distribution over hidden variables fixed*

$$\theta_k = \arg\max_{\theta} \int q_k(x) \log \frac{p(x, y \mid \theta)}{q_k(x)} \, dx \tag{7.21}$$

$$\theta_k = \arg\max_{\theta} \int q_k(x) \log p(x, y \mid \theta) \, dx. \tag{7.22}$$

Let us be sure about what happens for a dataset of N data points: In the E step, for each data point, the distribution over the hidden variables is set to the posterior for that data point $q_k^{(n)}(x) = p(x \mid y^{(n)}, \theta_{k-1})$, $\forall n$. In the M step, the single set of parameters is reestimated by maximizing the sum of the expected log likelihoods: $\theta_k = \arg\max_{\theta} \sum_n \int q_k^{(n)}(x) \log p(x, y^{(n)} \mid \theta) dx$.

Two things are still unclear: How does Equation 7.20 follow from Equation 7.19, and how is this algorithm guaranteed to increase the likelihood? The optimization in Equation 7.19 can be written as follows since $(x, y \mid \theta_{k-1}) = p(y \mid \theta_{k-1}) p(x \mid y, \theta_{k-1})$:

$$q_k(x) = \arg\max_{q(x)} \left[\log p(y|\theta_{k-1}) + \int q(x) \log \frac{p(x|y,\theta_{k-1})}{q(x)} dx \right] \quad (7.23)$$

Now, the first term is a constant with respect to $q(x)$, and the second term is the negative of the KL divergence:

$$\text{KL}(q(x) \| p(x|y,\theta_{k-1})) = \int q(x) \log \frac{q(x)}{p(x|y,\theta_{k-1})} dx \quad (7.24)$$

which we have seen in Equation 7.4 in its discrete form.

This is minimized at $q(x) = (x|y,\theta_{k-1})$, where the KL divergence is zero. Intuitively, the interpretation of this is that in the E step of EM, the goal is to find the posterior distribution of the hidden variables given the observed variables and the current settings of the parameters. We also see that since the KL divergence is zero, at the end of the E step, $F(q_k,\theta_{k-1}) = L(\theta_{k-1})$.

In the M step, F is increased with respect to θ. Therefore, $F(q_k,\theta_k) \geq F(q_k,\theta_{k-1})$. Moreover, $L(\theta_k) = F(q_{k+1},\theta_k) \geq F(q_k,\theta_k)$ after the next E step. We can put these steps together to establish that $L(\theta_k) \geq L(\theta_{k-1})$, establishing that the algorithm is guaranteed to increase the likelihood or keep it fixed (at convergence).

The EM algorithm can be applied to all the latent variable models described, that is, FA, probabilistic PCA, mixture models, and ICA. In the case of mixture models, the hidden variable is the discrete assignment s of data points to clusters; consequently, the integrals turn into sums if appropriate. EM has wide applicability to latent variable models, although it is not always the fastest optimization method [43]. Moreover, we should note that the likelihood often has many local optima, and EM will converge to some local optimum that may not be the global one [36].

7.3.4 Modeling Time Series and Other Structured Data

In the previous sections, we assumed that the data are unstructured, which means the observations are assumed to be independent and identically distributed. In fact, this assumption is unreasonable for many datasets in which the observations arrive in a sequence and subsequent observations are correlated. Sequential data can occur in time series modeling (as in financial data or the weather) and when the sequential nature of the data is not necessarily tied to time (as in protein data, which consist of sequences of amino acids).

In statistics, a time series is a sequence of data points, measured typically at successive time instants spaced at uniform time intervals. Time series analysis is comprised of methods for analyzing time series data in order to extract meaningful statistics and other characteristics of the data. Time series forecasting is the use of a model to predict future values based on previously observed values. Time series are frequently plotted via line charts.

As the most basic level, time series modeling consists of building a probabilistic model of the present observation given all past observations, $p(y_t \mid y_{t-1}, y_{t-2} \ldots)$. As the history of observations grows arbitrarily large, it is necessary to limit the complexity of such a model. There are two ways of doing this [36]:

- The first approach is to limit the window of past observations. Thus, one can simply model $p(y_t \mid y_{t-1})$ and assume that this relation holds for all t. This is known as a first-order Markov model. A second-order Markov model would be $p(y_t \mid y_{t-1}, y_{t-2})$ and so on. Such Markov models have two limitations:
  - First, the influence of past observations on present observations vanishes outside this window, which can be unrealistic.
  - Second, it may be unnatural and cumbersome to model directly the relationship between raw observations at one time step and raw observations at a subsequent time step. For example, if the observations are noisy images, it would make more sense to denoise them; extract some description of the objects, motions, and illuminations; and then try to predict from that.
- The second approach is to make use of latent or hidden variables. Instead of modeling directly the effect of y_{t-1} on y_t, we assume that the observations were generated from some underlying hidden variable x_t that captures the dynamics of the system. For example, y might be noisy sonar readings of objects in a room, and x might be the actual locations and

sizes of these objects. We usually call this hidden variable x the state variable as it is meant to capture all the aspects of the system relevant to predicting the future dynamical behavior of the system [36].

In order to understand more complex time series models, it is essential that one be familiar with SSMs and HMMs. These two classes of models have played a historically important role in control engineering, visual tracking, speech recognition, protein sequence modeling, and error decoding. They form the simplest building blocks from which other, richer time series models can be developed, in a manner completely analogous to the role that FA and mixture models play in building more complex models for iid data.

7.3.4.1 State-Space Models In an SSM, the sequence of observed data $y_1, y_2, y_3, \ldots$ is assumed to have been generated from some sequence of hidden state variables $x_1, x_2, x_3, \ldots$. Letting $x_{1:T}$ denote the sequence $x_1, \ldots, x_T$, the basic assumption in an SSM is that the joint probability of the hidden states and observations factors in the following way [36]:

$$p(x_{1:T}, y_{1:T} \mid \theta) = \prod_{t=1}^{T} p(x_t \mid x_{t-1}, \theta) p(y_t \mid x_t, \theta). \qquad (7.25)$$

In other words, the observations are assumed to have been generated from the hidden states via $p(y_t \mid x_t, \theta)$, and the hidden states are assumed to have first-order Markov dynamics captured by $p(x_t \mid x_{t-1}, \theta)$. We can consider the first term, $p(x_1 \mid x_0, \theta)$, to be a prior on the initial state of the system x_1.

The simplest kind of SSM assumes that all variables are multivariate Gaussian distributed, and all the relationships are linear. In such linear Gaussian SSMs, it can be written

$$y_t = Cx_t + v_t \qquad (7.26)$$

$$x_t = Ax_{t-1} + w_t \qquad (7.27)$$

where the matrices C and A define the linear relationships, and v and w are zero-mean Gaussian noise vectors with covariance matrices R and Q, respectively. If we assume that the prior on the initial state

$p(x_1)$ is also Gaussian, then all subsequent x's and y's are also Gaussian due to the fact that Gaussian densities are closed under linear transformations. This model can be generalized in many ways, for example, by augmenting it to include a sequence of observed inputs $u_1, \ldots, u_T$ as well as the observed model outputs $y_1, \ldots, y_T$.

By comparing Equations 7.12 and 7.26, we see that linear Gaussian SSMs can be thought of as a time series generalization of FA in which the factors are assumed to have linear Gaussian dynamics over time.

The parameters of this model are $\theta = (A, C, Q, R)$. To learn ML settings of these parameters, one can make use of the EM algorithm. The E step of the algorithm involves computing $q(x_{1:T} =) p(x_{1:T} \mid y_{1:T}, \theta)$, which is the posterior over hidden state sequences. In fact, this whole posterior does not have to be computed or represented; all that is required are the marginals $q(x_t)$ and pairwise marginals $q(x_t, x_{t+1})$. These can be computed via the Kalman smoothing algorithm, which is an efficient algorithm for inferring the distribution over the hidden states of a linear Gaussian SSM. Since the model is linear, the M step of the algorithm requires solving a pair of weighted linear regression problems to reestimate A and C; Q and R are estimated from the residuals of those regressions. This is analogous to the M step of FA, which also involves solving a linear regression problem.

7.3.4.2 Hidden Markov Models The HMM is a powerful statistical tool for modeling generative sequences that can be characterized by an underlying process generating an observable sequence. HMMs have found applications in many areas interested in signal processing, in particular speech processing, but have also been applied with success to low-level NLP (natural language processing) tasks such as part-of-speech tagging, phrase chunking, and extracting target information from documents. Andrei Markov gave his name to the mathematical theory of Markov processes in the early twentieth century [44], but it was Baum and his colleagues who developed the theory of HMMs in the 1960s [45].

Figure 7.12 shows an example of a Markov process. The model describes a simple model for a stock market index. The model has three states (Bull, Bear, and Even) and three index observations (up, down, and unchanged). This model is a finite-state automaton, with probabilistic transitions between states. Given a sequence of observations, for

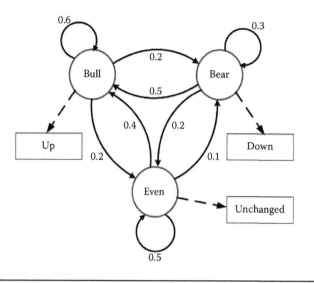

Figure 7.12 Markov process example.

example up-down-down, we can easily verify that the state sequence that produced those observations was Bull-Bear-Bear, and the probability of the sequence is simply the product of the transitions, in this case $0.2 \times 0.3 \times 0.3$.

Figure 7.13 shows an example of how the model of Figure 7.12 can be extended into an HMM. The new model now allows all observation symbols to be emitted from each state with a finite probability. This change makes the model much more expressive and able to better represent our intuition, in this case, that a bull market would have both good days and bad days, but there would be more good ones. The key difference is that now if we have the observation sequence up-down-down, then we cannot say exactly what state sequence produced these observations; thus, the state sequence is "hidden." We can calculate the probability that the model produced the sequence as well as which state sequence was most likely to have produced the observations [46].

Let us discuss more details of HMMs. HMMs are similar to SSMs in that the sequence of observations is assumed to have been generated from a sequence of underlying hidden states. The main difference is that in HMMs, the state is assumed to be discrete rather than a continuous random vector. Let s_t denote the hidden state of an HMM at time t. We assume that s_t can take discrete values in $\{1, \ldots, K\}$. The model can again be written as in (25):

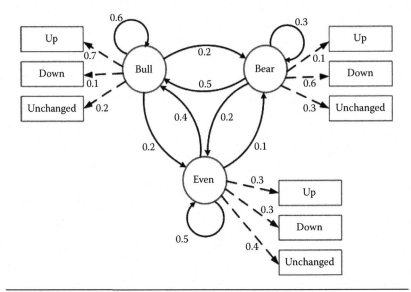

Figure 7.13   Hidden Markov model example.

$$P(s_{1:T}, y_{1:T}|\theta) = \prod_{t=1}^{T} P(s_t|s_{t-1}, \theta)P(y_t|s_t, \theta) \qquad (7.28)$$

where $P(s_1 \mid s_0, \theta)$ is simply some initial distribution over the K settings of the first hidden state; we can call this discrete distribution π, represented by a $K \times 1$ vector. The state transition probabilities $P(s_t \mid s_{t-1}, \theta)$ are captured by a $K \times K$ transition matrix A, with elements $A_{ij} = P(s_t = i \mid s_{t-1} = j, \theta)$. The observations in an HMM can be either continuous or discrete. For continuous observations y_t, one can choose, for example, a Gaussian density; thus, $P = (y_t \mid s_t = i, \theta)$ would be a different Gaussian for each choice of $i \in \{1, \dots, K\}$. This model is the dynamical generalization of a mixture of Gaussians. The marginal probability at each point in time is exactly a mixture of K Gaussians—the difference is which component generated data point y_t and which component generated y_{t-1} are not independent random variables, but certain combinations are more and less probable depending on the entries in A. For y_t, a discrete observation, let us assume that it can take on values $\{1, \dots, L\}$. In that case, the output probabilities $P(y_t \mid s_t, \theta)$ can be captured by an $L \times K$ emission matrix E.

The model parameters for a discrete observation HMM are $\theta = (\pi, A, E)$. Maximum likelihood learning of the model parameters can be approached using the EM algorithm, which in the case of HMMs is known as the Baum–Welch algorithm. The E step involves computing $Q(s_t)$ and $Q(s_t, s_{t+1})$, which are marginals of $Q(s_{1:T}) = P(s_{1:T} \mid y_{1:T}, \theta)$. These marginals are computed as part of the forward-backward algorithm, which, as the name suggests, sweeps forward and backward through the time series, and applies the Bayes rule efficiently using the Markov conditional independence properties of the HMM, to compute the required marginals. The M step of HMM learning involves reestimating π, A, and E by adding and normalizing expected counts for transitions and emissions that were computed in the E step [36].

7.3.4.3 Modeling Other Structured Data We have considered the case of iid data and time series data. The observations in real-world datasets can have many other possible structures as well. A few examples are presented next.

In spatial data, the points are assumed to live in some metric, often Euclidean, space. Three examples of spatial data include epidemiological data, which can be modeled as a function of the spatial location of the measurement; data from computer vision, for which the observations are measurements of features on a two-dimensional (2D) input to the camera; and functional neuroimaging, for which the data can be physiological measurements related to neural activity located in three-dimensional (3D) voxels defining coordinates in the brain. Generalizing HMMs, one can define Markov random field models in which there is a set of hidden variables correlated to neighbors in some lattice and related to the observed variables.

Hierarchical or tree-structured data contain known or unknown tree-like correlation structure between the data points or measured features. For instance, the data points may be features of animals related through an evolutionary tree. A very different form of structured data is if each data point itself is tree structured, for example, if each point is a parse tree of a sentence in the English language.

Finally, one can take the structured dependencies between variables and consider the structure itself as an unknown part of the model. Such models are known as probabilistic relational models and are closely related to graphical models (which is discussed in Section 7.3.7) [36].

7.3.5 Nonlinear, Factorial, and Hierarchical Models

All models that we have discussed so far are relatively simple to understand and learn. This simplicity is considered a limitation instead of an advantage since the intricacies of real-world data are unlikely to be well captured by a simple statistical model. Hence, it would be useful to know about much more flexible models.

A simple combination of two of the ideas we have described for iid data is the mixture of factor analyzers [47–49]. This model performs simultaneous clustering and dimensionality reduction on the data by assuming that the covariance in each Gaussian cluster can be modeled by an FA model. Thus, it becomes possible to apply a mixture model to very high-dimensional data while allowing each cluster to span a different subspace of the data.

As their name implies, linear Gaussian SSMs are limited by assumptions of linearity and Gaussian noise. In many realistic dynamical systems, there are significant nonlinear effects, which make it necessary to consider learning in nonlinear SSMs. Such models can also be learned using the EM algorithm, but the E step must deal with inference in non-Gaussian and potentially very complicated densities (since nonlinearities will turn Gaussians into non-Gaussians), and the M step is nonlinear regression rather than linear regression [50]. There are many methods of dealing with inference in nonlinear SSMs, including methods such as particle filtering [51–56], linearization [57], the unscented filter [58, 59], the EP algorithm [60], and embedded HMMs [61].

When we are to consider generalizing simple dimensionality reduction models such as PCA and FA, nonlinear models are also important. These models are limited in that they can only find a linear subspace of the data to capture the correlations between the observed variables. There are many interesting and important nonlinear dimensionality reduction models, including generative topographic mappings (GTMs) [62] (a probabilistic alternative to Kohonen maps); multidimensional scaling (MDS) [63, 64]; principal curves [65]; isomap [66]; and locally linear embedding (LLE) [67].

There are also limitations in HMMs. Even though they can model nonlinear dynamics by discretizing the hidden state space, an HMM with K hidden states can only capture $\log_2 K$ bits of information in its state variable about the past of the sequence. HMMs can be extended by allowing a vector of discrete state variables in an architecture known as a factorial HMM [68]. Thus, a vector of M variables, each of which can take K states, can capture K^M possible states in total and $M \log_2 K$ bits of information about the past of the sequence. The problem is that such a model, if dealt with naively as an HMM, would have exponentially many parameters, and it would take exponentially long to do inference in it. Both the complexity in time and the number of parameters can be alleviated by restricting the interactions between the hidden variables at one time step and at the next time step. A generalization of these ideas is the notion of a dynamical Bayesian network (DBN) [36, 68].

A relatively old but still quite powerful class of models for binary data is the Boltzmann machine (BM) [69]. This is a simple model inspired from Ising models in statistical physics. A BM is a multivariate model for capturing correlations and higher-order statistics in vectors of binary data. Consider data consisting of vectors of M binary variables (the elements of the vector may, for example, be pixels in a black-and-white image). Clearly, each data point can be an instance of one of 2^M possible patterns. An arbitrary distribution over such patterns would require a table with $2^M - 1$ entries, again intractable in number of parameters, storage, and computation time. A BM allows one to define flexible distributions over the 2^M entries of this table using $O(M^2)$ parameters defining a symmetric matrix of weights connecting the variables. This can be augmented with hidden variables to enrich the model class without adding exponentially many parameters. These hidden variables can be organized into layers of a hierarchy as in the Helmholtz machine [70]. Other hierarchical models include recent generalizations of ICA designed to capture higher-order statistics in images [71].

7.3.6 Intractability

The problem with the models described in the previous section is that learning their parameters is in general computationally intractable. In a model with exponentially many settings for the hidden states, doing the E step of an EM algorithm would require computing appropriate marginals of a distribution over exponentially many possibilities.

Let us consider a simple example. Imagine we have a vector of N binary random variables, $s = \{s_1, \ldots, s_N\}$, where $s_i \in \{0,1\}$, and a vector of N known integers $(r_1, \ldots, r_N)$ where $r_i \in \{0,1,3,\ldots,10\}$. Let the variable $= \sum_{i=1}^{N} r_i s_i$. Assume that the binary variables are all iid with $P(s_i = 1) = 1/2$, $\forall i$. Let N be 100. Now imagine that we are told $Y = 430$. How do we compute $P(s_i = 1 \mid Y = 430)$? The problem is that even though the s_i were independent *before* we observed the value of Y, now that we know the value of Y, not all settings of s are possible anymore. To figure out for some s_i, the probability of $P(s_i = 1 \mid Y = 430)$ requires that we enumerate all potentially exponentially many ways of achieving $Y = 430$ and counting how many of those had $s_i = 1$ vs $s_i = 0$.

This example illustrates the following ideas: Even if the prior is simple, the posterior can be complicated. Whether two random variables are independent or not is a function of one's state of knowledge. Thus, s_i and s_j may be independent if we are not told the value of Y but are certainly dependent given the value of Y. These types of phenomena are related to "explaining away," which refers to the fact that if there are multiple potential causes for some effect, observing one explains away the need for the others [36, 72].

Intractability can thus occur if we have a model with discrete hidden variables that can take on exponentially many combinations. Intractability can also occur with continuous hidden variables if their density is not simply described or if they interact with discrete hidden variables. Moreover, even for simple models, such as a mixture of Gaussians, intractability occurs when we consider the parameters to be unknown as well and we attempt to do Bayesian inference on them. To deal with intractability, it is essential to have good tools for representing multivariate distributions, such as graphical models [36].

7.3.7 Graphical Models

A graphical model is a probabilistic model for which a graph denotes the conditional independence structure between random variables. They are commonly used in probability theory, statistics—particularly Bayesian statistics—and ML.

Graphical models are important for two reasons:

- Graphs are an intuitive way of visualizing dependencies. We are used to graphical depictions of dependency, for example, in circuit diagrams and in phylogenetic trees.
- By exploiting the structure of the graph, it is possible to devise efficient message-passing algorithms for computing marginal and conditional probabilities in a complicated model.

The main statistical property represented explicitly by the graph is conditional independence between variables. We say that X and Y are conditionally independent given Z if $P(X,Y|Z) = P(X|Z)P(Y|Z)$ for all values of the variables X, Y, and Z where these quantities are defined [i.e., except settings z where $P(Z = z) = 0$]. We use the notation $X \perp Y|Z$ to denote the conditional independence relation. Conditional independence generalizes to sets of variables in the obvious way, and it is different from marginal independence, which states that $P(X,Y) = P(X)P(Y)$ and is denoted $X \perp Y$.

There are many different graphical formalisms for depicting conditional independence relationships, but let us focus on three of the major categories:

- Undirected graphs
- Factor graphs
- Directed graphs

7.3.7.1 Undirected Graphs   Each random variable in an undirected graphical model is represented by a node, and the edges of the graph indicate conditional independence relationships. Specifically, let X, Y, and Z be sets of random variables. Then, $X \perp Y|Z$ if every path on the graph from a node in X to a node in Y has to go through a node in Z. Thus, a variable X is conditionally independent of all other variables given the neighbors of X, and we say that the neighbors separate X from the rest of the graph. An example of an undirected graph is shown in Figure 7.14, left. In this graph, $A \perp B|C$ and $B \perp E|\{C, D\}$, for example, and the neighbors of D are B, C, E.

A clique is a fully connected subgraph of a graph. A maximal clique is not contained in any other clique of the graph. It turns out that the set of conditional independence relations implied by the separation

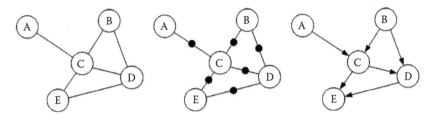

Figure 7.14 Three kinds of probabilistic graphical model: (left) undirected graphs, (center) factor graphs, and (right) directed graphs.

properties in the graph are satisfied by probability distributions, which can be written as a normalized product of nonnegative functions over the variables in the maximal cliques of the graph (this is known as the Hammersley–Clifford Theorem [73]). In the example in Figure 7.14, this implies that the probability distribution over (A, B, C, D, E) can be written as

$$P(A, B, C, D, E) = c g_1(A, C) g_2(B, C, D) g_3(C, D, E) \qquad (7.29)$$

Here, c is the constant that ensures that the probability distribution sums to 1, and g_1, g_2, and g_3 are nonnegative functions of their arguments. For example, if all the variables are binary, the function g_2 is a table with a nonnegative number for each of the $8 = 2 \times 2 \times 2$ possible settings of the variables B, C, D. These nonnegative functions are supposed to represent how compatible these settings are with each other, with a 0 encoding logical incompatibility. For this reason, the g's are sometimes referred to as compatibility functions, other times as potential functions. Undirected graphical models are also sometimes referred to as Markov networks [36].

7.3.7.2 Factor Graphs There are two kinds of nodes in a factor graph:

- Variable nodes
- Factor nodes

These are usually denoted as open circles and filled dots (Figure 7.14, center). A factor graph is like an undirected model, which represents a factorization of the joint probability distribution: Each factor is a nonnegative function of the variables connected to the corresponding factor node. Thus, for the factor graph in Figure 7.14, center, we have

$$P(A,B,C,D,E) = cg_1(A,C)g_2(B,C)g_3(B,D),$$
$$g_4(C,D)g_5(C,E)g_6(D,E) \tag{7.30}$$

Sometimes, factor nodes are called function nodes. Again, as in an undirected graphical model, the variables in a set X are conditionally independent of the variables in a set Y given Z if all paths from X to Y go through variables in Z. Note that the factor graph in Figure 7.14 has exactly the same conditional independence relations as the undirected graph, even though the factors in the former are contained in the factors in the latter. Factor graphs are particularly elegant and simple when it comes to implementing message-passing algorithms for inference (which is discussed further in the chapter) [36].

7.3.7.3 Directed Graphs In directed graphical models, also known as probabilistic DAGs, belief networks, and BNs, the nodes represent random variables, and the directed edges represent statistical dependencies. If there exists an edge from A to B, we say that A is a parent of B; conversely, B is a child of A. A directed graph corresponds to the factorization of the joint probability into a product of the conditional probabilities of each node given its parents. For the example in Figure 7.14, right, we write

$$P(A, B, C, D, E) = P(A)P(B)P(C|A,B)P(D|B,C)P(E|C,D) \tag{7.31}$$

In general, we would write

$$P(X_1,...,X_N) = \prod_{i=1}^{N} P(X_i| X_{pa_i}) \tag{7.32}$$

where X_{pa_i} denotes the variables that are parents of X_i in the graph.

Assessing the conditional independence relations in a directed graph is slightly less trivial than in undirected and factor graphs. Rather than simply looking at separation between sets of variables, one has to consider the directions of the edges. The graphical test for two sets of variables being conditionally independent given a third is called *d*-separation [72]. The *d*-separation takes into account the fact about *v-structures* of the graph, which consist of two (or more) parents of a child, as in the $A \rightarrow C \leftarrow B$ subgraph in Figure 7.14, right. In such a v-structure, $A \perp B$, but it is not true that $A \perp B | C$. That is, A and B are marginally independent, but conditionally dependent given C. This can be easily checked by writing out $P(A, B, C) = P(A)P(B)P(C|A,B)$. Summing out C leads to $P(A, B) = P(A)P(B)$. However, given the value of C, $P(A, B|C) = P(A)P(B)P(C|A,B)/P(C)$, which does not factor into separate functions of A and B. As a consequence of this property of v-structures, in a directed graph a variable X is independent of all other variables given the parents of X, the children of X, and the parents of the children of X. This is the minimal set that *d-separates* X from the rest of the graph and is known as the Markov boundary for X.

It is possible; although not always appropriate, to interpret a directed graphical model as a causal generative model of the data. The following procedure would generate data from the probability distribution defined by a directed graph: Draw a random value from the marginal distribution of all variables that do not have any parents [e.g., $a \sim P(A)$, $b \sim P(B)$], then sample from the conditional distribution of the children of these variables [e.g., $c \sim P(C|A = a, B = a)$] and continue this procedure until all variables are assigned values. In the model, $P(C|A, B)$ can capture the causal relationship between the causes A and B and the effect C. Such causal interpretations are much less natural for undirected and factor graphs since even generating a sample from such models cannot easily be done in a hierarchical manner starting from "parents" to "children" except in special cases. Moreover, the potential functions capture mutual compatibilities rather than cause–effect relations [36].

A useful property of directed graphical models is that there is no global normalization constant c. This global constant can be computationally intractable to compute in undirected and factor graphs. In directed graphs, each term is a conditional probability and is therefore already normalized $\sum_{x} P\left(X_i = x | X_{pa_i}\right) = 1$.

7.3.7.4 Expressive Power Directed, undirected, and factor graphs are complementary in their ability to express conditional independence relationships. Consider the directed graph consisting of a single v-structure $A \rightarrow C \leftarrow B$. This graph encodes $A \perp B$ but not $A \perp B | C$. There exists no undirected graph or factor graph over these three variables that captures exactly these independencies. For example,

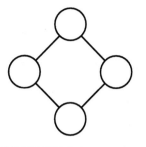

Figure 7.15   No directed graph over four variables can represent the set of conditional independence relationships represented by this undirected graph.

in $A - C - B$, it is not true that $A\perp B$, but it is true that $A\perp B|C$. On the other hand, if we consider the undirected graph in Figure 7.15, we see that some independence relationships are better captured by undirected models (and factor graphs) [36].

7.3.8 Exact Inference in Graphs

The problem of probabilistic inference in graphical models is the problem of computing a conditional probability of some variable X_i given the observed values of some other variables $X_{obs} = x_{obs}$ while marginalizing out all other variables. Starting from a joint distribution $P(X_1, \ldots, X_N)$, we can divide the set of all variables into three exhaustive and mutually exclusive sets $\{X_1, \ldots, X_N\} = \{X_i\} \bigcup X_{obs} \bigcup X_{other}$. We wish to compute

$$P(X_i| X_{obs} = x_{obs}) = \frac{\sum_x P(X_i, X_{other} = x, X_{obs} = x_{obs})}{\sum_{x'} \sum_x P(X_i = x', X_{other} = x, X_{obs} = x_{obs})} \qquad (7.33)$$

The problem is that the sum over x is exponential in the number of variables in X_{other}. For example, if there are M variables in X_{other} and each is binary, then there are 2^M possible values for x. If the variables are continuous, then the desired conditional probability is the ratio of two high-dimensional integrals, which could be intractable to compute. Probabilistic inference is essentially a problem of computing large sums and integrals.

There are several algorithms for computing these sums and integrals that exploit the structure of the graph to get the solution efficiently for certain graph structures (namely, trees and related graphs). For general graphs, the problem is fundamentally hard [74].

7.3.8.1 Elimination The simplest algorithm conceptually is variable elimination. It is the easiest to explain with an example. Consider computing $P(A = a|D = d)$ in the directed graph in Figure 7.14, right. This can be written as

$$P(A = a|D = d) \quad \propto \sum_c \sum_b \sum_e P(A = a, B = b, C = c, D = d, E = e)$$

$$= \sum_c \sum_b \sum_e P(A = a)P(B = b)P(C = c|A = a, B = b)$$

$$P(D = d|C = c, B = b)P(E = e|C = c, D = d)$$

$$= \sum_c \sum_b P(A = a)P(B = b)P(C = c|A = a, B = b)$$

$$P(D = d|C = c, B = b)\sum_e P(E = e|C = c, D = d)$$

$$= \sum_c \sum_b P(A = a)P(B = b)P(C = c|A = a, B = b)$$

$$P(D = d|C = c, B = b)$$

What we did was (a) exploit the factorization, (b) rearrange the sums, and (c) eliminate a variable E. We could repeat this procedure and eliminate the variable C. When we do this, we will need to compute a new function,

$$\varphi(A = a, B = b, D = d) \overset{\text{def}}{=} \sum_c P(C = c|A = a, B = b)$$
$$P(D = d \mid C = c, B = b)$$

resulting in

$$P(A = a|D = d) \propto \sum_b P(A = a)P(B = b)\phi(A = a, B = b, D = d)$$

Finally, we eliminate B by computing

$$\phi'(A = a, D = d) \overset{\text{def}}{=} \sum_b P(B = b)\phi(A = a, B = b, D = d)$$

to get our final answer, which can be written as

$$P(A = a|D = d) \propto P(A = a)\phi'(A = a, D = d)$$

$$= \frac{P(A = a)\phi'(A = a, D = d)}{\sum_a P(A = a)\phi'(A = a, D = d)}$$

The functions we get when we eliminate variables can be thought of as messages sent by that variable to its neighbors. Eliminating transforms the graph by removing the eliminated node and drawing (undirected) edges between all the nodes in the Markov boundary of the eliminated node.

The same answer is obtained no matter in what order we eliminate variables; however, the computational complexity can depend dramatically on the ordering used [36].

7.3.8.2 Belief Propagation Algorithm   Belief propagation (BP) is a message-passing algorithm proposed by Judea Pearl in 1982 for performing inference on graphical models, such as BNs and Markov random fields. It is inherently a Bayesian procedure, which calculates the marginal distribution for each unobserved node, conditioned on the observed nodes. BP was supposed to work only for tree-like graphs, but it has demonstrated empirical success in networks with cycles such as error-correcting codes. It has also been shown to converge to a stationary point of an approximate free energy, known as the Bethe free energy in statistical physics. The BP algorithm follows from the rules of probability and the conditional independence properties of the graph. Whereas variable elimination focuses on finding the conditional probability of a single variable X_i given $X_{obs} = x_{obs}$, BP can compute at once all the conditionals $p(X_i | X_{obs} = x_{obs})$ for all i not observed.

First, we should define singly connected directed graphs. A directed graph is singly connected if between every pair of nodes there is only one undirected path. An undirected path is a path along the edges of the graph ignoring the direction of the edges; in other words, the path can traverse edges both upstream and downstream. If there is more than one undirected path between any pair of nodes, then the graph is said to be multiply connected or loopy (since it has loops) [36].

Singly connected graphs have an important property that BP exploits. Let us call the set of observed variables the evidence $e = X_{obs}$.

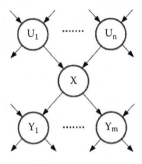

Figure 7.16 Belief propagation in a directed graph.

Every node in the graph divides the evidence into upstream e_X^+ and downstream e_X^- parts. For example, in Figure 7.16, the variables $U_1,...,U_n$, their parents, ancestors, and children and descendents (not including X, its children, and descendents) and anything else connected to X via an edge directed toward X are all considered to be upstream of X; anything connected to X via an edge away from X is considered downstream of X (e.g., Y_1, its children, the parents of its children, etc.). Similarly, every edge $X \rightarrow Y$ in a singly connected graph divides the evidence into upstream and downstream parts. This separation of the evidence into upstream and downstream components does not generally occur in multiply connected graphs.

The BP algorithm uses three key ideas to compute the probability of some variable given the evidence $p(X|e)$, which we can call the "belief" about X. First, the belief about X can be found by combining upstream and downstream evidence:

$$P(X|e) = \frac{P(X,e)}{P(e)} \propto P(X,e_X^+,e_X^-) \propto P(X|e_X^+)P(e_X^-|X) \quad (7.34)$$

The last proportionality results from the fact that given X the downstream and upstream evidence are conditionally independent: $P(e_X^-|X,e_X^+) = P(e_X^-|X)$. Second, the effect of the upstream and downstream evidence on X can be computed via a local message-passing algorithm between the nodes in the graph. Third, the message from X to Y has to be constructed carefully so that node X does not send back to Y any information that Y sent to X; otherwise, the message-passing algorithm would reverberate information between nodes amplifying and distorting the final beliefs.

Using these ideas and the basic rules of probability, we can arrive at the following equations, where $ch(X)$ and $pa(X)$ are children and parents of X, respectively:

$$\lambda(X) \overset{\text{def}}{=} P(e_X^-|X) = \prod_{j \in ch(X)} P(e_{XY_j}^-|X) \tag{7.35}$$

$$\pi(X) \overset{\text{def}}{=} P(X|e_X^+) = \sum_{U_1...U_n} P(X|U_1,...,U_n) \prod_{i \in pa(X)} P(U_i|e_{U_iX}^+) \tag{7.36}$$

Finally, the messages from parents to children (e.g., X to Y_j) and the messages from children to parents (e.g., X to U_i) can be computed as follows:

$$\pi_{Y_j}(X) \overset{\text{def}}{=} P(X|e_{XY_j}^+) \tag{7.37}$$

$$\propto \left[\prod_{k \neq j} P(e_{XY_k}^-|X) \right] \sum_{U_1...U_n} P(X|U_1...U_n) \prod_{i} P(U_i|e_{U_iX}^+)$$

$$\lambda_X(U_i) \overset{\text{def}}{=} P(e_{U_iX}^-|U_i) \tag{7.38}$$

$$= \sum_{X} P(e_X^-|X) \sum_{U_k:k \neq i} P(X|U_1...U_n) \prod_{k \neq i} P(U_k|e_{U_kX}^+)$$

It is important to notice that in the computation of both the top-down message (7.37) and the bottom-up message (7.38), the recipient of the message is explicitly excluded. Pearl's [72] mnemonic of calling these messages λ and π messages is meant to reflect their role in computing "likelihood" and "prior" terms [36].

BP includes as special cases two important algorithms:

- Kalman smoothing for linear Gaussian SSMs, and
- The forward-backward algorithm for HMMs.

Although BP is only valid on singly connected graphs, there is a large body of research on its application to multiply connected graphs—the use of BP on such graphs is called loopy BP and has been analyzed by several researchers [75, 76]. Interest in loopy BP arose out of its impressive performance in decoding error-correcting codes [77–80]. Although the beliefs are not guaranteed to be correct on loopy graphs, interesting connections can be made to approximate inference procedures inspired by statistical physics known as the Bethe and Kikuchi free energies [81].

7.3.8.3 Factor Graph Propagation In the BP algorithm, there is an asymmetry between the messages a child sends its parents and the messages a parent sends to its children. Propagation in singly connected factor graphs is conceptually much simpler and easier to implement. In a factor graph, the joint probability distribution is written as a product of factors. Consider a vector of variables $x = (x_1, \ldots, x_n,)$:

$$p(x) = p(x_1, \ldots, x_n) = \frac{1}{Z} \prod_j f_j(x_{S_j}) \qquad (7.39)$$

where Z is the normalization constant, S_j denotes the subset of $\{1, \ldots, n\}$ that participates in factor f_j and $X_{S_j} = \{x_i : i \in S_j\}$.

Let $n(x)$ denote the set of factor nodes that are neighbors of x and let $n(f)$ denote the set of variable nodes that are neighbors of f. We can compute probabilities in a factor graph by propagating messages from variable nodes to factor nodes and vice versa. The message from variable x to function f is

$$\mu_{x \to f}(x) = \prod_{h \in n(x) \setminus \{f\}} \mu_{h \to x}(x) \qquad (7.40)$$

and the message from function f to variable x is

$$\mu_{f \to x}(x) = \sum_{x \setminus x} \left(f(x) \prod_{y \in n(f) \setminus \{x\}} \mu_{y \to f}(y) \right) \qquad (7.41)$$

Once a variable has received all messages from its neighboring factor nodes, we can compute the probability of that variable by multiplying all the messages and renormalizing:

$$p(x) \propto \prod_{y \in n(x)} \mu_{h \to x}(x) \qquad (7.42)$$

Again, these equations can be derived by using Bayes rule and the conditional independence relations in a singly connected factor graph. For multiply connected factor graphs (where there is more than one path between at least one pair of variable nodes), one can apply a loopy version of factor graph propagation. Since the algorithms for directed graphs and factor graphs are essentially based on the same ideas, we also call the loopy version of factor graph propagation loopy BP [36].

7.3.8.4 Junction Tree Algorithm   For multiply connected graphs, the standard exact inference algorithms are based on the notion of a junction tree [82]. The junction tree algorithm is one of the most widely used algorithms, the basic idea of this algorithm is to group variables to convert the multiply connected graph into a singly connected undirected graph (tree) over sets of variables and do inference in this tree [36].

An overview of the steps involved in these algorithms is presented here. Starting from a directed graph, undirected edges are introduced between every pair of variables that share a child. This step is called *moralization* in a tongue-in-cheek reference to the fact that it involves marrying the unmarried parents of every node. All the remaining edges are then changed from directed to undirected. We now have an undirected graph that does not imply any additional conditional or marginal independence relations not present in the original directed graph (although the undirected graph may easily have many fewer conditional or marginal independence relations than the directed graph). The next step of the algorithm is "triangulation," which introduces an edge cutting across every cycle of length 4. For example, the cycle A-B-C-D-A, which would look like Figure 7.15, would be triangulated either by adding an edge A-C or an edge B-D. Once the graph has been triangulated, the maximal cliques of the graph are organized into a tree, where the nodes of the tree are cliques, by placing edges in the tree between some of the cliques with an overlap in variables (placing edges between all overlaps may not result in a tree). In general, it may be possible to build several trees in this way, and triangulating the graph means then there exists a tree with the "running intersection property." This property ensures that none of the variables is represented in disjoint parts of the tree as this would cause the algorithm to come up with multiple possibly inconsistent beliefs about the variable. Finally, once the tree with the running intersection property is built (the junction tree), it is possible to introduce the evidence into the tree and apply what is essentially a variant of BP to this junction tree. This BP algorithm is operating on sets of variables contained in the cliques of the junction tree, rather than on individual variables in the original graph. As such, the complexity of the algorithm scales exponentially with the size of the largest clique in the junction tree. For example, if moralization and triangulation results in a clique containing K binary variables, the junction tree algorithm would have to store and manipulate tables of size 2^K. Moreover, finding the optimal triangulation to get the most efficient junction tree for a particular graph is NP-complete [83, 84].

7.3.8.5 Cutset Conditioning   In certain graphs, the simplest inference algorithm is cutset conditioning, which is related to the idea of "reasoning by assumptions." The basic idea is straightforward: Find some small set of variables such that if they were given (i.e., you knew their values) it would make the remainder of the graph singly connected. For example, in the undirected graph in Figure 7.14, given C or D, the rest of the graph is singly connected. This set of variables is called the cutset. For each possible value of the variables in the cutset, run BP on the remainder of the graph to obtain the beliefs on the node of interest. These beliefs can be averaged with appropriate weights to obtain the true belief on the variable of interest. To make this more concrete, assume you want to find $P(X|e)$ and you discover a cutset consisting of a single variable C. Then, the following holds [36]:

$$P(X|e) = \sum_c P(X|C = c, e) P(C = c|e) \qquad (7.43)$$

where the beliefs $P(X|C = c, e)$ and corresponding weights $P(C = c|e)$ are computed as part of BP, run once for each value of c.

7.3.9 Learning in Graphical Models

In the previous section, we described exact algorithms for inferring the value of variables in a graph with known parameters and structure. If the parameters and structure are unknown, they can be learned from the data [85]. The learning problem can be divided into learning the graph parameters for a known structure and learning the model structure (i.e., which edges should be present or absent).

Here, we focus on directed graphs with discrete variables, although some of these issues become much more subtle for undirected and factor graphs [86]. The parameters of a directed graph with discrete variables parameterize the CPTs, $P(X_i \mid X_{pa_i})$. For each setting of X_{pa_i}, this table contains a probability distribution over X_i. For example, if all variables are binary and X_i has K parents, then this CPT has 2^{K+1} entries; however, since the probability over X_i has to sum to 1 for each setting of its parents, there are only 2^K independent entries. The most general parameterization would have a distinct parameter for each entry in this table, but this is often not a natural way to parameterize the dependency between variables. Alternatives (for binary data) are the noisy-or or sigmoid parameterization of the dependencies [87]. Whatever the specific parameterization, let θ_i denote the parameters relating X_i to its parents and let θ denote all the parameters in the model. Let m denote the model structure, which corresponds to the set of edges in the graph. More generally, the model structure can also contain the presence of additional hidden variables [88].

7.3.9.1 Learning Graph Parameters First, consider the problem of learning graph parameters when the model structure is known and there are no missing or hidden variables. The presence of missing/hidden variables complicates the situation.

7.3.9.1.1 The Complete Data Case Assume that the parameters controlling each family (a child and its parents) are distinct and that we observe N iid instances of all K variables in our graph. The dataset is therefore $D = \{X^{(1)} \ldots X^{(N)}\}$, and the likelihood can be written as

$$P(D|\theta) = \prod_{n=1}^{N} P(X^{(n)}|\theta) = \prod_{n=1}^{N} \prod_{i=1}^{K} P(X_i^{(n)}|X_{pa_i}^{(n)}, \theta_i) \quad (7.44)$$

Clearly, maximizing the log likelihood with respect to the parameters results in K decoupled optimization problems, one for each family, since the log likelihood can be written as a sum of K independent terms. Similarly, if the prior factors over the θ_i, then the Bayesian posterior is also factored: $P(\theta|D) = \prod_{i} P(\theta_i \mid D)$

7.3.9.1.2 The Incomplete Data Case   When there is missing/hidden data, the likelihood no longer factors over the variables. Divide the variables in $X^{(N)}$ into observed and missing components, $X_{obs}^{(n)}$ and $X_{mis}^{(n)}$, respectively. The observed data are now $D = \{X_{obs}^{(1)} \ldots X_{obs}^{(n)}\}$, and the likelihood is

$$P(D|\theta) = \prod_{n=1}^{N} P\left(X_{obs}^{(n)}|\theta\right) \tag{7.45}$$

$$= \prod_{n=1}^{N} \sum_{X_{mis}^{(n)}} P(X_{mis}^{(n)} = x_{mis}^{(n)}, X_{obs}^{(n)} \mid \theta) \tag{7.46}$$

$$= \prod_{n=1}^{N} \sum_{X_{mis}^{(n)}} \prod_{i=1}^{K} P(X_{i}^{(n)} \mid X_{pa_i}^{(n)}, \theta_i) \tag{7.47}$$

where, in the last expression, the missing variables are assumed to be set to the values $X_{mis}^{(n)}$. Because of the missing data, the cost function can no longer be written as a sum of K independent terms, and the parameters are all coupled. Similarly, even if the prior factors over the θ_i, the Bayesian posterior will couple all the θ_i.

One can still optimize the likelihood by making use of the EM algorithm (see Section 7.3.3). The E step of EM infers the distribution over the hidden variables given the current setting of the parameters. This can be done with BP for singly connected graphs or with the junction tree algorithm for multiply connected graphs. In the M step, the objective function being optimized conveniently factors in exactly the same way as in the complete data case (compare with Equation 7.22). Whereas for the complete data case the optimal ML parameters can often be computed in closed form, in the incomplete data case, an iterative algorithm such as EM is usually required.

Bayesian parameter inference in the incomplete data case is also substantially more complicated. The parameters and missing data are coupled in the posterior distribution, as can be seen by multiplying Equation 7.46 by the parameter prior and normalizing. Inference can be achieved via approximate inference methods such as MCMC methods [89] like Gibbs sampling.

7.3.9.2 Learning Graph Structure There are two main components to learning the structure of a graph from data: scoring and search. Scoring refers to computing a measure that can be used to compare different structures m and m' given a dataset D. Search refers to searching over the space of possible model structures, usually by proposing changes to the current model, to find the model with the highest score. This view of structure learning presupposes that the goal is to find a single structure with the highest score, although of course in the Bayesian inference framework it is desirable to infer the probability distribution over model structures given the data.

7.3.9.2.1 Scoring Metrics Assume that you have a prior $P(m)$ over model structures, which is ideally based on some domain knowledge. The natural score to use is the probability of the model given the data or some monotonic function of this:

$$s(m, D) = P(m \mid D) \propto P(D \mid m)P(m). \qquad (7.48)$$

This score requires computing the *marginal likelihood*,

$$P(D \mid m) = \int P(D \mid \theta, m) P(\theta \mid m) d\theta. \qquad (7.49)$$

For directed graphical models with fully observed discrete variables and factored Dirichlet priors over the parameters of the CPTs, the integral in Equation 7.49 is analytically tractable.

7.3.9.2.2 Search Algorithms Given a way of scoring models, one can search over the space of all possible valid graphical models for the one with the highest score [90]. The space of all possible graphs is very large (exponential in the number of variables), and for directed graphs, it can be expensive to check whether a particular change to the graph will result in a cycle being formed. Thus, intelligent heuristics are needed to search the space efficiently [91]. Alternatives to trying to find the most probable graph are methods that sample over the posterior distribution of graphs [92]. This has the advantage that it avoids the problem of overfitting, which can occur for algorithms that select a single structure with the highest score of exponentially many [36].

7.3.10 Bayesian Model Comparison and Occam's Razor

In all the previous sections, we have seen many different kinds of models. In fact, one of the most important problems in unsupervised learning is automatically determining which models are appropriate for a given data set. Model selection and comparison questions include all of the following:

- Are there clusters in the data, and if so, how many? What are their shapes (e.g., Gaussian, t distributed)?
- Do the data live on a low-dimensional manifold? What is the dimensionality? Is this manifold flat or curved?
- Are the data discretized? If so, to what precision?
- Are the data time series? If so, is it better modeled by an HMM, an SSM? Linear or nonlinear? Gaussian or non-Gaussian noise? How many states should the HMM have? How many state variables should the SSM have?
- Can the data be modeled well by a directed graph? What is the structure of this graph? Does it have hidden variables? Are these continuous or discrete?

Clearly, this list could be expanded more. A human being may be able to answer these questions via careful use of visualization, hypothesis testing, and guesswork. But ultimately, an intelligent unsupervised learning system should not be able to answer all these questions automatically.

Fortunately, the framework of Bayesian inference can be used to provide a rational, coherent, and automatic way of answering all of these questions. This means that, given a complete specification of the prior assumptions, there is an automatic procedure (based on Bayes rule) that provides a unique answer. Of course, as always, if the prior assumptions are very poor, the answers obtained could be useless. Therefore, it is essential to think carefully about the prior assumptions before turning the automatic Bayesian handle.

Let us go over this automatic procedure. Consider a model m_i coming from a set of possible models, $\{m_1, m_2, m_3, \ldots\}$. For instance, the model m_i might correspond to a Gaussian mixture model with i components. The models need not be nested, and the space of models does not need to be discrete (although we focus on that case). Given data D, the natural way to compare models is via their probability:

$$P(m_i|D) = \frac{P(D|m_i)P(m_i)}{P(D)}. \tag{7.50}$$

To compare models, the denominator, which sums over the potentially huge space of all possible models,

$$P(D) = \sum_j P(D|m_j)P(m_j)$$

is not required. Prior preference for models can be included in $P(m_i)$. However, it is interesting to look closely at the *marginal likelihood* term (sometimes called the *evidence* for model m_i). Assume that model m_i has parameters θ_i (e.g., the means and covariance matrices of the i Gaussians along with the mixing proportions). The marginal likelihood integrates over all possible parameter values,

$$P(D|m_i) = \int P(D|\theta_i, m_i)P(\theta|m_i)d\theta_i \tag{7.51}$$

where $P(\theta|m_i)$ is the prior over parameters, which is required for a complete specification of the model m_i.

The marginal likelihood has an interesting interpretation. It is the probability of generating dataset D from parameters that are randomly sampled from under the prior for m_i. This should be contrasted with the maximum likelihood for m_i, which is the probability of the data under the single setting of the parameters $\hat{\theta}_i$ that maximizes $P(D|\theta_i, m_i)$. A more complicated model will have a higher maximum likelihood, which is the reason why maximizing the likelihood results in overfitting (i.e., a preference for more complicated models than necessary). In contrast, the marginal likelihood can decrease as the model becomes more complicated. In a more complicated model, sampling random parameter values can generate a wider range of possible datasets, but since the probability over datasets has to integrate to 1 (assuming a fixed number of data points) spreading the density to allow for more complicated datasets necessarily results in some simpler datasets having lower density under the model. The decrease in the marginal likelihood as additional parameters are added has been called the automatic Occam's razor [93–95].

In theory, all the questions posed at the beginning of this section could be addressed by defining appropriate priors and carefully computing marginal likelihoods of competing hypotheses. However, in practice, the integral in Equation 7.51 is usually very high dimensional and intractable. It is therefore necessary to approximate it [36].

In these sections, we discussed the most important algorithms in unsupervised learning. For more details, readers are encouraged to consult the references mentioned.

7.4 Concluding Remark

The intent of this chapter was to present various signature generation algorithms that could be used for our purpose. To give readers appropriate pointers and directions toward various aspects related to the subject matter of this book, we used the necessary technical details on various related issues.

References

1. Gusfield, D. *Algorithms on Strings, Trees and Sequences: Computer Science and Computational Biology.* Cambridge: Cambridge University Press, 1997.
2. Pattern matching. Lecture slides of Frank Ruskey. Available at http://www.csc.uvic.ca/~ruskey/classes/326/slides/Chpt9PatternMatching.ppt (accessed September 3, 2012).
3. Aho, A.V., and Corasick, M.J. Efficient string matching: An aid to bibliographic search. *Communications of the ACM*, 1975, Volume 18, Issue 6, pp. 333–340.
4. Aho, A.V. Algorithms for finding patterns in strings. In *Handbook of Theoretical Computer Science*, Volume A., Jan van Leeuwen, Ed., Cambridge, MA: MIT Press, 1990, pp. 255–300.
5. Knuth, D., Morris, J.H., and Pratt, J.V. Fast pattern matching in strings. *SIAM Journal on Computing*, 1977, Volume 6, Issue 2, pp. 323–350.
6. Cormen, T.H., Leiserson, C.E., Rivest, R.L., and Stein, C. Section 32.4: The Knuth-Morris-Pratt algorithm. In *Introduction to Algorithms*, 2nd ed. New York: MIT Press and McGraw-Hill, 2001, pp. 923–931.
7. Harris, B. Approximate string matching. Available at http://www.denison.edu/academics/departments/mathcs/harris.pdf (accessed September 9, 2012).

8. Eddy, S.R. What is dynamic programming? *Nature Biotechnology*, 2004, Volume 22, pp. 909–910.

9. Pinzon, Y. Algorithms for approximate string matching. Presentation slides. Available at http://dis.unal.edu.co/~fgonza/courses/2006-II/algoritmia/approx_string_matching.pdf (accessed September 5, 2012).

10. Aldous, D., and Persi, D. Longest increasing subsequences: From patience sorting to the Baik-Deift-Johansson theorem. *Bulletin of the American Mathematical Society*, 1999, Volume 36, Issue 4, pp. 413–432.

11. Wohlfarter, A. Distribution properties of generalized van der Corput sequences. September 10, 2009. Available at http://www.geometrie.tuwien.ac.at/drmota/Diss_vdC.pdf (accessed September 5, 2012).

12. Kotsiantis, S., Patriarcheas, K., and Xenos, M. A combinational incremental ensemble of classifiers as a technique for predicting students' performance in distance education. *Knowledge-Based Systems*, 2010, Volume 23, Issue 6, pp. 529–535.

13. Ratsch, G. *A Brief Introduction into Machine Learning*. Tuebingin, Germany: Friedrich Miescher Laboratory of the Max Planck Society, 2005.

14. Kotsiantis, S.B., Zaharakis, I.D., and Pintelas, P.E. Supervised machine learning: A review of classification techniques. In *Emerging Artificial Intelligence Applications in Computer Engineering: Real Word AI Systems with Applications in eHealth, HCI, Information Retrieval and Pervasive Technologies*, ed. I. Maglogiannis. Amsterdam: Ios Press, 2007, pp. 3–24.

15. Batista, G., and Monard, M.C. An analysis of four missing data treatment methods for supervised learning. *Applied Artificial Intelligence*, 2003, Volume 17, pp. 519–533.

16. Hodge, V., and Austin, J. A survey of outlier detection methodologies. *Artificial Intelligence Review*, 2004, Volume 22, Issue 2, pp. 85–126.

17. Liu, H., and Hiroshi, M., eds. *Instance Selection and Construction for Data Mining*. Boston: Kluwer, 2001.

18. Reinartz T. A unifying view on instance selection. *Data Mining and Knowledge Discovery*, 2002, Volume 6, Issue 2, pp. 191–210.

19. Dietterich, T.G. Approximate statistical tests for comparing supervised classification learning algorithms. *Neural Computation*, 1998, Volume 10, Issue 7, pp. 1895–1924.

20. Nadeau, C., and Bengio, Y. Inference for the generalization error. *Machine Learning*, 2003, Volume 52, Issue 3, pp. 239–281; doi: 10.1023/A:1024068626366.

21. Hunt, E.B., Martin J., and Stone, P.J. *Experiments in Induction*. New York: Academic Press, 1966.

22. Breiman, L., Friedman, J.H., Stone C.J., and Olshen, R.A. *Classification and Regression Trees*. New York: Chapman and Hall/CRC, January 1, 1984.

23. Kononenko, I. Estimating attributes: Analysis and extensions of Relief. In *Machine Learning: ECML-94*, ed. L. De Raedt and F. Bergadano. New York: Springer-Verlag, 1994, pp. 171–182.

24. Elomaa, T., and Rousu, J. General and efficient multisplitting of numerical attributes. *Machine Learning*, 1999, Volume 36, Issue 3, pp. 201–244; doi: 10.1023/A:1007674919412.

25. Quinlan, J.R. *C4.5: Programs for Machine Learning.* San Francisco: Morgan Kaufmann, 1993.

26. Zheng, Z. Constructing conjunctions using systematic search on decision trees. *Knowledge Based Systems Journal,* 1998, Volume 10, Issue 7, pp. 421–430.

27. Gama, J., and Brazdil, P. Linear tree. *Intelligent Data Analysis,* 1999, Volume 3, Issue 1, pp. 1–22.

28. Markovitch S., and Rosenstein, D. Feature generation using general construction functions. *Machine Learning,* 2002, Volume 49, Issue 1, pp. 59–98; doi: 10.1023/A:1014046307775.

29. Cohen, W. Fast effective rule induction. *Proceedings of ICML-95,* July 9–12, 1995, Tahoe City, CA, pp. 115–123.

30. Rosenblatt, F. *The Perceptron—A Perceiving and Recognizing Automaton.* Report 85-460-1. Ithaca, NY: Cornell Aeronautical Laboratory, 1957.

31. Cestnik, B., Kononenko, I., and Bratko, I. Assistant 86: A knowledge elicitation tool for sophisticated users. *European Conference on Machine Learning and Principles and Practice of Knowledge Discovery in Databases - ECML,* May 1987, pp. 31–45.

32. Cestnik, B. Estimating probabilities: A crucial task in machine learning. *Proceedings of the European Conference on Artificial Intelligence,* 1990, Stockholm, Sweden, pp. 147–149.

33. Su, C., Ding, S., Jia, W., Wang, X., and Xu, X. Some progress of supervised learning. In *Lecture Notes in Computer Science,* Volume 5227, ed. D.-S. Huang et al. New York: Springer-Verlag, 2008, pp. 661–666.

34. Cowell, R.G. Conditions under which conditional independence and scoring methods lead to identical selection of Bayesian network models. *Proceedings of the 17th International Conference on Uncertainty in Artificial Intelligence,* August 2–5, 2001, Seattle, WA, pp. 91–97.

35. Ghahramani, Z., and Jordan, M.I. Factorial hidden Markov models. *Machine Learning,* 1997, Volume 29, pp. 245–273.

36. Ghahramani, Z. Unsupervised learning. Gatsby Computational Neuroscience Unit, University College, London. September 16, 2004. Available at mlg.eng.cam.ac.uk/zoubin/papers/ul.pdf (accessed September 10, 2012).

37. Hinton, G., and Sejnowski, T.J. *Unsupervised Learning: Foundations of Neural Computation (Computational Neuroscience).* Bradford Book, Cambridge, MA: MIT Press, 1999.

38. Wei, X. Information theory and machine learning. University of Illinois at Chicago. Available at http://www.ece.uic.edu/~devroye/courses/ECE534/project/Xiaokai.pdf (accessed September 11, 2012).

39. MacKay, D.J.C. *Information Theory, Inference, and Learning Algorithms.* Cambridge: Cambridge University Press, 2003.

40. Suhr, D.D. Principal component analysis vs. exploratory factor analysis. Paper presented at SUGI 30 Proceedings, April 10–13, 2005, Philadelphia. Available at http://www2.sas.com/proceedings/sugi30/203-30.pdf (accessed September 11, 2012).

41. Aggarwal, C.C., and Yu, P.S. Outliner detection for high dimensional data. *Proceedings of the ACM SIGMOD Conference*, Santa Barbara, CA, May 21–24, 2001, pp. 37–46.

42. MacQueen, J.B. Some methods for classification and analysis of multivariate observations. *Proceedings of 5th Berkeley Symposium on Mathematical Statistics and Probability*, Vol. 1. Berkeley: University of California Press, 1967, pp. 281–297.

43. Salakhutdinov, R., Roweis, S.T., and Ghahramani, Z. Optimization with EM and expectation-conjugate-gradient. In *International Conference on Machine Learning (ICML-2003)*, Washington, DC, August 21–24, 2003, pp. 672–679.

44. Markov, A. An example of statistical investigation in the text of "Eugene Onyegin" illustrating coupling of "tests" in chains. *Proceedings of the Academy of Sciences*, Vol. 7 of VI, 1913, pp. 153–162.

45. Petrie, T., Soules, G., and Weiss, N. A maximization technique occurring in the statistical analysis of probabilistic functions of Markov chains. *Annals of Mathematical Statistics*, 1970, Volume 41, Issue 1, pp. 164–171.

46. Blunsom, P. Hidden Markov models. August 19, 2004. Available at http://citeseerx.ist.psu.edu/viewdoc/summary?doi=10.1.1.123.1016 (accessed September 13, 2012).

47. Tipping, M.E., and Bishop, C.M. Mixtures of probabilistic principal component analyzers. *Neural Computation*, 1999, Volume 11, Issue 2, pp. 443–482.

48. Ghahramani, Z., and Hinton, G.E. *The EM Algorithm for Mixtures of Factor Analyzers*. Technical Report CRG-TR-96-1. Toronto, Ontario, Canada: University of Toronto, 1996.

49. Hinton, G.E., Dayan, P., and Revow, M. Modeling the manifolds of images of handwritten digits. *IEEE Transactions on Neural Networks*, 1997, Volume 8, Issue 1, pp. 65–74.

50. Ghahramani, Z., and Roweis, S.T. Learning nonlinear dynamical systems using an EM algorithm. *Proceedings of the 1998 Conference on Advances in Neural Information Processing Systems II*, November 30–December 5, 1998, Denver, CO, pp. 431–437.

51. Handschin, J.E., and Mayne, D.Q. Monte Carlo techniques to estimate the conditional expectation in multi-stage non-linear filtering. *International Journal of Control*, 1969, Volume 9, Issue 5, pp. 547–559.

52. Gordon, N.J., Salmond, D.J., and Smith, A.F.M. A novel approach to nonlinear/non-Gaussian Bayesian state space estimation. *IEE Proceedings F: Radar and Signal Processing*, 1993, Volume 140, Issue 2, pp. 107–113.

53. Kanazawa, K., Koller, D., and Russell, S.J. Stochastic simulation algorithms for dynamic probabilistic networks. In *Uncertainty in Artificial Intelligence. Proceedings of the Eleventh Conference*, ed. P. Besnard and S. Hanks. San Francisco: Morgan Kaufmann, 1995, pp. 346–351.

54. Kitagawa, G. Monte Carlo filter and smoother for non-Gaussian nonlinear state space models. *Journal of Computational and Graphical Statistics*, 1996, Volume 5, Issue 1, pp. 1–25.

55. Isard, M., and Blake, A. Condensation—Conditional density propagation for visual tracking. *International Journal of Computer Vision*, 1998, Volume 29, Issue 1, pp. 5–28.

56. Doucet, A., de Freitas, J.F.G., and Gordon, N.J. *Sequential Monte Carlo Methods in Practice (Statistics for Engineering and Information Science)*. New York: Springer, June 21, 2001.

57. Anderson, B.D.O., and Moore, J.B. *Optimal Filtering*. Englewood Cliffs, NJ: Prentice Hall, 1979.

58. Julier, S.J., and Uhlmann, J.K. A new extension of the Kalman filter to nonlinear systems. In *The Proceedings of AeroSense: The 11th International Symposium on Aerospace/Defense Sensing, Simulation and Controls, Multi Sensor Fusion, Tracking and Resource Management II*. SPIE, April, 1997, Orlando, FL, pp. 182–193.

59. Wan, E.A., Merwe, R. van der, and Nelson, A.T. Dual estimation and the unscented transformation. In Solla, S. Leen, T., and Müller, K.R., Eds., *Advances in Neural Information Processing Systems*, Vol. 12. Cambridge, MA: MIT Press, pp. 666–672.

60. Minka, T.P. Expectation propagation for approximate Bayesian inference. *Proceedings of the 17th Conference in Uncertainty in Artificial Intelligence (UAI-2001)*. San Francisco: Morgan Kaufmann, 2001, pp. 362–369.

61. Neal, R.M., Beal, M.J., and Roweis, S.T. Inferring state sequences for non-linear systems with embedded hidden Markov models. In Thrun, S., Saul, L.K., and Schölkopf, Eds., *Advances in Neural Information Processing Systems*, Vol. 16, Cambridge, MA: MIT Press, 2004.

62. Bishop, C.M., Svensen, M., and Williams, C.K.I. GTM: The generative topographic mapping. *Neural Computation*, 1998, Volume 10, Issue 1, pp. 215–234.

63. Shepard, R.N. The analysis of proximities: Multidimensional scaling with an unknown distance function. I. *Psychometrika*, 1962, Volume 27, Issue 2, pp. 125–140.

64. Kruskal, J.B. Multidimensional scaling by optimizing goodness of fit to a nonmetric hypothesis. *Psychometrika*, 1964, Volume 29, Number 1, pp. 1–27.

65. Hastie, T., and Stuetzle, W. Principle curves. *Journal of the American Statistical Association*, 1989, Volume 84, Issue 406, pp. 502–516.

66. Tenenbaum, J.B., Silva, V. de, and Langford, J.C. A global geometric framework for nonlinear dimensionality reduction. *Science*, 2000, Volume 290, Issue 5500, pp. 2319–2323.

67. Roweis, S.T., and Saul, L.K. Nonlinear dimensionality reduction by locally linear embedding. *Science*, 2000, Volume 290, Issue 5500, pp. 2323–2326.

68. Murphy, K.P. Dynamic Bayesian networks: Representation, inference and learning. PhD thesis, University of California, Berkeley, Computer Science, 2002.

69. Ackley, D.H., Hinton, G.E., and Sejnowski, T.J. A learning algorithm for Boltzmann machines. *Cognitive Science*, 1985, Volume 9, pp. 147–169.

70. Hinton, G.E., Dayan, P., Frey, B.J., and Neal, R.M. The wake-sleep algorithm for unsupervised neural networks. *Science*, 1995, Volume 268, Issue 5214, pp. 1158–1161.

71. Karklin, Y., and Lewicki, M.S. Learning higher-order structures in natural images. *Network: Computation in Neural Systems*, 2003, Volume 14, pp. 483–499.

72. Pearl, J. *Probabilistic Reasoning in Intelligent Systems: Networks of Plausible Inference*. San Mateo, CA: Morgan Kaufmann, 1988.

73. Besag, J. Spatial interaction and the statistical analysis of lattice systems. *Journal of the Royal Statistical Society*, Series B, 1974, 6, pp. 192–236.

74. Cooper, G.F. The computational complexity of probabilistic inference using Bayesian belief networks. *Artificial Intelligence*, 1990, Volume 42, Issue 2–3, pp. 393–405.

75. Weiss, Y. Correctness of local probability propagation in graphical models with loops. *Neural Computation*, 2000, Volume 12, Issue 1, pp. 1–41.

76. Weiss, Y., and Freeman, W.T. On the optimality of solutions of the max-product belief-propagation algorithm in arbitrary graphs. *IEEE Transactions on Information Theory*, Special Issue on codes on graphs and iterative algorithms, 2001, Volume 47, Issue 2, pp. 736–744.

77. Gallager, R.G. *Low-Density Parity-Check Codes*. Cambridge, MA: MIT Press, 1963.

78. Berrou, C., Glavieux, A., and Thitimajshima, P. Near Shannon limit error-correcting coding and decoding: Turbo-codes. 1. *IEEE International Conference on Communications (ICC 93)*, May 23–26, 1993, Geneva, Switzerland, pp. 1064–1070.

79. McEliece, R.J., MacKay, D.J.C., and Cheng, J.-F. Turbo decoding as an instance of Pearl's belief propagation algorithm. *IEEE Journal on Selected Areas in Communications*, 2006, Volume 16, Issue 2, pp. 140–152.

80. MacKay, D.J.C., and Neal, R.M. Good error-correcting codes based on very sparse matrices. *IEEE Transactions on Information Theory*, 1999, Volume 45, Issue 2, pp. 399–431.

81. Yedidia, J.S., Freeman, W.T., and Weiss, Y. Generalized belief propagation. In *Advances in Neural Information Processing Systems*, Vol. 13, Leen, T.K., Dietterich, T.G., and Tresp, V., Eds., Cambridge, MA: MIT Press, 2001.

82. Lauritzen, S.L., and Spiegelhalter, D.J. Local computations with probabilities on graphical structures and their application to expert systems. *Journal of the Royal Statistical Society*, Series B (Methodological), 1988, Volume 50, Issue 2, pp. 157–224.

83. Arnborg, S., Corneil, D.G., and Proskurowski, A. Complexity of finding embeddings in a k-tree. *SIAM Journal of Algebraic and Discrete Methods*, 1987, Volume 8, Issue 2, pp. 277–284.

84. Kjaerulff, U. *Triangulation of Graphs: Algorithms Giving Small Total State Space*. Aalborg, Denmark: University of Aalborg, Institute for Electronic Systems, Department of Mathematics and Computer Science, 1990.

85. Heckerman, D. *A Tutorial on Learning with Bayesian Networks*. Technical Report MSR-TR-95-06. Redmond, WA: Microsoft Research, 1996.

86. Murray, I., and Ghahramani, Z. Bayesian learning in undirected graphical models: Approximate MCMC algorithms. In *Proceedings of the 20th Conference on Uncertainty in Artificial Intelligence (UAI 2004)*. July 7–11, 2004, Banff, Canada: AUAI Press, pp. 392–399.

87. Neal, R.M. Connectionist learning of belief networks. *Artificial Intelligence*, 1992, Volume 56, Issue 1, pp. 71–113.

88. Elidan, G., Lotner, N., Friedman, N., and Koller, D. Discovering hidden variables: A structure-based approach. In *Advances in Neural Information Processing Systems,* Vol. 13, Leen, T.K., Dietterich, T.G., and Tresp, V., Eds., 2000, pp. 479–485.

89. Neal, R.M. *Probabilistic Inference Using Markov Chain Monte Carlo Methods.* Technical report. Toronto, Ontario, Canada: Department of Computer Science, University of Toronto, September 1993.

90. Friedman, N. The Bayesian structural EM algorithm. *Proceedings of the Fourteenth Conference on Uncertainty in Artificial Intelligence (UAI '98),* July 24–26, 1998, Madison, WI, pp. 129–138.

91. Moore, A., and Wong, W.-K. Optimal reinsertion: A new search operator for accelerated and more accurate Bayesian network structure learning. In *Proceedings of the 20th International Conference on Machine Learning (ICML '03),* ed. T. Fawcett and N. Mishra. Menlo Park, CA: AAAI Press, August 2003, pp. 552–559.

92. Friedman, N., and Koller, D. Being Bayesian about network structure: A Bayesian approach to structure discovery in Bayesian networks. *Machine Learning,* 2003, Volume 50, pp. 95–126.

93. Jefferys, W.H., and Berger, J.O. Ockham's razor and Bayesian analysis. *American Scientist*, 1992, Volume 80, pp. 64–72.

94. MacKay, D.J.C. Probable networks and plausible predictions—a review of practical Bayesian methods for supervised neural networks. *Network: Computation in Neural Systems,* 1995, Volume 6, pp. 469–505.

95. Rasmussen, C.E., and Ghahramani, Z. Occam's razor. In *Advances in Neural Information Processing Systems*, Vol. 13, Leen, T.K., Ditterich, T.G., and Tresp, V., Eds., Cambridge, MA: MIT Press, 2001, pp. 294–300.

8

ZERO-DAY POLYMORPHIC WORM COLLECTION METHOD

8.1 Introduction

We have learned that we need mainly two steps to generate signatures for zero-day polymorphic worms:

- First, we should collect zero-day polymorphic worm samples. To do this, we have to propose a new sample collection method.
- After collecting zero-day polymorphic worm samples, we should develop new algorithms to generate signatures for the collected samples.

This chapter and the next chapter present examples of how the collection process and generation of signatures can be performed. The zero-day polymorphic worm collection method described in this chapter (i.e., double-honeynet system) and the developed signature generation algorithms: substring extraction algorithm (SEA), modified Knuth–Morris–Pratt algorithm (MKMPA), and modified principal component analysis (MPCA) algorithm described in the next chapter were worked out by Mohammed et al. in material like References 1–3.

This chapter contains two parts. The first part discusses the design of a double-honeynet system in detail. The second part discusses the following:

- Information about the software used to implement the double-honeynet system.
- Double-honeynet system configurations using VMware.

8.2 Motivation for the Double-Honeynet System

Unknown Internet worms pose a major threat to Internet infrastructure security, and their destruction causes losses of millions of dollars.

Security experts manually generate the IDS (intrusion detection system) signatures by studying the network traces after a new worm has been released. Unfortunately, this job takes a lot of time. We propose a double-honeynet system that could automatically detect unknown worms without any human intervention. In our system, interaction between the two honeynets works by forming a loop that allows us to collect all polymorphic worm instances, which enables the system to produce accurate worm signatures. The double-honeynet system is a hybrid system with both network-based and host-based mechanisms. This allows us to collect polymorphic worm instances at the network and host levels, which reduces false positives and false negatives dramatically.

8.3 Double-Honeynet Architecture

The purpose of the double-honeynet system is to detect unknown (i.e., previously unreported) worms automatically. A key contribution of this system is the ability of distinguishing worm activities from normal activities without any involvement of experts in the field.

Figure 8.1 shows the main components of the double-honeynet system. First, the incoming traffic goes through the local router, which samples the unwanted inbound connections and redirects the samples' connections to honeynet 1. As the redirected packets pass through the local router, a packet capture (PCAP) library is used to capture the packets and then to analyze their payloads to contribute to the signature generation process.

The local router is configured with publicly accessible addresses, which represent wanted services. Connections made to other addresses are considered unwanted and redirected to honeynet 1 through the internal router. Once honeynet 1 is compromised, the worm will attempt to make outbound connections to attack another network. The internal router is implemented to separate the double honeynet from the local-area network (LAN). This router intercepts all outbound connections from honeynet 1 and redirects those to honeynet 2, which does the same task, forming a loop. The looping mechanism allows us to capture different instances of the polymorphic worm as it mutates on each loop iteration.

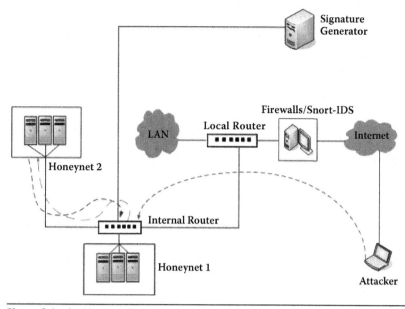

Figure 8.1 Double-honeynet system.

We stop the loop after a considerable amount of time to collect polymorphic worms. More details about how much time is taken to collect such types of attacks are presented in Section 8.5.

Only those packets that make outbound connections are considered polymorphic worms; hence, the double-honeynet system forwards only the packets that make outbound connections. This policy is in place due to the fact that benign users do not try to make outbound connections if they are faced with nonexisting addresses. In fact, our system collects other malicious activities that do not intend to propagate themselves but to attack targeted machines only. Such malicious attack is out of our work scope.

When enough instances of worm payloads are collected by honeynet 1 and honeynet 2, they are forwarded to the signature generator component, which generates signatures automatically using specific algorithms. These algorithms are discussed in the next chapter.

For example, as shown in the scenario in Figure 8.1, if the local router suspects packet 1 (P_1), packet 2 (P_2), and packet 3 (P_3) are malicious, it redirects them to honeynet 1 through the internal router. Among these three packets, P_1 and P_2 make outbound connections, and the internal router redirects these outbound connections to honeynet 2. In honeynet 2, P_1 and P_2 change their payloads and become P_1' and P_2', respectively (i.e., P_1' and P_2' are the instances of P_1 and P_2, respectively). Therefore, in this case, P_1' and P_2' make outbound connections, and the internal router redirects these connections to honeynet 1. In honeynet 1, P_1' and P_2' change their payloads and become P_1'' and P_2'', respectively (i.e., P_1'' and P_2'' are also other instances of P_1 and P_2, respectively).

Now, P_1 and P_2 are found malicious because of the outbound connections. Therefore, honeynet 1 forwards P_1, P_1'', P_2, and P_2'' to the signature generator for the signature generation process. Similarly, honeynet 2 forwards P_1' and P_2' to the signature generator for the signature generation process.

In this scenario, P_3 does not make any outbound connection when it gets to honeynet 1. Therefore, P_3 is not considered malicious.

8.4 Software

The software tools used in the double-honeynet system are introduced next.

8.4.1 Honeywall Roo CD-ROM

The Honeywall Roo CD-ROM version 1.4 is downloaded from the Honeynet Project and Research Alliance. It provides data capture, control, and analysis capabilities [4, 5]. Most important, it monitors all traffic that goes in and out of the honeynet. Honeywall Roo CD-ROM runs Snort-inline, an intrusion prevention system based on the IDS Snort. Snort-inline either drops unwanted packets or modifies them to make them harmless. It records information on all the activities in the honeynet using Sebek. It runs the Sebek server; the Sebek clients run on the honeypots. The clients then send all captured information to the server. For management and data analysis, it uses the Walleye Web interface. Walleye also works as a maintenance interface, but there is a command line tool and a dialog menu that can also be used to configure and maintain the honeywall.

8.4.2 Sebek

Sebek is a data capture tool that mainly records keystrokes but also all other types of sys_read data [6]. It records and copies all activity on the machine, including changes to files, network communications, and so on. The main method it uses is to capture network traffic and reassemble the Transmission Control Protocol (TCP) flow. This is in the case of unencrypted data. Encrypted data are another problem because Sebek can only reassemble it in its encrypted form. Instead of breaking the encryption, Sebek circumvents it by getting the data from the operating system's kernel. Sebek has a client-server architecture. On the client side, it resides entirely in the operating system kernel. Whenever a system call is made, Sebek hijacks it by redirecting it to its own *read()* call. This way, Sebek can capture the data prior to encryption and after decryption.

After capturing the data, the client sends it to the server, which saves it in a database or simply logs the records. The server is normally on the honeywall machine in the case of a honeynet, and it collects data from all the honeypots and puts them all together for analysis.

To prevent detection by intruders, Sebek employs some obfuscation methods. On the client, it is completely hidden from the user and therefore from an intruder on the system as well. However, this is not enough because the data that are captured have to be sent to the server, thereby exposing itself (i.e., the server). Sebek uses a covert channel to communicate with the server. It generates packets to be sent inside Sebek without using the TCP/IP (Internet Protocol) stack, and the packets are sent directly to the driver, bypassing the raw socket interface. The packets are then invisible to the user, and Sebek modifies the kernel to prevent the user from blocking transition of the packets. Figure 8.2 shows Sebek deployment.

In the case of multiple clients, there is a risk of the clients seeing each other's packets. Sebek configures its own raw socket interface on the clients to ignore all incoming Sebek packets. Only the server can receive Sebek packets. Due to its comprehensive log capabilities, it can be used as a tool for forensics data collection. It has a Web interface that can perform data analysis.

8.4.3 Snort_inline

Snort_inline is a modified version of Snort. It is "an Intrusion Prevention System (IPS) that uses existing Intrusion Detection System (IDS) signatures to make decisions on packets that traverse snort_inline." The decisions are usually drop, reject, modify, or allow [7].

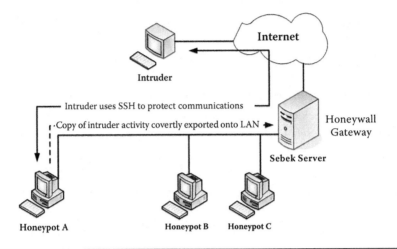

Figure 8.2 Sebek deployment. (Adapted from Honeynet Project. *Know your enemy: Sebek, a kernel based data capture tool.* November 17, 2003. http://old.honeynet.org/papers/sebek.pdf.)

8.5 Double-Honeynet System Configurations

In this section, we discuss the double-honeynet system architecture and configuration using VMware.

8.5.1 Implementation of Double-Honeynet Architecture

Figure 8.3 shows the architecture of the double-honeynet system, implemented using VMware Workstation version 7 on a personal computer (PC) with Intel Pentium 4, 3.19-GHZ central processing unit (CPU), 8-GB RAM, and the PC running on Windows XP 64 bit. The operating system of that personal computer is referred to as the host operating system in Figure 8.3. The host machine was connected to our home router, and it accessed the Internet through it.

We used a virtual machine to deploy the double-honeynet system due to the lack of resources and to keep the establishment low cost. One PC was used, and VMware Workstation was installed on it. The VMware Workstation is a software package that gives its users the opportunity to create virtual machines that constitute virtual networks interconnected with each other. Thus, we created the double-honeynet system as a virtual network seen from the outside world as an independent network. Attackers could locate the honeypot and attack it. The honeypot was transparently connected to the Internet

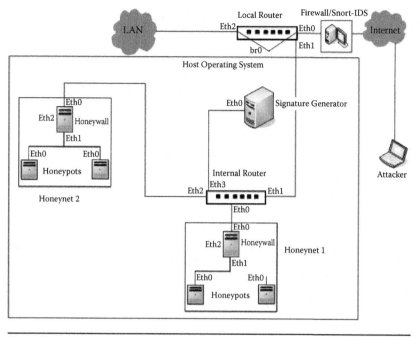

Figure 8.3 Double-honeynet architecture.

through the honeywall, which in turn intercepted all outbound and inbound traffic. Therefore, malicious traffic targeting the honeypot (inbound) or malicious traffic generated by the compromised honeypot (outbound) was available to us from the honeywall for further analysis and investigation. As mentioned in Section 8.3, honeynet 1 and honeynet 2 were configured to deliver unlimited outbound connections. The *internal router* was used to protect our local network by redirecting all outbound connections from honeynet 1 to honeynet 2 and vice versa.

8.5.2 Double-Honeynet Configurations

Our double-honeynet system contains six components: local router, internal router, LAN, honeynet 1, honeynet 2, and signature generator. The subnet mask for each subnet (whether local router, internal router, LAN, honeynet 1, honeynet 2, or signature generator) is consequently 255.255.255.0. The following sections discuss the configurations of each component.

8.5.2.1 Local Router Configuration As mentioned in Section 8.3, the local router's function is to pass unwanted traffic to honeynet 1 through the internal router. For example, if the IP address space of our LAN is 212.0.50.0/24, with one public Web server, the server's IP address is 212.0.50.19. If an attacker outside the network launches a worm attack against 212.0.50.0/24, the worm scans the IP address space of victims. It is highly probable that an unused IP address (e.g., 212.0.50.10) will be attempted before 212.0.50.19. Therefore, the local router will redirect the packet to honeynet 1 through the internal router. After the worm compromises honeynet 1, the worm will try to make an outbound connection to harm another network. We configured the internal router to protect the LAN from worms' outbound connections. The internal router intercepts all outbound connections from honeynet 1 and redirects them to honeynet 2, which performs the same task being done by honeynet 1 forming loop connections. The following are the details of the local router machine properties and iptables configuration.

- Machine properties:
  - Operating system: Ubuntu Linux 9.10
  - Number of network cards:
      Three network cards (Eth0, Eth1, and Eth2).
      Eth0 and Eth2 are a bridged LAN port.
      The function of Eth1 is to connect the local router with honeynet 1 through the internal router.
- IP addresses:
    Eth1: 192.168.50.20
- Prior to the iptables setting, we enabled IP forwarding in the local router.
    Edit /etc/sysctl.conf file as follows:
    Net.ipv4.ip_frowrd = 1
- IPtables configuration
    The settings of the network address translator (NAT) in the kernel using iptables are as follows:
    1. Do not translate packets going to the real public server:
       ```
       # iptables -t nat -A PREROUTING -m
       physdev—physdev-in eth0 -d 212.0.50.19 -j
       RETURN
       ```

2. Translate all other packets going to the public LAN to the internal router:

```
# iptables -t nat -A PREROUTING -m phys-
dev—physdev-in eth0 -d 212.0.50.0/24 -j
DNAT—to 192.168.50.22
```

8.5.2.2 Internal Router Configuration Again, as mentioned in Section 8.3, the internal router's function is to protect the LAN from worms' outbound connections and to redirect the outbound connections from honeynet 1 to honeynet 2 and vice versa. Let us investigate more about the internal router machine properties and iptables configuration:

- Machine properties
  - Operating system: Ubuntu Linux 9.10
  - Number of network cards:

    Four network cards (Eth0, Eth1, Eth2, and Eth3).

    Eth0 function is to connect the internal router to the honeynet 1 clients.

    Eth1 function is to connect the internal router with the local router.

    Eth2 function is to connect the internal router with the honeynet 2 clients.

    Eth3 function is to connect the internal router with the signature generator.
  - IP addresses:

    Eth0: 192.168.51.20

    Eth1: 192.168.50.22

    Eth2: 192.168.58.20

    Eth3 192.168.55.20
  - Before we set the IPtables rules, we enable the IP forwarding in the internal router:

    Edit /etc/sysctl.conf file as follows: Net.ipv4.ip_frowrd = 1
  - IPtables configuration:

    The settings of the NAT in the kernel using iptables are as follows:

    1. Translate packets coming in from eth1 to honeynet 1: `# iptables -t nat -A PREROUTING -i eth1 -j DNAT—to 192.168.51.22`

2. From honeynet 1, do not translate packets to the signature generator: `# iptables -t nat -A PREROUTING -i eth0 -s 192.168.51.22 -d 192.168.55.22 -j RETURN`

3. From honeynet 1, translate all other packets to honeynet 2: `# iptables -t nat -A PREROUTING -i eth0 -j DNAT—to 192.168.58.22`

4. From honeynet 2, do not translate packets to the signature generator: `# iptables -t nat -A PREROUTING -i eth0 -s 192.168.58.22 -d 192.168.55.22 -j RETURN`

5. From honeynet 2, translate all other packets to honeynet 1: `# iptables -t nat -A PREROUTING -i eth0 -j DNAT—to 192.168.51.22`

8.5.2.3 LAN Configuration   As described in Section 8.5.2.1, we have one public Web server in our LAN with this IP address: 212.0.50.19. The following are the details of the public Web server machine properties:

- Machine properties:
  - Operating system: Ubuntu Linux 9.10
  - Number of network cards:
    One network card Eth0.
  - IP address:
    Eth0: 212.0.50.19.

8.5.2.4 Honeynet 1   As shown in Figure 8.3, honeynet 1 contains the honeywall and two honeypots. The main function of honeynet 1 is to capture polymorphic worm instances. The following are the details of the honeywall machine properties and configuration:

- Machine properties:
  - Number of network cards:
    Three network cards (Eth0, Eth1, and Eth2).
    Eth0 function is to connect honeynet 1 with honeynet 2 through the internal router.
    Eth1 function is to connect honeynet 1 with its clients (honeypots).
    Eth2 is used for the management interface.

- IP addresses:
  Eth0: 192.168.51.22
  Eth1: 192.168.52.20
  Eth2: 192.168.40.7
- Honeywall configurations:
  1. Honeynet public IP addresses
     In the following, we type the external IP addresses for the honeypots. These are the IP addresses that are the attackers:
     IP addresses: 192.168.52.22, 192.168.52.23
  2. Honeynet network
     In the following, we type the honeynet network in CIDR (classless interdomain routing) notation:
     Honeynet Network CIDR: 192.168.52.0/24
  3. Broadcast address of the honeynet: 192.168.52.255
  4. Management interface:
     Third interface will be used for remote management. This interface helps us to remotely manage the honeywall through the secure shell (SSH) and Walleye Web interfaces. We use Eth2 for the management interface.
     IP address of the management interface: 192.168.40.7
     Network mask of the management interface: 255.255.255.0
     Default gateway for the management interface: 198.168.40.1
     DNS server IP for honeywall gateway:192.168.40.2
     Secure shell daemon (SSHD) listening port: 22
     Space-delimited list of TCP ports allowed into the management interface: 22 443
     Space-delimited list of IP addresses that can access the management interface: 192.168.40.0/24
  5. Firewall restrictions:
     The double honeynet is configured to perform unlimited outbound connections as mentioned in Section 8.3.
  6. Configure Sebek variables
     Sebek is a data capture tool designed to capture the attackers' activities on a honeypot. It has two

components. The first is a client that runs on the honeypots; its purpose is to capture all of the attackers' activities (keystrokes, file uploads, passwords), then covertly send the data to the server. The second component is the server, which collects the data from the honeypots. The server normally runs on the honeywall gateway.

Destination IP address of the Sebek packets: 192.268.52.20

Destination User Datagram Protocol (UDP) port of the Sebek packets: 1101

7. Honeypots configuration: The following are the details of the honeypot machines' properties and configuration.
   - Honeypot 1
     - Machine properties
       Operating system: Windows XP
       Number of network cards: We use one network card Eth0.
       IP address: Eth0: 192.168.52.22
   - Honeypot 2
     - Machine properties
       Operating system: Ubuntu Linux 9.10
       Number of network cards: We use one network card Eth0.
       IP address: Eth0: 192.168.52.23

8.5.2.5 Honeynet 2 Configuration   Honeynet 2 contains a honeywall and two honeypots. The function of honeynet 2 is to capture polymorphic worm instances. The following are the details of the honeywall machine properties and configuration:

- Machine properties:
  - Number of network cards:
    Three network cards (Eth0, Eth1, and Eth2).
    Eth0 function is to connect honeynet 2 with honeynet 2 through the internal router.
    Eth1 function is to connect honeynet 2 with his clients (honeypots).
    Eth2 used for management interface.

- IP addresses:
    Eth0: 192.168.58.22
    Eth1: 192.168.59.20
    Eth2: 192.168.40.8
- Honeywall configuration
    1. Honeynet public IP addresses
       In the following, we type the external IP addresses for the honeypots. These are the IP addresses that are attackers:
       IP addresses: 192.168.59.22, 192.168.59.23
    2. Honeynet network
       In the following, we type the honeynet network in CIDR notation:
       Honeynet network CIDR: 192.168.59.0/24
    3. Broadcast address of the honeynet: 192.168.59.255
    4. Management interface:
       Third interface will be used for remote management. This interface helps us to remotely manage the honeywall through SSH and Walleye Web interfaces. We use Eth2 for the management interface.
       IP address of the management interface: 192.168.40.8
       Network mask of the management interface: 255.255.255.0
       Default gateway for the management interface: 198.168.40.1
       DNS server IP for honeywall gateway: 192.168.40.2
       SSHD listening port: 22
       Space-delimited list of TCP ports allowed into the management interface: 22 443
       Space-delimited list of IP addresses that can access the management interface: 192.168.40.0/24
    5. Firewall restrictions:
       The double honeynet is configured to perform unlimited outbound connections as mentioned in Section 8.3.
    6. Configure Sebek variables
       Destination IP address of the Sebek packets: 192.68.59.20
       Destination UDP port of the Sebek Packets: 1101

7. Honeypot configuration

The following are the details of the honeypot machine properties.

- Honeypot 1
  - Machine properties:
    Operating system: Windows XP
    Number of network cards: We use one network card, Eth0.
    IP address: 192.168.59.22
- Honeypot 2
  - Machine properties:
    Operating system: Ubuntu Linux 9.10
    Number of network cards: We use one network card.
    IP address: 192.168.59.23

8.5.2.6 Signature Generator Configuration   The function of the signature generator is to generate signatures for polymorphic worm samples using algorithms discussed in the next chapter.

- Machine properties:
  - Operating system: Ubuntu Linux 9.10
  - Number of network cards: One network card, Eth0.
  - IP address: Eth0: 192.168.55.22

8.6 Chapter Summary

This chapter discussed two parts. In the first part, we gave full details of the double-honeynet system. In the second part, we gave a brief introduction to the software used to implement the double-honeynet system and double-honeynet configurations using VMware.

References

1. Mohammed, M.M.Z.E., Chan, H.A., Ventura, N., Hashim, M., and Amin, I. A modified Knuth-Morris-Pratt algorithm for zero-day polymorphic worms detection. In *Proceedings of the 2009 International Conference on Security & Management (SAM 2009)*, July 13–16, 2009, Las Vegas, NV, 2 vol. CSREA Press, Las Vegas, NV, 2009, pp. 652–657.

2. Mohammed, M.M.Z.E., and Chan, H.A. Honeycyber: Automated signature generation for zero-day polymorphic worms. In *Proceedings of the IEEE Military Communications Conference (MILCOM),* San Diego, CA, November 17–19, 2008, pp. 1–6.
3. Mohssen, M.Z.E.M, Chan, H.A., Ventura, N., Hashim, M., and Amin, I. Accurate signature generation for polymorphic worms using principal component analysis. In *Proceedings of IEEE Globecom 2010 Workshop on Web and Pervasive Security (WPS 2010),* Miami, FL, December 6–10, 2010, pp. 1555–1560.
4. The Honeynet Project. *Know your enemy. Honeywall CD-ROM Roo.* Available at https://projects.honeynet.org/honeywall/ (accessed August 18, 2012).
5. The Honeynet Project. *Roo CD-ROM User's Manual.* Available at http://old.honeynet.org/tools/cdrom/roo/manual/index.html (accessed August 18, 2012).
6. The Honeynet Project. *Know your enemy: Sebek, a kernel based data capture tool.* November 17, 2003. Available at http://old.honeynet.org/papers/sebek.pdf (accessed August 18, 2012).
7. Snort—The de facto standard for intrusion detection/prevention. Available at http://blog.joelesler.net/2006/01/snort-de-facto-standard-for-intrusion_27.html (accessed December 06, 2012).

9

Developed Signature Generation Algorithms

9.1 Introduction

In Chapter 8, we discussed the double-honeynet system theory and configurations for zero-day polymorphic worm sample collection. If you are able to do the configurations mentioned using VMware and connect your computer to the Internet for a considerable amount of time (i.e., at least 1 week as we suggest, but less time may be enough depending on your location and Internet connectivity), you would be able to collect zero-day polymorphic worms. Now, we assume that you have implemented the double-honeynet system and collected zero-day polymorphic worm samples. The next step would be to generate signatures for the collected samples using some algorithms. This chapter discusses how to generate signatures for polymorphic worms.

The discussion has two main parts:

a. The first part presents our proposed substring exaction algorithm (SEA), modified Knuth–Morris–Pratt algorithm (MKMPA), and modified principal component analysis (MPCA), which are used to generate worm signatures for zero-day polymorphic worms. Also, we present the pseudocodes for these algorithms.

To explain how our proposed algorithms generate signatures for polymorphic worms, we assume that we have a polymorphic worm A that has n instances $(A_1, A_2, \ldots, A_n)$. Generating a signature for polymorphic worm A involves two steps:

- First, we generate the signature itself.
- Second, we test the quality of the generated signature using mixed traffic (new variants of polymorphic worm A and normal traffic).

Before stating the details of our contributions and the subsequent analysis, we briefly mention an introduction about the string-matching search method and the original Knuth–Morris–Pratt algorithm (KMPA) to give a clear picture of the subject topic.

b. The second part discusses the implementation results of our proposed algorithms.

9.2 An Overview and Motivation for Using String Matching

After presenting the double-honeynet system and its functions in Chapter 8, we now describe the SEA, MKMPA, and MPCA to highlight our contributions.

String matching [1] is an important subject in the wider domain of text processing. String-matching algorithms are basic components used in practical software implementations used in most of the available operating systems. Moreover, they emphasize programming methods that serve as paradigms in other fields of computer science (e.g., system or software design). Finally, they also play an important role in theoretical computer science by providing challenging problems.

String matching generally consists of finding a substring (called a pattern) within another string (called the text). The pattern is generally denoted as

$$x = x[0...m-1]$$

whose length is m, and the text is generally denoted as

$$y = y[0...n-1]$$

whose length is n. Both the strings—pattern and text—are built over a finite set of characters, called the alphabet and denoted by Σ, whose size is denoted by σ.

The string-matching algorithm plays an important role in network intrusion detection systems (IDSs), which can detect malicious attacks and protect the network systems. In fact, at the heart of almost every modern IDS, there is a string-matching algorithm. This is a crucial technique because it allows detection systems to base their actions on the content that is actually flowing to a machine. From a vast number of packets, the string identifies those packets that contain data matching the fingerprint of a known attack. Essentially, the string-matching algorithm compares the set of strings in the rule set with the data seen in the packets, which flow across the network.

Our work uses the SEA and MKMPA (which are based on string-matching algorithms) to generate signatures for polymorphic worm attacks. The SEA aims at extracting substrings from the polymorphic worm, whereas the MKMPA aims at finding out multiple invariant substrings that are shared between polymorphic worm instances and using them as signatures.

9.3 The Knuth–Morris–Pratt Algorithm

The basic idea of the KMPA and some information were presented in Chapter 7. Let us again review our understanding. The KMP string-searching algorithm (or KMPA) [1] searches for occurrences of a "word" W within a main "text string" S by employing the observation that when a mismatch occurs, the word itself embodies sufficient information to determine where the next match could begin, thus bypassing reexamination of previously matched characters.

Let us use an example to illustrate how the algorithm works. To illustrate the algorithm's working method, we go through a sample run (relatively artificial) of the algorithm. At any given time, the algorithm is in a state determined by two integers, m and i. Here, m denotes the position within S that is the beginning of a prospective match for W, and i denotes the index in W denoting the character currently under consideration. This is depicted at the start of the run, like

```
m:  0123456789012345678 9012
S:  ABC ABCDAB ABCDABCDABDE
W:  ABCDABD
i:  0123456
```

We proceed by comparing successive characters of W to "parallel" positional characters of S, moving from one to the next if they match. However, in the fourth step in our noted case, we obtain that $S[3]$ is a space and $W[3]$ is equal to the character D (i.e., $W[3]$ = "D"), which is a mismatch. Rather than beginning to search again at the position $S[1]$, we note that no "A" occurs between positions 0 and 3 in S except at 0. Hence, having checked all those characters previously, we know that there is no chance of finding the beginning of a match if we check them again. Therefore, we simply move on to the next character, setting $m = 4$ and $i = 0$.

```
m:  01234567890123456789012
S:  ABC ABCDAB ABCDABCDABDE
W:      ABCDABD
i:      0123456
```

We quickly obtain a nearly complete match "ABCDAB," but at $W[6]$ (that is, $S[10]$), we again have a discrepancy. However, just prior to the end of the current partial match, we passed an "AB," which could be the beginning of a new match, so we must take this into consideration. As we already know that these characters match the two characters prior to the current position, we need not check them again; we simply reset $m = 8$, $i = 2$, and continue matching the current character. Thus, we omit not only previously matched characters of S but also previously matched characters of W.

```
m:  01234567890123456789012
S:  ABC ABCDAB ABCDABCDABDE
W:          ABCDABD
i:          0123456
```

We continue with the same method of matching until we match the word W.

9.3.1 Proposed Substring Extraction Algorithm

In this section, we show how our proposed SEA is used to extract substrings from one of the polymorphic worm variants that are collected by the double-honeynet system.

This section and the next (9.3.2) show the signature generation process for polymorphic worm A using the SEA and an MKMPA. The procedure of testing the quality of the generated signature is discussed in Section 9.3.3.

Let us assume that we have a polymorphic worm A that has n instances $(A_1, \ldots , A_n)$, and A_i has length M_i for $i = 1, \ldots , n$. Assume that A_1 is selected to be the instance from which we extract substrings, and the A_1 string contains $a_1\ a_2\ a_3 \ldots a_{m1}$. Let X be the minimum length of a substring that we are going to extract from A_1. The first substring from A_1 with length X is $(a_1 \ a_2 \ldots a_x)$. Then, we shift one position to the right to extract a new substring, which will be $(a_2 \ a_3 \ldots a_{x+1})$. Continuing this way, the last substring from A_1 will be $(a_{m1-X+1} \ldots a_{m1})$. In general, if instance A_i has length equal to M, and letting a minimum length of the substring that we are going to extract from A_1 be equal to X, then the total number of substrings (TNS) that will be extracted from A_i could be obtained by this equation:

$$TNS(A_i) = M - X + 1$$

The next step is to increase X by one and start new substring extraction from the beginning of A_1. The first substring will be $(a_1 \ a_2 \ldots a_{x+1})$. The substring extraction will continue satisfying this condition, $X < M$.

Figure 9.1 and Table 9.1 show all substring extraction possibilities using the proposed SEA from the string ZYXCBA assuming the minimum length of X is equal to three.

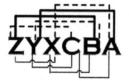

Thin solid line X=3, The substrings are ZYX, YXC, XCB, CBA
Dashed line X=4, The substrings are ZYXC, YXCB, XCBA
Thick solid line X=5, The substrings are ZYXCB, YXCBA

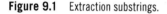

Figure 9.1   Extraction substrings.

Table 9.1   Substring Extraction

NO. OF SUBTRACTIONS	LENGTH OF X	SUBSTRINGS
S1,1	3	ZYX
S1,2	3	YXC
S1,3	3	XCB
S1,4	3	CBA
S1,5	4	ZYXC
S1,6	4	YXCB
S1,7	4	XCBA
S1,8	5	ZYXCB
S1,9	5	YXCBA

The output of the SEA will be used by both the MKMPA and the MPCA method. The MKMPA uses the substrings extracted by the SEA to search the occurrences of each substring in the remaining instances $(A_2, A_3, \dots, A_n)$. The substrings that occur in all the remaining instances will be considered the worm's signature. To clarify some of the points noted here, we present the details of the MKMPA in the next section.

9.3.2 A Modified Knuth–Morris–Pratt Algorithm

In this section, we describe our modification of the KMPA. As mentioned, the KMPA searches for occurrences of W (word) within S (text string). Our modification of the KMPA is to search for the occurrence of different words $(W_1, W_2, \dots, W_n)$ within string text S. For example, say we have a polymorphic worm A with n instances $(A_1, A_2, \dots, A_n)$. Let us select A_1 to be the instance from which we would extract substrings. If nine substrings are extracted from A_1, each substring will be W_i for $i = 1$ to 9. That means A_1 has nine words $(W_1, W_2, \dots, W_9)$, whereas the remaining instances $(A_2, A_3, \dots, A_n)$ are considered the S text string.

Considering this example, the MKMPA searches the occurrences of W_1 in the remaining instances of S $(A_2, A_3, \dots, A_n)$. If W_1 occurs in all remaining instances of S, then we consider it a signature; otherwise, we ignore it. The other words $(W_2, W_3, \dots, W_9)$ are similarly handled. Just as an example, if W_1, W_5, W_6, and W_9 occur in all remaining instances of S, then W_1, W_5, W_6, and W_9 are considered a signature of the polymorphic worm A.

9.3.3 Testing the Quality of the Generated Signature for Polymorphic Worm A

We test the quality of the generated signature for polymorphic worm A by using mixed traffic (new variants of polymorphic worm A and normal traffic, i.e., innocuous packets). The new variants of polymorphic worm A are not the same variants that are used to generate the signature. Let us assume that our system received a packet P (where P contains either malicious or innocuous data). The MKMPA compares P payload against the generated signature to determine whether P is a new variant of polymorphic worm A or not. The MKMPA considers

P as a new variant of the polymorphic worm A if all the substrings of the generated signature appear in P.

9.4 Modified Principal Component Analysis

Before introducing MPCA, we present a brief introduction to and motivation for using the PCA statistical method in our work. Then, we illustrate the MPCA, which contains our contributions to the PCA.

9.4.1 An Overview of and Motivation for Using PCA in Our Work

In general, when presented with the need to analyze a high-dimensional structure, a commonly employed and powerful approach is to seek an alternative lower-dimensional approximation to the structure that preserves its important properties. A structure that can often appear complex because of its high dimension may be largely governed by a small set of independent variables and so can be well approximated by a lower-dimensional representation. Dimension analysis and dimension reduction techniques attempt to find these simple variables and can therefore be useful tools to understand the original structures. The most commonly used technique to analyze high-dimensional structures is the PCA method [2, 3]. Given a high-dimensional object and its associated coordinate space, PCA finds a new coordinate space that is the best one to use for dimension reduction of the given object. Once the object is placed into this new coordinate space, projecting the object onto a subset of the axes can be done in a way that minimizes error. When a high-dimensional object can be well approximated in this way in a smaller number of dimensions, we refer to the smaller number of dimensions as the object's intrinsic dimensionality.

9.4.2 Our Contributions in the PCA

This section, Section 9.4.3, and Section 9.4.4 show the signature generation process for polymorphic worm A using MPCA. Testing the quality of the generated signature is discussed in Section 9.4.5.

In our work, instead of applying PCA directly, we have made appropriate modifications to it to fit it with our mechanism. Our contribution in the PCA method is in combining the PCA (i.e., extending) with the proposed SEA to obtain more accurate and relatively faster signatures for polymorphic worms. The extended method (SEA and PCA) is termed modified principle component analysis (MPCA). We have previously mentioned that the polymorphic worm evades the IDSs by changing its payload in every infection attempt; however, there are some invariant substrings that will remain fixed (i.e., some substrings will not change) in all polymorphic worm variants, so the SEA extracts substrings from a polymorphic worm in a good way (i.e., it will extract all the possibilities of substrings from a polymorphic worm variant that contain worm signature) that helps us obtain accurate signatures. After the SEA extracts the substrings, it will pass those to the PCA, thus easing the heavy burden to the PCA in terms of time (i.e., the PCA will start directly by determining the frequency count of each substring in the rest of the instances without doing the substring extraction process).

After the PCA receives the substrings from the SEA, it will determine the frequency count of each substring in the remaining instances $(A_2, A_3, \ldots, A_n)$. Last, the PCA will determine the most significant data on the polymorphic worm instances and use them as a signature. We present the details in the next section.

9.4.3 Determination of Frequency Counts

Here, we determine the frequency count of each substring S_i (A_1 substrings) in each of the remaining instances $(A_2, \ldots, A_n)$. Then, we apply PCA on the frequency count data to reduce the dimension and obtain the most significant data.

9.4.4 Using PCA to Determine the Most Significant Data for Polymorphic Worm Instances

The methodology of employing PCA for the given problem on determining the most significant data for polymorphic worm instances is outlined next.

Let F_i denote the vector of frequencies ($F_{i1}, \ldots, F_{iN}$) of the substring S_i in the instances $(A_1, \ldots, A_n)$, $i = 1, \ldots, L$.

We construct the frequency matrix F by letting F_i be the ith row of F, provided that F_i is not the zero vector.

$$F = \begin{pmatrix} f_{11} & \cdots & f_{1N} \\ \vdots & \ddots & \vdots \\ f_{L1} & \cdots & f_{LN} \end{pmatrix}$$

9.4.4.1 Normalization of Data The normalization of the data is applied by normalizing the data in each row of the matrix F, yielding a matrix D (L x N).

$$D = \begin{pmatrix} d_{11} & \cdots & d_{1N} \\ \vdots & \ddots & \vdots \\ d_{L1} & \cdots & d_{Ln} \end{pmatrix}$$

$$d_{ik} \leftarrow \frac{f_{ik}}{\sum_{j=1}^{N} f_{ij}}$$

9.4.4.2 Mean Adjusted Data To adjust the data around the zero mean, we use the formula

$$g_{ik} \leftarrow d_{ik} - \overline{d}_i \quad \forall i, k$$

where $\overline{d}_i$ = mean of the ith vector:

$$= \frac{1}{N} \sum_{j=1}^{N} d_{ij}$$

The data-adjusted matrix G is given by

$$G = \begin{pmatrix} g_{11} & \cdots & g_{1N} \\ \vdots & \ddots & \vdots \\ g_{L1} & \cdots & g_{LN} \end{pmatrix}$$

9.4.4.3 Evaluation of the Covariance Matrix   Let g_i denote the ith row of G, then the covariance between any two vectors g_i and g_j is given by

$$\text{Cov}(g_i, g_j) = C_{ij} = \frac{\sum_{k=1}^{L} (d_{ik} - \bar{d}_i)(d_{jk} - \bar{d}_j)}{N-1}$$

Then, the covariance matrix C ($N \times N$) is given by

$$C = \begin{pmatrix} C_{11} & \cdots & C_{1N} \\ \vdots & \ddots & \vdots \\ C_{N1} & \cdots & C_{NN} \end{pmatrix}$$

9.4.4.4 Eigenvalue Evaluation   Evaluate the eigenvalues of matrix C from its characteristic polynomial $|C - \lambda I| = 0$ and then compute the corresponding eigenvectors.

9.4.4.5 Principal Component Evaluation   Let $L_1, L_2, \ldots, L_N$ be the eigenvalues of matrix C obtained by solving the characteristic equation $|C - \lambda I| = 0$. If necessary, re-sort the eigenvalues of C in a descending order such that $|L_1| \geq \ldots \geq |L_N|$. Let $V_1, V_2, \ldots, V_N$ be the eigenvectors of matrix C corresponding to the eigenvalues $L_1, L_2, \ldots, L_N$. The k principal components are given by $V_1, V_2, \ldots, V_K$ where $K \leq N$.

9.4.4.6 Projection of Data Adjust Along the Principal Component   Let V be the matrix that has the k principal components as its columns. That is,

$$V = [V_1, V_2, \ldots, V_K]$$

Then, the feature descriptor is obtained from the equation

$$\text{Feature Descriptor} = V^T \times F.$$

To determine the threshold of polymorphic worm A, we use a distance function (Euclidean distance) to evaluate the maximum distance between the rows of F and the rows of FD. The maximum distance R works as a threshold. The Euclidean distance theory is discussed in Section 9.5.

9.4.5 *Testing the Quality of the Generated Signature for Polymorphic Worm A*

In the preceding section, we calculated the *FD* and threshold for polymorphic worm *A*. In this section, we test the quality of the generated signature for polymorphic worm *A* using mixed traffic (new variants of polymorphic worm and normal traffic, i.e., innocuous packets). The new variants of polymorphic worm *A* are not the same variants used to generate the signature.

Let us assume that our system received a packet *P* (where *P* contains either malicious or innocuous data). MPCA performs the following steps to determine whether *P* is a new variant of polymorphic worm *A*:

- Determine frequencies of the substrings of the *W* array in *P* (the *W* array contains extracted substrings of A_1 as mentioned previously). This will produce a frequency matrix F_1.
- Calculate the distance between the polymorphic worm *FD* and F_1 using Euclidean distance. This will produce a distance matrix D_1.
- Compare the distances in D_1 to the threshold *R* of polymorphic worm *A*. If any are less than or equal to the threshold, classify *P* as a new variant of polymorphic worm *A*.

9.5 Clustering Method for Different Types of Polymorphic Worms

When our network receives different types of polymorphic worms (mixed polymorphic worms), we must first separate them into clusters and then generate signatures for each cluster the same as in Sections 9.3 and 9.4. To perform the clustering, we use the Euclidean distance, which is the most familiar distance metric. Euclidean distance is frequently used as a measure of similarity in the nearest-neighbor method [2]. Let $X = (X_1, X_1, \ldots, X_p)'$ and $Y = (Y_1, Y_2, \ldots, Y_p)'$. The Euclidean distance between *X* and *Y* is

$$d(x, y) = \sqrt{(x - y)'(x - y)}.$$

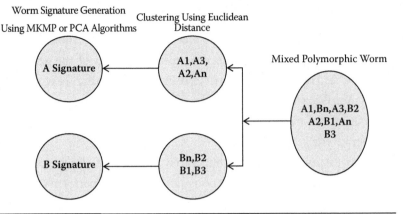

Figure 9.2   Clustering and signature generation for mixed polymorphic worms.

Clustering and Signature Generation Process Example

Now, let us explain how our algorithms deal with mixed polymorphic worm environments. First, we separate the mixed polymorphic worms into clusters, and then we generate signatures for each cluster using the MKMPA and MPCA. Figure 9.2 shows clustering and signature generation processes for two mixed polymorphic worms.

9.6 Signature Generation Algorithm Pseudocodes

In this section, we describe the signature generation algorithm (SEA, MKMPA, and MPCA) pseudocodes. These algorithms were discussed previously, and as mentioned previously, generating a signature for polymorphic worm A involves two main steps:

- First, we generate the signature itself.
- Second, we test the quality of the generated signature using mixed traffic (new variants of polymorphic worm A and normal traffic).

9.6.1 Signature Generation Process

This section presents the pseudocodes for generating a signature for polymorphic worm A using the SEA, the MKMPA, and MPCA.

9.6.1.1 Substring Extraction Algorithm Pseudocode The goal of SEA (as discussed in Section 9.3.1) is to extract substrings from the first instance of polymorphic worm A and then to put them in an array W.

SEA Pseudocode

```
1. Function SubstringExtraction:
2. Input (a file A1: First instance of polymorphic
      worm A, x: minimum substring length)
3. Output: (W: array of substrings of A1 with a minimum
      substring length x)
4. Define variables:
         Integer M : Length of file A1
         Integer X: Maximum substring length
         Integer z: (x<=z<=X) takes the lengths x to X
         Integer Tz: Total number of substrings of file
            A1 with a substring length z
         Integer position: the position of the first
            character of a substring of A1 with length z.
         Array of characters S: a substring of A1 with
            length z
5. X= M-1
6.  For  z := x to X Do
7.            Set Tz = M-z+1
8.            Set position = 0
9.                 While  position <= Tz
10.                     S = A1 (position) to
   A1(position+z-1)
11.                     Append (W, S)
12.                     position←position +1
13.                 EndWhile
      EndFor
14. Return W.
```

9.6.1.2 Modified Knuth–Morris–Pratt Algorithm Pseudocode Let us consider the example mentioned in Section 9.3.1 that we have a polymorphic worm with N instances $(A_1, A_2, \ldots, A_n)$. We select A_1 to be the instance from which we extract substrings. If G substrings are extracted from A_1, each substring will be equal to W_i for $i = 1$ to G. That means A_1 has G words $(W_1, W_2, \ldots, W_G)$, whereas the remaining instances $(A_2, A_3, \ldots, A_n)$ are considered as S text string.

The MKMPA contains two functions:

a. *kmpfound* Function. The kmpfound function is an MKMPA, which receives a word w from W array $(W_1, W_2, \ldots, W_G)$ and a file S (one file of the remaining instances $A_2, \ldots, A_n$) and determines whether w can be found in S.

b. *SignatureFile* Function. The *SignatureFile* function is combined with the *kmpfound* function to retrieve the words $(W_1, W_2, \ldots, W_G)$ that appear in all of the remaining instances $(A_2, \ldots, A_n)$ and use them as worm signatures.

The MKMPA has two inputs:

- The first input is the substrings of the W array (the output of the SEA).
- The second input is the remaining instances $(A_2, \ldots, A_n)$.

The goal of the MKMPA is to determine which substrings of the W array appear in all remaining instances $(A_2, \ldots, A_n)$ and to use them as a suspected worm signature.

MKMPA Pseudocode: *kmpfound* Function

```
1. Function kmpfound
2. Inputs:
      S: an instance of polymorphic worm A (A2,..., An)
      w: a word from file W to be searched in file S/*
        W is the Output of the SEA */
3. Output:
      a boolean value (true if w is found in S, and false
      otherwise)
4. Define variables:
          an integer, m ← 0 (the beginning of the current
            match in S)
          an integer, i ← 0 (the position of the current
            character in w)
          an array of integers, T (the table, computed
            elsewhere)
5. while m+i is less than the length of S, do:
6.        if w[i] = S[m + i],
7.                        if i equals the (length of w)-1,
8.                                  return true
9.                    let i ← i + 1
10.        Otherwise,
```

```
11.             let m ← m + i - T[i],
12.             if T[i] is greater than -1,
13.                 let i ← T[i]
14.             else
15.                 let i ← 0
16.         Return false.
```

MKMPA Algorithm Pseudocode: *SignatureFile* Function

```
1. Function SignatureFile
2. Inputs:
            W: Array of substrings of A1
            A2,..., An: Instances of worm A
3. Output:
            SigFile : Array of substrings of A1 found
            in the rest instances (A2,..., An)
            (Signature file contains the signature
            of the polymorphic worm A)
4. Define variables:
    FoundInAll: boolean variables which takes the
    value true if a word w(j) is found in all files
    A2,..., An
5. SigFile = Null
6. For j : = 1 To the length of W
7.          FoundInAll = True
8.          For k := 2 To n
9.                  Use function KMPFound to check whether
                    word W(j) can be found in file Ak
10.             If W(j) is not found in file Ak
11.                     Set FoundInAll = False
12.                 EndIf
13.             If FoundInAll
14.             Append W(j) to file SigFile
15.                 EndIf
16.         EndFor
17.     EndFor
18. Return SigFile
```

9.6.1.3 MPCA Pseudocode Here, we present the pseudocode for the MPCA method, which contains two functions:

a. ***Compute Array of Frequencies Function.*** The goal of this function is to compute the frequencies of each substring in the W array in the remaining instances ($A_2, \ldots, A_n$). The W array contains the substrings extracted by the SEA.

The inputs to this function are the W array and the remaining instances $(A_2, \dots, A_n)$. The output of this function is the frequencies of each W substring in the remaining instances $(A_2, \dots, A_n)$.

b. ***Compute Principal Component Function.*** This function computes the most important components and uses them as the worm signature.

The goal of this function is to extract the feature descriptor, which contains the most important features of polymorphic worm A.

The input to this function is matrix *FFF*, which is the output of the *Compute Array of Frequencies* function. The output of this function is the feature descriptor of polymorphic worm A.

In the following, we describe the pseudocodes for the *Compute Array of Frequencies* function and the *Compute Principal Component* function.

Modified Principal Component Analysis:
Compute Array of Frequencies Function Pseudocode

1. **Function** ComputeArrayOfFrequencies
2. **Inputs:** (Instances A2,..,An, Array W)).
3. **Output** (Matrix FF of frequencies of substrings of A1 stored in array W in files A2,...,An), and a vector of integers Zr)
4. **Define variables:**
      Integers: X,j,k, Wlength
      Matrices of Real: FF, FFF (FFF is the matrix will be obtained by reducing all the zero rows of matrix FF)
5. **Set** x = Minimum substring length
6. **W** : = ***SubstringExtraction*** (A1, x)
7. **Wlength** : = Length (W) (number of substrings extracted in W array)
8. **FF** = Matrix (Wlength, n-1)/* n is the number of polymorphic worm A instances */
9. **for** j from 1 To Wlength Do
10.   **for** k from 1 to n-1 Do
11.   **set** FF(j, k) be the frequency of word W(j) in file A(k+1)

12.   EndFor
13. EndFor
14. Remove all zero rows from FF giving Matrix FFF of size Nx(n-1) and save indexes of zero rows in a vector Zr
15. **Return** FFF and Zr

Modified Principal Component Analysis:
Compute Principal Component Function Pseudocode

1.   **Function** ComputePrincipalComponents:
2.   **Inputs**(FFF, K: Number of most important feature)
3.   **Output** (FD: a matrix of feature descriptors)
4.   **Define variables:**
       Matrices of Real: D, G, C, evecs, evals, PC (**D:** matrix of normalized frequencies; **G:** matrix of Mean Adjusted Data; **C:** covariance Matrix; **evecs:** matrix of eigenvectors of covariance Matrix; **evals:** matrix of eigenvalues of covariance matrix; **PC:** matrix consisting set of principal component vectors)
5.   **FFF** = ComputeArrayofFrequnciesMatrix (A2,...An, W)
6.   **FFFRows** = Number of rows of FFF
7.   **FFFCols** = Number of columns of FFF
8.   **Compute** the matrix of normalized frequencies D =

       (dij) using dik $\leftarrow \dfrac{f_{ik}}{\sum_{j=1}^{N} f_{ij}}$

9.   **Set** $\bar{d}_i$ (mean of the ith row of D)
10. **Compute** matrix G = (gik) where gik = dik-$\bar{d}_i$
11. **Compute** the covariance matrix C (Ci,j) where Cij =

    $\dfrac{\sum_{k=1}^{L}(d_{ik}-\bar{d}_i)(d_{jk}-\bar{d}_j)}{N-1}$, (C is NxN matrix)

12. **Compute the eigenvalues of C** ($\lambda 1$, $\lambda 2$, ..., λn) by solving $|C-\lambda I|$ = 0, sorted in a descending order of their magnitudes.
13. **Compute** the eignvectors of C V1, V2,..., Vn corresponding to the eigenvalues of C.
14. **Let** matrix V be the matrix whose columns are the eigenvectors vj^T (j = 1,..,k)
15. **Compute** the Feature Descriptor FD = V^T x FFF
16. **Return** FD

Pseudocodes for testing the quality of the generated signature for polymorphic worm A are discussed in the following section.

9.6.2 Testing the Quality of the Generated Signature for Polymorphic Worm A

In this section, we show the MKMPA and MPCA pseudocodes for testing the quality of the generated signature for polymorphic worm A (this signature was generated in Section 9.6.1 using the SEA, the KMPA, and MPCA). To test the quality of the signature, we use mixed traffic (new variants of polymorphic worm and normal traffic, i.e., innocuous packets). The new variants of polymorphic worm A are not the same as the variants used to generate the signature (i.e., training set is $A_1, A_2, ..., A_n$; test set is $A_{n+1}, ..., A_m$, where $m > n$).

Now, we describe the pseudocodes of the MKMPA and MPCA that we use to test the quality of the generated signature for polymorphic worm A.

Modified Knuth–Morris–Pratt Algorithm Pseudocode for Testing the Generated Signature for Polymorphic Worm A

1. **Inputs:** a packet P (which can be suspicious
   (An+1,..,Am) or innocuous packet), and SigFile which
   contains the signature of Polymorphic Worm A that
   was generated using SignatureFile function)
2. **Output:** a boolean value (true if all substrings of
   SigFile are found in packet P, and false otherwise)
3. **If** *kmpFound* (P, SigFile)
          Return True
      Otherwise
          Return False.

MPCA Pseudocode for Testing the Quality of the Generated Signature for Polymorphic Worm A

1. **Inputs:** a packet P (which can be suspicious
   (An+1,..,Am) or innocuous packet), W array, the
   vector Zr; and the Polymorphic worm A's Feature
   Descriptor(FD) and threshold r which was calculated
   using the ComputePrincipalComponents function)

2. **Output:** a boolean value (true if the Euclidean distance between the FD and Packet P < = r, and false otherwise)

3. **Define Variable**
   Let k = number of rows of FD.

4. Use function *FunctionComputeArrayOfFrequencies* to compute the frequencies of substrings of W array in Packet P, save the frequencies in a vector Fj and remove components of Fj indexed by Zr (Dimension of Fj is as same as FD).

5. **Calculate** the Euclidean distance between rows of **FD** and **Fj** Then save it a matrix **Dt**.

6. **If for some j (1< = j< = k) the distance** Dt(j) **is less than the threshold value r, return** true, otherwise **return** False

9.7 Chapter Summary

The first part of this chapter discussed algorithms used to generate signatures for polymorphic worms. The SEA is used to extract substrings from one of the polymorphic worm instances. The chapter described a modified version of the KMPA called the MKMPA. The MKPMA is a signature generator algorithm that searches the occurrence of different words (extracted substrings) on string text (remaining instances). MPCA is a signature generator statistical approach that is used to reduce the dimension of the worm payload so that the most significant data appear and are used as the worm signature. Euclidean distance has been used to solve the clustering problem. The second-discussed pseudocodes for the signature generation algorithms are the MKMPA and MPCA.

9.8 Conclusion and Recommendations for Future Work

Polymorphic worms evade signature-based IDSs by changing their payloads in every infection attempt. This book presents the ways to design methods for the detection of polymorphic worm attacks. In addition to different directions of the research topic and investigation of the available works, we present our solutions and detection methods. The detection mechanisms are based on two different approaches. In the first approach, a double-honeynet system is proposed to collect all polymorphic worm instances. In the second approach, signatures are generated for the polymorphic worm instances that are collected by the double-honeynet system.

Then, two different methods, the MKMPA and MPCA, are used to generate signatures for the polymorphic worms.

The MKMPA compares the polymorphic worm substrings to find multiple invariant substrings shared among all polymorphic worm instances and are therefore used as the signatures of the polymorphic worm. MPCA is used to determine the most significant data shared among all the polymorphic worm instances and are then used as the signatures.

It is recommended that for any real-life deployment of our system, real physical machines should be used with a multitude of different honeypots (running different operating systems and software applications) that will give the overall system the maximum ability to detect new zero-day polymorphic worms.

As a future work, the system may be improved by using supervised machine learning algorithms.

References

1. Gusfield, D. *Algorithms on Strings, Trees and Sequences: Computer Science and Computational Biology.* Cambridge: Cambridge University Press, May 28, 1997.
2. Aggarwal, C.C., and Yu, P.S. Outliner detection for high dimensional data. *ACM SIGMOD Record,* 2001, Volume 30, Issue 2, pp. 37–46.
3. Wei, X., Ahmed, T., Chen, M., and Pathan, A.-S.K. PeerMate: A malicious peer detection algorithm for P2P systems based on MSPCA. *International Conference on Computing, Networking and Communications (IEEE ICNC 2012),* January 30–February 2, 2012, Maui, Hawaii, pp. 815–819.

Index